English Grammar

HARPERCOLLINS COLLEGE OUTLINE

English Grammar

Barbara J. Daniels
Camden County College

David I. Daniels
Camden County College

HarperPerennial
A Division of HarperCollins*Publishers*

An American BookWorks Corporation Production

Project Manager: Judith A.V. Harlan
Editor: Robert A. Weinstein

Library of Congress Cataloging-in-Publication Data

Daniels, Barbara. 1945–
   English grammar / Barbara Daniels, David I. Daniels.
     p.   cm.
   Includes index.
   ISBN 0-06-467109-7
   1. English language—Grammar—1950–   I. Daniels, David I., 1942–
   II. Title
PE1112.D26   1991
428.2—dc20   90-56015

94 95 ABW/RRD 10 9 8 7 6 5

Contents

Preface

Grammar describes how language works. The study of grammar, besides being interesting in itself, provides guideposts for clearer and more effective self-expression. By calling your attention to the way language functions in daily life, studying grammar helps you become a more effective reader, writer, and speaker.

In this book we have tried to describe English as educated speakers and writers actually use it. On the whole, we have concentrated on describing the written language, but the principles of good writing we describe apply to speech as well.

This book is organized into eight chapters. The first chapter provides an overview of the sentence—the basic unit of expression. The remaining chapters discuss the parts of speech: nouns and articles, pronouns, verbs, verbals, adjectives and adverbs, conjunctions, and prepositions.

You will find this book easy to use. Technical terms have been kept to a minimum. Headings divide the subject matter of each chapter into manageable segments, and convenient lists and charts are provided in each chapter.

This book is designed so that you can teach yourself grammar. Among the features that make the book especially useful are the following:

- **139 exercises** containing 1,390 sentences so that you can practice your new skills at every stage.

- **Answers** provided for every exercise, enabling you to check your progress as you proceed.

- **"Try It Out,"** a special section included in each chapter, enabling you to apply the skills you have learned in your own writing.

- **A glossary** at the back of the book providing easy access to definitions of more than 100 terms without your having to comb through previous chapters. Throughout the text, **boldface print** will alert you to terms defined in the glossary.

We would like to thank Robert A. Weinstein for his thoughtful perusal of the manuscript and many helpful suggestions.

This book is dedicated to Viola and Henry G. Bossman, whose intelligence, courage, and enthusiasm have been a constant inspiration.

Barbara J. Daniels
David I. Daniels

1

Sentence Basics

The sentence is the basic unit of grammar. In writing, each new sentence opens with a capital letter and closes with an end mark, such as a period or a question mark. Sentences contain subjects (which mention someone or something) and predicates (which tell something about their subjects). All sentences express complete ideas.

RECOGNIZING TYPES OF SENTENCES

Sentences can be classified into four types: declarative, interrogative, imperative, and exclamatory.

Declarative sentences make statements. A declarative sentence can be as short as two words:

John ran.

Short as this example is, it illustrates the usual word order in declarative sentences — a noun (or pronoun) followed by a verb. The vast majority of sentences are declarative.

Interrogative sentences ask questions. Some interrogative sentences begin with a question word (such as *who, what,* and *where*):

Who ran?

Many interrogative sentences reverse the word order of declarative sentences and begin with verbs:

Did John run?

Imperative sentences give orders. An imperative sentence appears to have no subject because *you* is assumed to be its subject. An imperative sentence can be as short as one word:

Run!

Exclamatory sentences express emotions. Consider the following example:

What a fast runner John is!

This sentence expresses astonishment or admiration. Exclamatory sentences close with exclamation points. They are much rarer than the other three types of sentences.

EXERCISE 1

NOTE: Answers to all the exercises are provided at the back of this book.

Directions: Identify the types of sentences below by using the following code:

D   declarative   INT   interrogative
IMP   imperative   E   exclamatory

Example:

_D_.   Early Friday morning 580,000 gallons of molasses leaked from a storage tank and spread across an area half a mile wide.

_____ 1. Why do the yolks of eggs cook faster in the microwave oven than the whites do?

_____ 2. You look wonderful!

_____ 3. Stay away from your hamsters when you are sick since hamsters can catch some of the same diseases humans do.

_____ 4. Bands that use prerecorded music during live performances may have trouble pacing their shows in response to their audiences.

_____ 5. Graham crackers were named after Sylvester Graham, a dietary reformer.

_____ 6. Did *Tyrannosaurus rex* use its short forelimbs to grasp its prey?

_____ 7. Our plan worked!

_____ 8. Should crying babies be allowed to disrupt religious services?

_____ 9. Wear your seat belt every time you drive.

_____10. A Wood County, West Virginia, court jailed a protester rather than accept twelve canvas bags filled with 44,100 pennies in payment of his $441 fine.

UNDERSTANDING SUBJECTS AND PREDICATES

One way to analyze sentences is to divide them into two parts. The first part of the sentence, the **subject**, mentions a person, place or thing. The second part, the **predicate**, says something about the subject:

subject   predicate
John / ran.

Not many sentences are as short as this one. In most sentences, both subject and predicate are much longer. The subject may consist of a single word or it may contain a key word and one or more words that describe it. Look at the following sentence:

subject
The hungry lions / ate everything except the bones.

The key word here is *lions*, but the word *hungry* helps to describe them. The word immediately following the subject, *ate*, tells what the lions did. Words that describe actions are called **verbs**. Predicates consist of verbs and any other words that may follow them. Look at the sentence again:

predicate
The hungry lions / *ate everything except the bones*.

In this sentence the remainder of the predicate explains what the lions ate.

In the sentence above, the verb describes an action. Here is a sentence with a different kind of verb:

linking verb
The manager of our department *was* my uncle.

The various forms of the verb *to be* (*am, is, are, was,* and *were*) as well as some other verbs (for example, *appear, feel,* and *seem*) describe not actions but conditions. These verbs are called **linking verbs** because they link subjects to words that describe or rename them. Sentences with linking verbs can also be divided into subjects and predicates:

subject   predicate
The manager of our department / was my uncle.

This, then, is the basic pattern for sentences: a subject followed by a predicate. Other word orders are possible, some of them rather complicated, but keeping the basic pattern in mind will help you understand more difficult sentences.

Analyzing a sentence will be easier if you begin by finding the verb. Usually, the part before the verb will be the subject, and the verb and whatever follows it will be the predicate.

EXERCISE 2   **Directions:** Draw a line between the subject and the predicate in each sentence below.

Example:

    Bill / carried his tools in a five-gallon plastic bucket.

1. Lidia often buys snacks at the university store.

2. All of Glencoe's buses are equipped with safety belts.

3. Paulette wore the same brand of blue jeans for twenty years.

4. A team of divers retrieved the body of a drowned man from a pool of water about ninety feet below the falls.

5. Most people choose a television set for the quality of its picture.

6. Corn sweeteners are cheaper than table sugar.

7. The city of New York spent 100 million dollars to renovate the Times Square subway station.

8. Part of the appeal of doing jigsaw puzzles is creating order out of disorder.

9. Several inches of water flooded the basement of the library during the night.

10. Sometimes an exploding battery sprays acid onto skin and clothing.

RECOGNIZING PARTS OF SPEECH

Words can be divided into categories according to the roles they play in sentences. These categories are called the **parts of speech**. One piece of information a dictionary provides about a word is its part of speech. For example, if you look up the word *trivet* in a dictionary, you will find out not only how to spell it and what it means ("a small metal plate with short legs") but also what part of speech it is — a noun.

Parts of speech are very important in grammar. In fact, it would be impossible to describe how languages work without dividing words into categories. However, the categories are sometimes very flexible. For example, consider the word *book* in the following sentences:

1. The *book* is on the table.

2. Carlton Hotel? *Book* me a single room for tomorrow, please.

3. The *book* value of this used car is $4,000, but I bought it for only $3,200.

Book is a noun in the first sentence, a verb in the second sentence, and an adjective in the third one. What part of speech a word in a specific sentence belongs to depends on how it is used in that sentence.

Fortunately, a skill you acquire naturally as you learn a language is the ability to sort words into categories based on their positions in sentences. Look at the nonsense word *mixim* in this sentence, for example:

Put the *mixim* back on the table.

You may not know what a mixim is, but you know that grammatically it is similar to words like *apple* and *book* because it has the word *the* in front of it and because of its position in the sentence. You know that if you had more than one mixim you would probably have mixims, and that if a mixim had legs you could write about "a mixim's legs" or "the legs of the mixim." In short, you expect the word *mixim* to behave exactly like other nouns, even though you have never seen the word before and do not know what it means.

Below is a list of the parts of speech and a brief description of each one. Each chapter of this book provides additional information about one or more parts of speech.

Nouns name people, places, and things. *Dorothy, Kansas,* and *tornado* are all nouns. Here, the word *things* is used in the broadest possible way to include abstract ideas such as *anger, capitalism,* and *philosophy.*

EXERCISE 3   **Directions:** Circle the nouns in the sentences below. The number of nouns in each sentence is indicated in parentheses.

Example:

Faith reviewed chemistry almost every day last summer. (4)

1. Martin orders all his clothes from catalogues. (3)

2. The guests on the show were interested only in their own opinions. (3)

3. At outdoor concerts the quality of the sound is not always satisfactory. (3)

4. A typical supermarket sells more than 18,000 products. (2)

5.   The outside of the building will be cleaned and restored. (2)

6.   One flea can lay 500 eggs. (2)

7.   Mike is the best quarterback the team has ever had. (3)

8.   Caryl shampooed the little rug on both sides. (3)

9.   Squirrels eat bulbs, rob nests, and get into attics. (4)

10.   Aluminum is lighter than steel, so greater use of aluminum in cars should lead to lower costs for fuel. (7)

Articles introduce nouns. That is, an article signals that a noun is coming up shortly in the sentence. (One or more words may come between an article and the noun it refers to.) *A, an,* and *the* are articles.

EXERCISE 4   **Directions:** Circle the articles in the sentences below. The number of articles in each item is indicated in parentheses.

Example:

(The) team took (a) risk by drafting Miles Sheehan in (the) third round. (3)

1.   The parsonage has a wood-burning stove shaped like an old-fashioned church. (3)

2.   After the picnic Linda washed the plastic knives, forks, and spoons, the plastic tablecloth, and the plastic sandwich bags. (4)

3.   W. B. Tallman was the master of ceremonies at the tap dancing recital. (2)

4.   Some people have trouble accepting the idea that alcoholism is a disease. (2)

5.   Credit card companies may charge interest from the day of a purchase until the day a payment arrives. (4)

6.   Drinking milk is a better way to recover from eating a hot chili pepper than drinking water is. (2)

7.   As part of her research project, Doreen is collecting all the trash one person discards in a year. (2)

8.   Thunderstorms are generated by temperature imbalances in the atmosphere. (1)

9.   Gas leaks out of the car when it is parked on a hill. (2)

10.   Amateur astronomers can find out about the orbits of artificial satellites by contacting the National Aeronautics and Space Administration. (2)

Pronouns replace nouns. In the sentence "Sarah entered the room, but *she* didn't say anything," the word *she*, a pronoun, refers to Sarah. (Repeating the noun *Sarah* would sound a little clumsy.) *I, you, his, it,* and *themselves* are examples of pronouns.

EXERCISE 5   **Directions:** Circle the pronouns in the sentences below. The number of pronouns in each sentence is indicated in parentheses.

Example:

Marian's son has tattoos of dragons on his shoulders and a tattoo of a barn owl on his right arm. (2)

1. You must accept yourself before you can have good relationships with other people. (3)

2. The toll collectors have air conditioners and radios in their toll booths. (1)

3. I was invited to join the task force because of my background in marketing. (2)

4. Fran kept looking for an affordable apartment where she could keep her six cats. (2)

5. Parents should make their expectations for their children as clear as they can. (3)

6. Annette was very shy as a teenager, but now she is the most outgoing person in her group of friends. (2)

7. Mom works in her garden whenever she can. (2)

8. Justin's hands were covered with ink before he had finished reading the first page of his newspaper. (2)

9. Chimney swifts use their sticky saliva to attach their nests to the inner walls of chimneys. (2)

10. Arthur is considered a poor credit risk because he does not have a telephone. (1)

Verbs describe actions or conditions. *Jump* and *exist* are verbs. It is often important to distinguish between main verbs and verbals. A **main verb** describes an action or condition with reference to a specific subject:

verb

The cat *jumped* off the refrigerator.

verb

A dangerous situation *exists* in the Near East.

Verbals are derived from verbs, but they are used in sentences as nouns, adjectives or adverbs. Some verbals (such as *to jump* and *to exist*) are called **infinitives**. Verbals also include words ending in *-ing*, such as *jumping* and *existing*. Verbals cannot function as the main verbs in sentences.

EXERCISE 6   **Directions:** Circle the verbs in the following sentences. Each sentence contains one verb.

Example:

> The heavy garbage bag burst open.

1. A pair of baby shoes dangled from the rear view mirror.

2. Elliott first met Olivia in the snack section of a supermarket.

3. Mr. Pandolfo wrote his own will.

4. Our new Miracle Antenna actually makes our television reception worse.

5. Every kitchen or office contains at least one drawer full of odds and ends.

6. Many of my neighbors hide their house keys in the same kind of imitation rock.

7. Malcolm prefers a manual can opener to an electric one.

8. A large snow thrower removes more snow than a compact model.

9. Louise bought a rhinestone necklace for her cat.

10. Gloria owns her own business, a truck wash.

Adjectives describe (the technical term is **modify**) nouns and pronouns. *House* is a noun that names a kind of structure, but to indicate a specific house, you might want to describe it further by calling it a "*small, white* house." *Small* and *white* are adjectives.

EXERCISE 7   **Directions:** Circle the adjectives in the sentences below. The number of adjectives in each sentence is indicated in parentheses.

Example:

> Marina wore a black silk blouse and white shorts with gold buttons on them. (4)

1. Joe covered his flat roof with fresh asphalt and gravel. (2)

2. Allergies can cause watery eyes, itchy skin, and a runny nose. (3)

3. Julieta chose her car for its quick acceleration and powerful brakes. (2)

4. Bright colors and big letters decorate the packaging of foods intended for young children. (3)

5. Teenagers may argue over fine points more than younger children do because the teenagers are testing their new ability to think abstractly. (3)

6. Gina has a good background in sales. (1)

7. My old glasses had large frames. (2)

8. Fred has an excellent understanding of nutrition. (1)

9. Jason still uses a black telephone with a rotary dial. (2)

10. Sanding a wooden floor is a dusty job. (2)

Adverbs modify verbs, adjectives or other adverbs. To expand the simple sentence "Daksha slept" you might add the descriptive detail "Daksha slept *soundly*." *Soundly*, the word describing how Daksha slept, is an adverb. Many other adverbs also end in *-ly*. Adverbs answer questions such as the following about verbs, adjectives, and other adverbs: "How?" "When?" and "Where?" For example, in the sentence "I am very happy," *very* is an adverb that answers the question "How?" about the adjective *happy*.

EXERCISE 8   **Directions:** Circle the adverbs in the sentences below. The number of adverbs in each sentence is indicated in parentheses.
Example:

The protesters want the new tax repealed (immediately) (1)

1. Douglas finally bought a radon detector. (1)

2. Because Olga had previously filed for bankruptcy, she was very careful with her money. (2)

3. What is the best type of car for a teenager who has recently begun to drive? (1)

4. Americans typically consume much more protein than they need. (2)

5. Unlike a piano, an electric keyboard never needs tuning. (1)

6. The Ashers have already replaced the muffler in their new car three times. (1)

7. Chain saws are less dangerous now than they once were. (3)

8. Mrs. Loughlin bounced heavily on the sofa to see if it had been solidly made. (2)

9. In Canada the health care system is financed entirely by the government. (1)

10. Extremely dry conditions persist in the Southwest. (1)

Conjunctions connect words, phrases, and clauses. In the three examples below, the same conjunction, *and,* first connects two words, then two phrases, and last, two clauses:

Reggie both <u>worked</u> *and* <u>played</u> with great intensity.

I lost <u>my new gloves</u> *and* <u>my briefcase</u> on the same day.

<u>Susan was the best student in the English class</u>, *and* <u>she also excelled in gymnastics</u>.

Coordinating conjunctions connect words, phrases, and clauses of roughly equal importance. *And, but, or, nor, yet, for,* and *so* are coordinating conjunctions. Coordinating conjunctions do not usually begin sentences.

Subordinating conjunctions connect clauses and indicate that one of the two clauses is more important than the other. *After, although, as, because, if, since, unless, when,* and *while* are some of the many subordinating conjunctions. A subordinating conjunction appears at the beginning or in the middle of a sentence.

EXERCISE 9

Directions: Circle the conjunctions in the sentences below. Each sentence contains one conjunction.

Example:

Nail polish remover (and) liquid soap had been spilled on the bathroom floor.

1. Anita prefers wild peach sherbet, but Trudy likes mango ice cream.

2. Dominic likes to put his feet in a pail of hot water when he comes home from a hard day at work.

3. If you store rice in the refrigerator, it will not develop a rancid flavor.

4. Bunions do not require surgery unless they make walking difficult.

5. Many truckers will signal when a passing car can move safely back into the right lane.

6. Anxiety, rapid panting, trembling, and staggering may be signs a dog is suffering from heat prostration.

7. Although Jan broke her collarbone, her bicycle helmet probably saved her life.

8. Contrary to popular belief, sitting in a draft or getting wet does not increase one's chances of getting a cold.

9. Leslie hid the dirty dishes in a cabinet before her mother came into the kitchen.

10. The speed of sound increases as air grows warmer.

Prepositions connect nouns, pronouns, and noun phrases to other words in sentences and indicate the relationships between them. Consider this example:

Stephen left his baseball glove *on* the kitchen counter.

In this sentence the preposition *on* connects the noun *glove* to the noun phrase "the kitchen counter" and indicates the position of the glove in relation to the counter. A list of prepositions is provided in chapter 8.

EXERCISE 10 **Directions:** Circle the prepositions in the sentences below. The number of prepositions in each sentence is indicated in parentheses.

Example:

Sonja traveled to Moscow with a group from her college. (3)

1. Molly and Luis opened a restaurant in an old cabin on Barr Lake. (2)

2. A change from one work shift to another, a big meal or a dose of medication can make a driver sleepy. (3)

3. Solar-powered cars built by college students raced from Orlando, Florida, to Warren, Michigan. (3)

4. Patricia dries her laundry on a line in her backyard. (2)

5. In 1990 the state of Wisconsin apologized for a massacre of Sac and Fox Indians which occurred in 1832. (5)

6. After take-off, the last message to a pilot from an airport control tower is "Roger, good day." (3)

7. Angela's grandmother saw Halley's Comet in 1910 and again in 1986. (2)

8. Ray's recipe for baked beans is famous in our neighborhood. (2)

9. Writing on a dollar bill can result in a fine of $100 and a jail sentence of six months. (4)

10. In 1988 almost one and a half million acres in Yellowstone Park were destroyed by fire. (3).

Interjections express emotions. They have no grammatical connection with the other words in their sentences. Interjections are most common in informal writing. Consider the following examples:

Oh, darn, I forgot my watch again.

Why, I haven't done that sort of thing for years.

Oh, darn and *Why* are interjections.

EXERCISE 11   **Directions:** Circle the interjections in the sentences below. Each sentence contains one interjection.

Example:

"(Oh,) be quiet!" shouted Perry.

1. Great! Now we have enough players to start the game.

2. Aha! I caught you trying to take the last cookie!

3. "I remember, well, more than I'd like to about my first job," said Kim.

4. "Yech, anchovies," Michael complained. "I'll just have a salad."

5. "Wow, you look wonderful in that hat," said Jorge.

6. Teresa muttered "Ouch!" as she brushed against her hot travel iron.

7. "Shh," whispered Josh. "We want to surprise Dad."

8. Hey, you shouldn't drink that water until it's been tested.

9. Darn! I left my sunglasses at work.

10. Whew! I thought we'd never get the car packed.

EXERCISE 12   **Directions:** Identify the underlined word in each sentence below by writing the correct part of speech on the line at the left. Choose among the following terms:

noun   verb   conjunction
article   adverb   preposition
pronoun   adjective   interjection

Example:

interjection   Oh, Jan, your plastic rain hat melted in the dryer.

_____ 1. <u>Good</u> loudspeakers need not be expensive.

_____ 2. Melissa <u>is</u> too short to get a good view of the road from the driver's seat.

_____ 3. Using skim <u>milk</u> on cereal keeps the total fat content low.

_____ 4. Ralph <u>rarely</u> balances his checkbook.

_____ 5. My old Barbie doll has pink plastic high heels, <u>but</u> your doll has running shoes.

_____ 6. Dorothy never opens <u>her</u> junk mail.

_____ 7. Cortisone <u>reduces</u> inflammation.

_____ 8. Fossil evidence suggests that whales once had hind <u>feet</u>.

_____ 9. Julie made <u>a</u> braided rug out of discarded clothes.

_____ 10. The kidnappers demanded a ransom <u>of</u> $2 million.

EXERCISE 13 **Directions:** Identify the part of speech of each capitalized nonsense word in the sentences below by using the following code:

N   noun   V   verb
ADJ   adjective   ADV   adverb

Example.

__<u>V</u>__   The glass museum GRUDACS at nine o'clock every morning.

_____ 1. Attendance at national BEPS has almost doubled during the last three years.

_____ 2. Mr. Grove often SEGABLES his ideas at public meetings.

_____ 3. If you encounter a bear while you are hiking, back away SERIFALLY.

_____ 4. The "Danielle Carr Show" was dropped because its OCILACS were so low.

_____ 5. Installing NINWROC blinds makes it easier to control how much light enters a room.

_____ 6. Conrad wants to sell a waterbed, a RECHERTION rug, and an old drum set.

_____ 7. One of the warning signs of an ONDEAB is pain in the center of the chest behind the breastbone.

_____ 8. The NATLAC way to save money is to deposit a specific amount in a bank account each month.

_____ 9. Ed's German Shepherd, Arrow, ZINBAZZES trips in Ed's new car.

_____ 10. The TRESPOOF countries are seeking increases in the aid they receive from the world's richest nations.

RECOGNIZING PHRASES

Some combinations of words within sentences seem to go together. **Phrases** are combinations that belong together because they express a single idea, just as a single word might. Unlike sentences, phrases do not contain both subjects and predicates. Look at the following sentence:

> phrase
> *A tall, dark-haired man* entered the room.

The phrase "A tall, dark-haired man" functions exactly as a noun would in its place. Compare this sentence with the sentence "*Simon* entered the room." "A tall, dark-haired man" and *Simon* function in the same way.

Here is another example:

> phrase
> I *should have gone* with her yesterday.

The phrase "should have gone" functions as a one-word verb would. Compare this sentence with the similar one "I *go* with her whenever I can." The kind of phrase that acts like a noun is a **noun phrase**, and the kind that acts like a verb is a **verb phrase**.

A third kind of phrase is called a **prepositional phrase** because it contains a preposition. Here are some examples of sentences containing prepositional phrases:

> prepositional phrase
> Robert is engaged *to Roxanne*.

> prepositional phrase
> *In the morning*, everything will look more cheerful.

prepositional phrases

Going *to work by public transportation* can be frustrating.

Prepositional phrases usually function as adverbs or adjectives.

EXERCISE 14   **Directions:** Identify the underlined phrase in each of the sentences below by using the following code:

NP   noun phrase

VP   verb phrase

PP   prepositional phrase

Example:

VP   The head librarian has been studying requests for a special section of the library devoted to ecology.

_____ 1.   Joanne considered the pool too cold for a swim.

_____ 2.   Smallpox was a worldwide problem when Dr. Yost began practicing in 1940.

_____ 3.   Marci is searching the classified advertisements for an affordable car.

_____ 4.   The grand opening of the new bowling center is scheduled for next week.

_____ 5.   Charles May traced his ancestry back to Charlemagne.

_____ 6.   Evelyn lost a certified check.

_____ 7.   Very few of our customers have complained.

_____ 8.   Why do people put lit firecrackers into mail boxes?

_____ 9.   The president believes that informal meetings among world leaders increase the chances for world peace.

_____ 10.   The mayor has installed a shower in her office.

RECOGNIZING CLAUSES

Other word combinations that occur frequently in sentences are called clauses. Unlike phrases, **clauses** contain subjects and predicates, just as sentences do. As a matter of fact, some clauses are complete sentences:

subject   predicate

The man / carried his little son on his shoulders.

In the next example the same clause is not a complete sentence:

The man carried his little son on his shoulders, and his daughter walked beside him.

In the second sentence, "The man carried his little son on his shoulders" fits the definition of a clause (it has a subject and a predicate), but it no longer fits the definition of a sentence (it does not close with an end mark). Almost the same may be said of the second part, "his daughter walked beside him," which has a subject and a predicate but does not begin with a capital letter. Taken together, however, the two clauses connected by the conjunction *and* do add up to a sentence. A sentence, then, may consist of a single clause or of two or more clauses.

Independent Clauses

Clauses that can stand alone as sentences are called **independent clauses.** A writer often may choose between expressing two closely related ideas as one sentence or as two:

A strong wind began to blow from the northeast. The sky grew dark.

A strong wind began to blow from the northeast, and the sky grew dark.

These two examples mean almost the same thing. The first version consists of two independent clauses punctuated as sentences. The second consists of the same two clauses joined by *and*.

Dependent Clauses

Some clauses, called **dependent clauses**, contain subjects and verbs but cannot stand alone as sentences. They begin with subordinating conjunctions such as *although, if* or *when*, which promise that a second clause will occur in the same sentence. For example, suppose the person who sold you this book had handed it over and said, "If you study this book carefully." You would look up expectantly, waiting for him or her to finish. The person might go on to say, "you'll learn a great deal about grammar." The promise made by the word *If* that a second clause would follow has now been fulfilled. The complete sentence consists of a dependent clause followed by an independent clause.

Another kind of dependent clause begins with a relative pronoun such as *who, which* or *that*:

I know a man *who speaks six languages*.

He often speaks to me in Greek, *which I consider very rude*.

I've told him a dozen times *that I don't understand Greek*.

Such clauses, known as relative clauses, can also occur in the middle of sentences. Look at the following example:

relative clause

The man *who spoke Greek to me just now* is my friend.

This is really two sentences in one:

1. The man is my friend.

2. He spoke Greek to me just now.

By changing the pronoun *He* to the pronoun *who*, you can insert the second sentence smoothly into the first one.

EXERCISE 15   **Directions:** Identify the underlined clause in each sentence below by using the following code:

I   independent clause

D   dependent clause

Example:

_*D*_   <u>Although bacon tastes good</u>, it contains fat, salt, and nitrosamines.

_____ 1. If Ruth knows she will be on her feet all day, <u>she refuses to wear uncomfortable shoes to work</u>.

_____ 2. As problems develop with pesticides, <u>more farmers are turning to natural ways of controlling pests, such as releasing predatory insects</u>.

_____ 3. <u>Until the construction at the airport is completed</u>, finding a place to park will take longer.

_____ 4. <u>Every move Lynette makes has been scrutinized</u> since she became Miss Oklahoma.

_____ 5. The egg shelf on the refrigerator door is the worst place to store eggs <u>because eggs kept there are constantly jostled</u>.

_____ 6. When her car broke down, <u>Marie used an old pair of pantyhose to repair the fan belt</u>.

_____ 7. Shoes should not be handed down from one child to another <u>though hand-me-down clothing is acceptable</u>.

_____ 8. Sugar-free soft drinks contain acids <u>that can harm the teeth</u>.

_____ 9. People <u>who want seats at the trial</u> must pass through metal detectors.

_____ 10. <u>After he looked through the unpaid bills</u>, Geoffrey cut up all his credit cards.

USING CLAUSES IN SENTENCES

A sentence consisting of a single independent clause is called a **simple sentence**:

The textbook was confusing.

A simple sentence can have more than one subject:

The *textbook* and the *lectures* were confusing.

It can also have more than one verb:

The textbook *looked* interesting but *proved* difficult to understand.

It can also have both more than one subject and more than one verb:

The *textbook* and the *lectures seemed* difficult but *were* really very useful.

Here, *seemed* and *were* both refer to *textbooks* and *lectures*, so this example is still a simple sentence.

Forming Compound Sentences

Any sentence with two subjects, each with its own verb, has two separate clauses and is not a simple sentence. Look at this example:

independent clause

The textbook seemed too difficult, but

independent clause

the lectures were clear and interesting.

Here the first subject, *textbook*, and the first verb, *seemed*, go together, as do the second subject, *lectures*, and the second verb, *were*. The two different subjects have two distinct predicates. Therefore, the sentence has two clauses.

A single sentence with two independent clauses is called a **compound sentence**. The coordinating conjunction that joins the clauses of a compound sentence suggests that the two clauses are equally important:

The weather was perfect, and *everything was ready for the picnic.*

The weather was perfect, but *Amanda didn't feel like going out.*

The weather was perfect, so *Alejandro returned to the house to put away his umbrella.*

Forming Complex Sentences

Combining an independent and a dependent clause produces a different effect. The independent clause is the more important of the two, and the dependent clause usually acts as a modifier. Sentences consisting of one independent clause and one or more dependent clauses are called **complex sentences**:

> dependent clause
>
> When we heard how much the repairs would cost,
>
> independent clause
>
> we decided to get a new TV set.
>
> dependent clause
>
> After we heard how much a new TV set would cost,
>
> independent clause
>
> we thought again about the repairs.
>
> independent clause
>
> We finally decided to get a new set,
>
> dependent clause
>
> although we couldn't really afford it.

Notice that the dependent clause can appear either at the beginning or at the end of a complex sentence.

Forming Compound - Complex Sentences

The most complicated sentence structures combine two (or more) independent clauses and at least one dependent clause. The results are called **compound-complex sentences**:

> dependent clause
>
> Although Jonathan didn't really want the responsibility,
>
> independent clause
>
> his friends persuaded him to run for sheriff,
>
> independent clause
>
> and since his election he has done an excellent job.

EXERCISE 16

Directions: Identify each of the sentences below by writing one of the following terms on the line at the left:

| simple | complex |
| compound | compound-complex |

Example:

_____*complex*_____   The tires on Martin's car squeal whenever he turns a corner.

_____   1. Mrs. Perez bought a new rug for her dining room.

_____   2. Carmine has a large collection of compact discs, but he rarely plays them.

_____ 3. Becky and Raymond often read to their children.

_____ 4. Before the game started, Mr. Wong made popcorn, and Mrs. Wong poured lemonade for everybody.

_____ 5. Adam keeps his money under his mattress, so he doesn't need a bank account.

_____ 6. Because the Levines have a good whole-house fan, they rarely use their air conditioner.

_____ 7. Some cough medicines contain alcohol.

_____ 8. After the Hamiltons bought a four-poster bed, they moved their old bed to the guest room.

_____ 9. Although Harriet likes the comfort of a big car, she drives a subcompact.

_____ 10. The Sesslers watched six movies last week, and Mrs. Sessler hated every one of them.

IDENTIFYING SENTENCE PATTERNS

The number of possible sentences is infinite, but most sentences belong to one of five basic types. Learning to recognize these types will help you to understand how sentences work and to construct better sentences yourself.

Often modifiers of various sorts (mostly adjectives, adverbs, and prepositional phrases) expand the basic sentence patterns and make them more interesting. For example, the following sentence illustrates Pattern A (subject-verb):

The man laughed.

Adding an adjective does not alter the basic pattern:

The *tall* man laughed.

Adding a second adjective does not affect the pattern either:

The tall, *skinny* man laughed.

A prepositional phrase can also appear as a modifier:

The tall, skinny man *in the gray suit* laughed.

And an adverb can modify the verb:

The tall, skinny man in the gray suit laughed *slyly*.

But after all the modifiers have been added, the basic pattern remains the same:

        subject   verb

The tall, skinny *man* in the gray suit *laughed* slyly.

When searching for these patterns in the exercises and in your own sentences, you should remember that subjects and verbs do not occur in prepositional phrases.

Pattern A. Subject-Verb (S-V)

The simplest type of sentence consists of a noun, pronoun or noun phrase serving as the <u>subject</u> followed by a <u>verb</u> standing alone in the predicate. "<u>John</u> <u>ran</u>" is a sentence of this type. Here are some additional examples:

S   V

<u>Alice</u> <u>arrived</u>.

<u>She</u> <u>arrived</u>.

<u>The women</u> <u>arrived</u>.

EXERCISE 17   **Directions:** The sentences below follow Pattern A. Identify the underlined elements in the sentences by using the following code:

S   subject   V   verb

Example:

  _V_   Several people <u>fainted</u> in the stifling heat.

_____ 1. <u>Our neighbor's dog</u> barked all afternoon.

_____ 2. We <u>travel</u> to the Pacific Coast nearly every year.

_____ 3. The speeding car almost <u>crashed</u>.

_____ 4. Our walking group <u>meets</u> at seven o'clock in the morning.

_____ 5. <u>The band</u> played all evening.

_____ 6. After the battle, many of the enemy <u>surrendered</u>.

_____ 7. <u>June</u> speaks at almost every staff meeting.

_____ 8. <u>The opening ceremonies</u> begin with a trumpet fanfare.

_____ 9. Hector and I <u>ride</u> to work together.

_____10. Tiffany <u>hid</u> behind the boxes in the corner of the basement.

Pattern B.
Subject-Verb-
Direct Object
(S-V-DO)

A direct object names the person or thing directly acted on by the action described by the verb. In the S-V-DO pattern, a direct object follows the verb:

S	V	DO
Alice	saw	*Charles.*
Alice	saw	*nobody.*
Alice	saw	*the rabbit.*

EXERCISE 18   **Directions:** Circle the direct objects in the sentences below. The subjects have been underlined once and the verbs twice.

Example:

Bill sharpened (his chisel) before work.

1. Mrs. Fagan cleans the gutters regularly.

2. Jeff easily unlatched the gate.

3. Mr. Petrucelli is refinancing his mortgage.

4. Most runners hit the ground with their heels first.

5. Daniel equipped his car with a motion detector, a trunk switch, a hood lock, and a siren.

6. Almost all home owners carry some insurance.

7. Few companies sell stock directly to the public.

8. Mr. Bancroft makes his own glass-cleaning liquid.

9. Penny burned the leaves in the back yard.

10. By keeping my eyes on the ground, I found forty-five cents last week.

Pattern C.
Subject-Verb-
Direct Object -
Object
Complement
(S-V-DO-OC)

In this pattern a noun or adjective, called an object complement, identifies or describes the direct object.

S	V	DO	OC
Alice	called	Charles	*Professor Miller.*
Alice	called	Charles	*amusing.*

EXERCISE 19   **Directions:** Indicate whether the object complements underlined in the sentences below are nouns or adjectives by using the following code:

N   noun   ADJ   adjective

Example:

ADJ   The storm makes driving underlined{dangerous}.

_____ 1. The new comic books should keep Cindy quiet for a while.

_____ 2. Margo named her daughter <u>Tamara</u>.

_____ 3. The storage compartments make our new car especially <u>convenient</u>.

_____ 4. Jerry considers his health his top <u>priority</u>.

_____ 5. I find jazz played on stereo headphones very <u>exciting</u>.

_____ 6. Being overweight can make high blood pressure <u>worse</u>.

_____ 7. The Cat Fanciers elected Sondra <u>treasurer</u> again.

_____ 8. Bernice called Alicia an <u>idiot</u>.

_____ 9. The judge declared Meredith <u>incompetent</u> to stand trial.

_____10. Your explanation of U.S. Treasury bonds is making me <u>sleepy</u>.

Pattern D. Subject-Verb-Indirect Object-Direct Object (S-V-IO-DO)

An indirect object tells to whom or for whom a direct object is intended. In the S-V-IO-DO pattern the indirect object immediately follows the verb and is followed by the direct object:

S	V	IO	DO
Alice	gave	*Charles*	the rabbit.
Alice	gave	*him*	the rabbit.
Alice	gave	*the professor*	the rabbit.

EXERCISE 20

Directions: In each sentence below circle the indirect object. The direct object has been underlined.

Example:

Kerry gave (Harvey) <u>a tire pressure gauge</u> for Christmas.

1. Colston left Rita <u>all his money</u>.

2. Allen served his sisters <u>jelly sandwiches</u>.

3. The same person asks the trainer <u>questions</u> at the end of each session.

4. Mrs. Fox frequently writes the mayor <u>angry letters</u>.

5. Mrs. Beckford sent her son <u>a large tin of oatmeal cookies</u>.

6. Philip sold Larry <u>his car</u>.

7. Carmen bought Stan <u>a book about how to make home repairs</u>.

8. I brought my sister <u>a basket full of scented soaps</u>.

9. Charlene told her lawyer <u>the truth</u>.

10.   Noel gave Susie <u>a gigantic inflatable dinosaur</u>.

**Pattern E.
Subject-Linking
Verb-Subject
Complement
(S-LV-SC)**

This pattern differs from Pattern B in that here what follows the verb is not a direct object but a word or phrase that renames or describes the subject. This word or phrase is a **subject complement**. The verb in this kind of sentence acts as an equal sign to show that both the subject and the subject complement refer to the same thing:

S   LV   SC

<u>Alice</u> <u>is</u> a child.   (Alice = a child.)

Such a verb is called a linking verb.

An adjective can also be a subject complement. In this pattern, the adjective does not rename the subject but describes it:

S   LV   SC

<u>Alice</u> <u>is</u> happy.

EXERCISE 21   **Directions:** Indicate whether the subject complements underlined in the sentences below are nouns or adjectives by using the following code:

N   noun

ADJ   adjective

Example:

ADJ   Kerosene heaters are not necessarily <u>safe</u>.

_____ 1.   Bran is a good <u>source</u> of fiber.

_____ 2.   The astronomers on the project are too <u>stubborn</u> to change their plans.

_____ 3.   Computer-assisted design is the <u>answer</u> to our company's main problems.

_____ 4.   My record in high school was <u>unremarkable</u>.

_____ 5.   Urban rats are <u>fatter</u> in the winter, when food spoils less easily.

_____ 6.   Linny Martin is an excellent <u>actress</u>.

_____ 7.   Our four-speed fan is fairly <u>noisy</u>.

_____ 8.   Empathy is the <u>ability</u> to share other people's feelings.

_____ 9.   Leo's new car looks <u>expensive</u>.

_____ 10. This software seems <u>adequate</u> for a small home office.

TRY IT OUT

Basic sentence patterns rarely exist in pure forms. In fact, writing becomes more vivid and memorable when the basic patterns are expanded. Look at this S-V-DO sentence:

S   V   DO

Loudspeakers reproduce sounds.

Like all the basic patterns, this one can be expanded through the addition of adjectives, adverbs, and prepositional phrases:

S   V

The best *loudspeakers* accurately *reproduce* very deep bass

DO

sounds even under adverse conditions.

Use the same approach to expand the following basic sentences:

1. Negotiations continue. (S-V)
2. Peg found money. (S-V-DO)
3. A girl sent Dennis a letter. (S-V-IO-DO)
4. The candidate is eager. (S-LV-SC)

MAKING SENTENCES COMPLETE

Occasionally, a series of words that opens with a capital letter and closes with an end mark appears to be a sentence but is missing a vital sentence element. At other times, two complete sentences are incorrectly punctuated as one sentence.

Correcting Sentence Fragments

A series of words punctuated as a sentence but missing a vital element is called a **sentence fragment**. Just as a fragment of a broken dish is only part of the dish, a sentence fragment is only part of a complete sentence.

CORRECTING SENTENCE FRAGMENTS WITH MISSING SUBJECTS

Sometimes what appears to be a complete sentence is missing a subject:

predicate

NOT: Charges no annual fee for a credit card.

Adding a subject corrects the situation:

subject   predicate
The bank around the corner charges no annual fee for a credit card.

An imperative sentence is assumed to have *you* as its subject:

subject   predicate
(you)   Please charge this purchase to Media Enterprises.

EXERCISE 22   **Directions:** Identify the items below by using the following code:

S   complete sentence   F   sentence fragment

Example:

__*S*__   Current interest rates are high.

_____ 1. I want to get rid of the mice without seeing, touching or harming them.

_____ 2. Advised against buying extra rustproofing for the new car.

_____ 3. All smoking in the building will be prohibited after July first.

_____ 4. Each year plants trees near the township's schools.

_____ 5. Karen is saving money to buy an air conditioner.

_____ 6. Gives the user a painful shock.

_____ 7. Did not understand the side effects of the medications that he took.

_____ 8. More than 1,000 acres of crops was lost to flooding in the Trinity Valley.

_____ 9. Requires a pregnant minor to consult her parents before getting an abortion.

_____ 10. Rolls back more than fifty odometers every day.

CORRECTING SENTENCE FRAGMENTS WITH MISSING OR INCOMPLETE VERBS

Sometimes a main verb is missing or incomplete. (Remember, every predicate requires at least one main verb; infinitives and verbals ending in *-ing* do not fulfill this requirement.) The following fragment is missing a main verb:

incomplete verb
NOT: Pat *reading* a book entitled *How to Apply for a Job*.

"Reading a book entitled *How to Apply for a Job*" is not a true predicate because it lacks a main verb. Changing the *-ing* word to a main verb solves the problem:

complete verb
Pat *read* a book entitled *How to Apply for a Job*.

Words ending in *-ing* can be parts of verb phrases that serve as main verbs. In the version below *reading* has become part of a verb phrase:

complete verb

Pat *was reading* a book entitled *How to Apply for a Job*.

EXERCISE 23   **Directions:** Identify each of the items below by using the following code:

S   complete sentence   F   sentence fragment

Example:

___F___   The Fitzgeralds actually installing a fireplace in their bathroom.

_____ 1. The movie begins at three o'clock in the morning.

_____ 2. A plastic hairbrush melting in the heat of the hair dryer.

_____ 3. Precautions to prevent accidental poisoning.

_____ 4. Coastal erosion constantly takes place.

_____ 5. Bob Denison often gets his picture taken with celebrities.

_____ 6. Fire ants commonly swarm on electrical relay switches, causing short circuits in air conditioners.

_____ 7. Cooler, drier air arriving this morning and a shower possible this afternoon.

_____ 8. Storehouses, workshops, and stables unchanged for more than 2,000 years.

_____ 9. A bomb exploding in the newspaper office.

_____10. The three-year-old twins to undergo blood tests.

CORRECTING SENTENCE FRAGMENTS WITH MISSING SUBJECTS AND VERBS

Sometimes both the subject and the verb are missing:

NOT: Many visual aids, such as bar graphs, pie charts, and line graphs.

Naturally, both subject and verb must be supplied in order to turn this type of fragment into a complete sentence:

subject   verb

Dora   *provided* many visual aids, such as bar graphs, pie charts, and line graphs.

EXERCISE 24   **Directions:** Identify each of the items below by using the following code:

S   complete sentence

F   sentence fragment

Example:

F   In the classroom, in stores, on television, and in magazines.

_____ 1. From publications on fuel oil spills to descriptions of the fat content of french fries.

_____ 2. Dropping scissors on the floor can destroy the alignment of the blades.

_____ 3. About oil spills, chemicals in foods, and air pollution.

_____ 4. The pricing structure leads to higher rates.

_____ 5. Just as expensive but half as large.

_____ 6. The dust bag on a small vacuum cleaner must be changed frequently.

_____ 7. Burglars prefer quiet ways of entering a home, such as picking a lock.

_____ 8. Only $3 for the razor, but $25 a year for the blades.

_____ 9. Food cooked on a gas grill tastes the same as food cooked on a charcoal grill.

_____ 10. Directly under a high-voltage power line.

CORRECTING SENTENCE FRAGMENTS THAT ARE DEPENDENT CLAUSES

Dependent clauses cannot stand alone as sentences. After hearing or reading the following dependent clause, you would certainly expect more information:

dependent clause

NOT: Even though Grant bought the chocolate bars for his children.

Supplying the missing independent clause corrects the error:

dependent clause

Even though Grant bought the chocolate bars for his

independent clause

children, *he ate most of them himself.*

EXERCISE 25   **Directions:** Identify the items below by using the following code:

S   complete sentence

F   sentence fragment

Example:

F   Because many young wage earners cannot afford to take vacations.

_____ 1. A person who is so obviously self-disciplined.

_____ 2. If you feel the left wheels of your vehicle lifting, you should steer to the right.

_____ 3. When motorists block the path of emergency vehicles, such as ambulances.

_____ 4. Since Anna forgot to recharge the flashlight.

_____ 5. Once Norman had the package wrapped and labeled, he had to decide which package-delivery service to use.

_____ 6. Although the doughnuts are labeled as "lite," they are hardly a diet food.

_____ 7. Because the state's rural areas did not experience the prosperity of its cities.

_____ 8. Since an accurate count of the population can be taken in the largest country in the world.

_____ 9. Objects that fit in the tube are too small to be sold as toys for children under three.

_____10. I never miss Anselmo's birthday, although most years he has to drop several hints before I remember.

CORRECTING FUSED SENTENCES AND COMMA SPLICES

Another common mistake is to fuse two separate sentences and write them as one sentence. Look at the following example:

> NOT: Henry and Rose are both in their late thirties they decided to pay for their own wedding.

The connection between these ideas is clear in the writer's mind: Henry and Rose are older than most people who get married for the first time. They both have jobs and make good salaries, so they decided not to ask their parents to pay for their wedding. However, running the two thoughts together makes them difficult for the reader to understand.

Adding a comma between the two clauses does not improve matters:

> NOT: Henry and Rose are both in their late thirties, they decided to pay for their own wedding.

A comma by itself cannot be used to connect two independent clauses. Trying to use a comma for this purpose creates an error known as a **comma splice**. Both types of run-on sentences, the **fused sentence** (without a comma) and the comma splice, are equally wrong. Repunctuating the two independent clauses as two separate sentences is correct:

Henry and Rose are both in their late thirties. They decided to pay for their own wedding.

Also, using a semicolon (a stronger mark of punctuation than a comma) between the two clauses helps show how closely the two ideas are connected:

Henry and Rose are both in their late thirties; they decided to pay for their own wedding.

However, connecting the two thoughts with a coordinating conjunction helps more:

Henry and Rose are both in their late thirties, *so* they decided to pay for their own wedding.

And using a subordinating conjunction to show the reader which of the two ideas is the more important is still more helpful:

Since Henry and Rose are both in their late thirties, they decided to pay for their own wedding.

CORRECTING RUN-ON SENTENCES JOINED BY CONJUNCTIVE ADVERBS

Conjunctive adverbs indicate the relationships between ideas, but, unlike coordinating conjunctions, they do not connect one independent clause to another. *Accordingly, however, meanwhile,* and *therefore* are examples of conjunctive adverbs. Look at the following example:

NOT: The Taylors won a new swimming pool, however, no one in the family knew how to swim.

The conjunctive adverb *however* does not connect the two clauses of this sentence as a coordinating conjunction would. A little repunctuating corrects the error:

The Taylors won a new swimming pool; however, no one in the family knew how to swim.

EXERCISE 26   **Directions:** Identify the items below by using the following code:

S   complete sentence

RO   run-on (fused sentence or comma splice)

Example:

RO   Mrs. Evans dreaded being audited, however, she did not have to pay any extra taxes.

_____ 1.   The chocolate chips can be melted in a microwave oven in less than two minutes then the four egg yolks can be added one at a time.

_____ 2.   David's cat cringed at the sight of the can of flea powder, still, she started purring as soon as David finished treating her.

_____ 3. Mountain lions roamed this area long before residents built their homes here.

_____ 4. Shop only once a week, also stick to a preplanned grocery list.

_____ 5. Answering the questionnaire honestly was difficult for Leland.

_____ 6. Children who do not produce enough human growth hormone never grow much taller than three or four feet.

_____ 7. Sarah, a geology major, is learning how to map mountains to determine their geological structure, meanwhile, I'm still struggling with my statistics class.

_____ 8. The township plans to fire its road crew and hire an outside contractor to collect recyclable trash and repair the streets.

_____ 9. Marnie loves scary movies, nevertheless, her boyfriend refuses to watch them.

_____10. Mrs. Zarilli won the Best Boss in the Business contest last year.

CORRECTING RUN-ON SENTENCES WITH PRONOUNS AS SUBJECTS

Pronouns often refer to nouns mentioned in previous sentences. However, the close connection of a noun or pronoun in one sentence and a pronoun in the next is no reason to write the two sentences as one:

NOT: Andy had attended painting classes for only a week,
        he realized that he wasn't destined to be a great artist.

Here, adding a subordinating conjunction solves the problem:

Andy had attended painting classes for only a week *when* he realized that he wasn't destined to be a great artist.

EXERCISE 27 **Directions:** Identify each of the items below by using the following code:

S   complete sentence
RO   run-on (fused sentence or comma splice)

Example:

_S_   Because Anita's stove had a broken dial, she had no idea how hot the oven was.

_____ 1. Revere Truck Service provides fleet maintenance and general service, it specializes in the repair and replacement of engines and transmissions.

_____ 2. Customers deserve full information about the products they buy, this is a basic consumer right.

_____ 3. Drew wanted to use his coupon for a free air freshener, but it had already expired.

_____ 4. Linda called the bank to arrange for a loan, her approval came through in less than two hours.

_____ 5. Before the tent sale we moved furniture from the warehouse into the parking lot, and it was a back-breaking job.

_____ 6. Kimberly put all her wedding pictures in a special album, which she has shown me at least four times.

_____ 7. Your buttermilk biscuits taste superb, they are the best I've ever tasted.

_____ 8. Because Kevin's design for a bookmark won first prize, his picture was in the local paper.

_____ 9. A storm knocked down the hundred-year-old tree in our yard, our insurance did not cover the damage.

_____ 10. Margarine costs less than butter, it contains less saturated fat.

*S*entences can be classified as declarative, interrogative, imperative, and exclamatory.

Each sentence contains a subject and a predicate.

Words can be divided into categories called parts of speech according to the roles they play in sentences.

The parts of speech are nouns, articles, pronouns, verbs, verbals, adjectives, adverbs, conjunctions, prepositions, and interjections.

Phrases are combinations of words that belong together but do not have both subjects and predicates.

Clauses are combinations of words that contain subjects and predicates.

Independent clauses can stand alone as sentences, but dependent clauses cannot.

Different combinations of clauses result in compound, complex, and compound-complex sentences.

The five basic sentence patterns are subject-verb, subject-verb- direct object, subject-verb-direct object-object complement, subject-verb-indirect object-direct object, and subject-linking verb-subject complement.

A sentence fragment is an incomplete sentence, and a run-on sentence is two sentences incorrectly punctuated as a single sentence.

A sentence fragment can be corrected by adding the missing element.

A run-on sentence can be corrected by adding a period and a capital letter, a semicolon or a conjunction.

2

Nouns and Articles

N*ouns are names. They indicate people (George Washington, Dracula), places (New York, Zambia), and objects (table, mountain). They also refer to a variety of abstract ideas (such as* friendship *and* biology).

One way to tell whether a word is a noun is to put the word the *in front of it. If the resulting combination sounds acceptable, the word is a noun. For example,* book *is a noun because the combination "the book" sounds right. On the other hand, the word* asked *is not a noun because the combination "the asked" does not sound right. Although this test is not infallible (for example, it works poorly with names of people and places), if you can make up a sentence in which* the *plus the word makes sense, the word is probably a noun.*

*Nouns appear in sentences as subjects, objects, and complements. Many nouns have both singular and plural forms (*boy *is singular,* boys *plural). Nouns can also be changed slightly to indicate possession, as in the* boy's *cap.*

EXERCISE 1

Directions: Circle the nouns in the sentences below. The number of nouns in each sentence is indicated in parentheses.

Example:

At high altitudes climbers tire easily. (2)

1. The older girls dislike the mushy vegetables in frozen dinners. (3)

2. Shorter campaigns might make voters more interested in politics. (3)

3. Interesting baskets can be made of straw, bark or roots. (4)

4. After a long, lonely winter, the ugly duckling emerged as a beautiful swan. (3)

5. Chicory tastes like coffee but contains no caffeine. (3)

6. For her class Juanita created a gigantic collage that included old shoes, silverware, and clippings from newspapers. (7)

7. Some people who have every pillow fluffed and in its proper place in their rooms never make an effort to organize their closets. (6)

8. Vera's salsa was delicious and contained very few calories. (3)

9. Detectors installed in the wrong places lead to frequent false alarms. (3)

10. Osteoporosis is the abnormal loss of bone. (3)

RECOGNIZING TYPES OF NOUNS

Nouns can be classified in various ways. Usually, these classes contrast with one another. For example, common nouns contrast with proper nouns, concrete nouns with abstract nouns, and count nouns with mass nouns. The same noun can belong to several classes. For example, the word *butterfly* is both a concrete noun and a count noun.

A **common noun** names any, some or all members of a group: *singer, continent,* and *car* are common nouns. Common nouns are not capitalized unless they begin sentences.

A **proper noun** names a specific member of a group: *Janet, Asia*, and *Cadillac* are proper nouns. Proper nouns are always capitalized.

A **concrete noun** names something we can perceive with our senses. That is, if it were present, we could see, hear, touch, taste or smell it. *Table, noise,* and *pineapple* are concrete nouns.

An **abstract noun** names something we cannot perceive with our senses. *Democracy, belief,* and *sadness* are abstract nouns.

A **count noun** names something that can be counted, at least in theory. *Dog* is a count noun because if we came into a room which contained a certain number of dogs, we could find out how many there were by counting them. *Dish, river,* and *star* are other examples of count nouns.

A **mass noun** names something that cannot be counted, even in theory. *Information, music,* and *water* are mass nouns. Mass nouns do not have plurals, and they cannot be used with *a* or *an*.

A **collective noun** names a group considered as a whole. *Team, committee,* and *flock* are collective nouns. Unlike mass nouns, collective nouns can be counted, as in "five teams" and "three committees."

A **compound noun** is a combination of two or more words to form a new word or phrase that functions as a single noun. Proper names are good examples of compound nouns: *George Washington,* for example, refers to a single person even though two nouns are involved. Some compounds are written as one word (*cowboy, mailbox*), some with hyphens (*eye-opener, mother-in-law*), and some as two words (*pogo stick, ice cream*). Dictionaries sometimes vary in their recommendations about how to write compounds.

EXERCISE 2   *Directions:* Identify the types of nouns underlined in the sentences below. Circle the correct answer for each one.

Example:

(count noun)   mass noun   Ethan can operate his new <u>camera</u> with only one hand.

proper noun   common noun   1. The <u>Gray Ranch</u> has been a working cattle ranch since the turn of the century.

proper noun   common noun   2. A baseball commissioner represents the interests of the fans as well as those of the <u>owners</u>.

concrete noun   abstract noun   3. Fay had trouble washing her <u>feet</u> with her soap-on-a-rope.

concrete noun   abstract noun   4. His <u>childhood</u> was ordinary, if a little lonely.

count noun   mass noun   5. Whipped <u>butter</u> contains fewer calories per serving than ordinary butter.

count noun   mass noun   6. Customers are not in the mood to accept major changes in styles of <u>clothing</u>.

concrete noun   mass noun   7. The <u>jacket</u> is long enough to wear as a dress.

collective noun   proper noun   8. At night the <u>Platypus Cafe</u> is almost always deserted.

compound noun   abstract noun   9. Jeanne's <u>earring</u> was found under the dog's dish.

collective noun   count noun   10. Randy installed a dashboard <u>fan</u> that runs on the power from his car's cigarette lighter.

UNDERSTANDING NOUN PHRASES

Often, the role a noun plays in a sentence can also be played by a phrase consisting of a noun and some additional, closely related words. These additional words extend the noun's meaning in various ways. For example, here are three ways the single noun *clowns* could be expanded:

> The clowns (definite article + noun)

> The funny clowns (definite article + adjective + noun)

> The clowns in the circus (definite article + noun + prepositional phrase)

Each of these **noun phrases** might occur in a sentence anywhere the single noun *clowns* might occur. For example, in the following sentence a noun is the subject:

> noun
> *Clowns* are funny.

However, in the sentence below a noun phrase plays the same role:

> noun phrase
> *The clowns in this circus* are funny.

In the following sentence *clowns* is the direct object:

> noun
> Children enjoy *clowns*.

But in the sentence below a noun phrase is the direct object:

> noun phrase
> The children enjoyed *the noisy clowns*.

In another kind of noun phrase one noun modifies another, as in *department store* and *silver dollar*. The first noun in this type of combination is being used as an adjective (see chapter 6). Noun phrases of this type are sometimes categorized as compound nouns.

TRY IT OUT

Using phrases instead of single nouns can make sentences more specific and more interesting. Consider the following sentence:

Chicks were released from a box.

It doesn't say much, does it? Expanding this basic sentence results in sentences like these:

1.   Rare peregrine falcon chicks were released from a nest box.

2.   Rare peregrine falcon chicks were released from an artificial nest box at the top of a twenty-three story office building.

Now, try writing some sentences of your own. Use the nouns in the groups below as the basis for interesting sentences:

1.   store, bread, lunch

2.   rain, window, night

3.   safari, elephant, camera

UNDERSTANDING NOUN CLAUSES

Sometimes an entire clause can act as a noun. (Remember, a clause is a group of related words that includes both a subject and a predicate.) A single noun is the direct object in the following sentence.

Many Americans like *baseball*.

But in the next sentence, which follows the same pattern, a **noun clause** is the direct object:

Many Americans think *that baseball was invented by Abner Doubleday in Cooperstown, NY, in 1839*.

Unlike a noun phrase, a noun clause does not necessarily contain a noun; it just functions as a noun.   Consider the following sentence:

They ate *whatever they could find*.

"Whatever they could find" is a noun clause. It functions as a noun (like the noun *cheese* in the sentence "They ate cheese"), but it does not contain a single noun.

EXERCISE 3   *Directions:* Circle the words that identify the noun phrases and noun clauses underlined in the sentences below.

Example:

noun phrase   (noun clause)   The council proposed <u>that all community residents be required to recycle</u>.

noun phrase   noun clause   1. <u>The glass cover of LeeAnne's electric skillet</u> allowed her to check the bacon without having to lift the lid.

noun phrase   noun clause   2. Truckers complain <u>that many low overpasses are incorrectly marked</u>.

noun phrase   noun clause   3. <u>The space shuttle lift-off</u> was delayed because of a technical problem.

noun phrase   noun clause   4. <u>Thirty-five million soccer balls</u> are manufactured in northern Pakistan each year.

noun phrase   noun clause   5. Early Egyptians believed <u>that scarab beetles were reborn each day at noon,</u> so the scarab became a symbol of eternal life.

noun phrase   noun clause   6. In a test market a company determines <u>how well a new product will sell</u>.

noun phrase   noun clause   7. Our sun may once have had <u>a small, dark companion star</u>.

noun phrase   noun clause   8. <u>Anyone you choose</u> is fine with me.

noun phrase   noun clause   9. In East Falls <u>an old carpet mill</u> was turned into an apartment complex.

noun phrase   noun clause   10. Randy's best friend kept repeating <u>whatever Randy said</u>.

USING NOUNS IN SENTENCES

Nouns can function in sentences as subjects, objects, complements, and appositives.

Nouns as Subjects

In most sentences, a noun or noun phrase functions as the subject. Bear in mind that in grammar books, **subject** means the grammatical subject, not what the sentence seems to be about. Consider the following sentence:

On rainy days the children played checkers.

Here, the grammatical subject is *children* because they are performing the action of the verb *played,* not *checkers* (which is the direct object) or *rainy days* or anything else the sentence seems to be about. An easy way to find the grammatical subject is to ask a question consisting of the phrase "who or what" and the verb. In other words, for this sentence ask the question "Who or what played?" The answer is *children*, the grammatical subject.

The noun or noun phrase serving as a subject usually appears before the verb. The following sentences are in this very common pattern:

noun   verb
Mary   won the race.

noun phrase   verb
The president   resigned.

noun phrase   verb
The quick brown fox   jumped over the lazy dog.

COMPLETE SUBJECTS

A noun phrase functioning as the subject of a verb is called the **complete subject**. In the following sentence the noun phrase "the tall, skinny boy in the yellow cap" is the complete subject of the verb *broke:*

The tall, skinny boy in the yellow cap broke the window.

SIMPLE SUBJECTS

Of all the words in the noun phrase "The tall, skinny boy in the yellow cap," the most important is *boy,* the noun itself. The other words all modify this noun in some way. The noun at the heart of a noun phrase is called the **simple subject**. The simple subject is the one-word answer to the question formed by adding "who or what" to the verb.

The simple subject never appears in a prepositional phrase. Therefore, when looking for a subject, first cross out all the prepositional phrases to make things clearer. This approach would help you locate the subject in the following sentence:

The owner of the car is my brother.

"Of the car" is a prepositional phrase, so it cannot contain the subject. Here is what remains after the prepositional phrase is eliminated:

The owner ~~of the car~~ is my brother.

Now it is much clearer that the subject of this sentence is *owner*. For more about prepositional phrases, see chapter 8.

EXERCISE 4   *Directions:* Underline the nouns used as simple subjects in the sentences below. The verbs have been underlined twice. Crossing out prepositional phrases will help you locate the subjects.

Example:

An unlisted telephone <u>number</u> <u>is</u> more expensive than a number printed in the telephone book.

1. The first step in repairing a broken window <u>is</u> to remove the broken glass.

2   For a ten dollar fee our employees <u>will deliver</u> your groceries to your door.

3. Today more men <u>are studying</u> home economics.

4. The breakup of a long-term relationship <u>can be</u> very painful.

5. After only three weeks of summer Belle already <u>longed</u> for cooler weather.

6. Large numbers of divorced fathers <u>lose</u> contact with their children.

7. Bicycling <u>strengthens</u> leg and hip muscles and <u>makes</u> them more flexible.

8. Many people <u>have transferred</u> old home movies to video tape.

9. Wool <u>wrinkles</u> easily.

10. The first income tax law in the United States <u>was passed</u> to pay for the Civil War.

COMPOUND SUBJECTS

Often the answer to the question formed by asking "who or what" with the verb is more than one person or thing. Look at the following sentence:

                              verb
Olaf and Sarah *live* in Cleveland.

Here, the answer to the question "Who or what live?" is "Olaf and Sarah." This is called a **compound subject**. It contains two nouns, *Olaf* and *Sarah*, which are both the subjects of the verb *live*.

EXERCISE 5   ***Directions:*** Underline the nouns used as compound subjects in the sentences below. The main verbs are underlined twice.
Example:

Fish and chicken are good for people with high cholesterol.

1. Weddings and formal teas are held in the Sundial Herb Garden.

2. Action films and comedies often open during the summer months.

3. Used sports cars and convertibles cost more than used family sedans that were originally just as expensive as the sportier cars.

4. Frozen dinners and baked potatoes can be prepared in toaster ovens.

5. A cupful of pencils and a photograph of Old Faithful sat on Martha's desk.

6. Several old friends and relatives from out of town attended my parents' anniversary dinner.

7. Shanghai and Mexico City rank among the largest cities in the world.

8. Fission and fusion are two ways of releasing atomic energy.

9. Toll-free hotlines and in-person counseling can help people who have become addicted to gambling.

10. Easy pedaling and reliable braking are crucial in a touring bike.

Nouns as Objects

Nouns often function as objects. They may be objects of verbs or of prepositions. Objects of verbs are of two kinds, direct and indirect. **Object complements** provide additional information about direct objects. Like the subjects of sentences, objects of verbs and object complements are never found in prepositional phrases.

NOUNS AS DIRECT OBJECTS

A very common sentence pattern consists of a noun, an action verb, and another noun, in that order:

noun   verb   noun
Elliott   kissed   Olivia.

noun phrase   verb   noun phrase
The captain   sank   the ship.

If a sentence contains only one object, it will always be a direct object. You can locate direct objects by asking a question beginning with the verb and followed by "whom or what?" In the first example, if you ask "Kissed whom or what?" the answer will be *Olivia.* In the second sentence, if you ask "Sank whom or what?" the answer is the *ship. Olivia* and *ship* are therefore direct objects. A traditional definition is that a **direct object** names the person, thing or idea directly acted upon by the action of the verb.

NOUNS AS INDIRECT OBJECTS

Sometimes an action verb is followed by more than one object. Look at the following sentence:

Ricardo bought his little brother an ice cream soda.

Both *brother* and *soda* are objects of the verb *bought.* What Ricardo really bought is an ice cream soda. *Soda* answers the question "Bought whom or what?" so it is the direct object. But he bought the soda *for* his little brother. *Brother* is the indirect object. An **indirect object** can always be changed into a phrase beginning with the prepositions *to* or *for*. To find an indirect object, ask the question "To or for whom or what?"

Compare the following pairs of sentences:

indirect object
The librarian gave   *Bob*   a book.
The librarian gave a book to Bob.

"Gave Bob a book" means the same as "gave a book to Bob." The answer to the question "To or for whom or what?" is "to Bob," so *Bob* is the indirect object in the first sentence.

indirect object
Victor made his   *father*   a cup of coffee.
Victor made a cup of coffee for his father.

The object *father* and the phrase "for his father" mean the same thing. The answer to the question "To or for whom or what?" is *father. Father* is therefore the indirect object in the first sentence of this pair.

When a sentence contains an indirect object and a direct object, the indirect object always comes first.

EXERCISE 6   *Directions*: Identify the types of objects circled in the sentences below. Use the following code:

DO   direct object

IO   indirect object

The verbs are underlined for you.

Example:

DO   Mozart <u>gave</u> his first public performance at the age of six.

_____ 1. Soft music can <u>relieve</u> stress.

_____ 2. Molly <u>told</u> Keith the best way to make watermelon pickles.

_____ 3. Mimi <u>bought</u> her father an Elvis Presley T-shirt.

_____ 4. Last month brush fires <u>destroyed</u> twenty-eight homes in southern California.

_____ 5. Manuel <u>left</u> Bonnie a message.

_____ 6. A roller-skating waitress <u>offered</u> Florence some fried catfish.

_____ 7. A committee of local business people <u>coordinated</u> the Turtle Creek Day festivities.

_____ 8. New federal laws <u>will give</u> middle-class workers some tax relief.

_____ 9. The Bronx Zoo recently <u>opened</u> a baboon exhibit.

_____ 10. A nearby commercial dairy <u>makes</u> mint chocolate chip ice cream.

NOUNS AS OBJECTS OF PREPOSITIONS

In the phrases "to Bob" and "for his father," the words *to* and *for* are prepositions. (For more on prepositions, see chapter 8.) A noun or noun phrase often follows a preposition to form a prepositional phrase. In a prepositional phrase, the noun is called the **object of the preposition**. The preposition is underlined in each of the following phrases:

noun	noun	noun phrase
<u>at</u> *home*	<u>in</u> *bed*	<u>on</u> *the kitchen table*

Prepositional phrases usually function in sentences as adjectives or adverbs.

EXERCISE 7   *Directions:* Circle the nouns used as the objects of the prepositions underlined in the sentences below.

Example:

Kites have been made and flown <u>for</u> 2,000 years.

1. <u>During</u> the night the Whitneys often hear Craig opening the refrigerator door.

2. Midori's favorite book is being made <u>into</u> a movie.

3. A gas station attendant was injured <u>in</u> an attempted robbery last night.

4. <u>On</u> his new album Jackson Bow performs only cheerful love songs.

5. The Winslow Board of Education trimmed 10 percent <u>from</u> the operating budget.

6. To qualify <u>for</u> the low fare you must buy your ticket this week.

7. Michael Lewis was the first player to arrive <u>at</u> training camp.

8. Extra sheets and towels are <u>in</u> the closet.

9. Lew Erwin composed music <u>for</u> silent films.

10. The video camera comes <u>with</u> a leather carrying case.

Nouns as Complements

Complement as a grammatical term means a word (or phrase) that completes the meaning of another word. That is, it clarifies the first word or adds to it in some way. This is indicated by the spelling "compl*E*ment," which suggests the idea "compl*E*te."

NOUNS AS SUBJECT COMPLEMENTS

The following sentence contains a **subject complement**:

subject complement

Greg is the   *chairperson*.

Greg is the subject, which we can verify by asking the question "Who or what is?" (Answer: Greg.) But the verb *is* describes not an action but a condition. It tells not what Greg is doing but what his position on the committee is. This kind of verb is called a linking verb. Linking verbs are followed not by objects but by subject complements, words that provide more information about subjects.

EXERCISE 8　　*Directions:* Circle the nouns that function as simple subjects and subject complements in the sentences below. Then draw an arrow to connect them. The verbs are underlined for you.

Example:

The (workers) on the night shift <u>are</u> all (robots).

1. The sun <u>is</u> the single biggest cause of cancer in the United States.

2. Neil's letters <u>are</u> brief notes jotted down on scrap paper.

3. Uncle Julius <u>was</u> a peculiar man.

4. A common request made by cable television viewers <u>is</u> for more sports programming.

5. Ross eventually <u>became</u> an expert electrician.

6. The antismog regulations in Los Angeles <u>are</u> the toughest environmental rules in the nation.

7. Tara Pederson <u>would be</u> a good choice for team captain.

8. The name of the first bubble gum <u>was</u> Blibber-Blubber.

9. Phyllis <u>is</u> your mother's cousin.

10. At Canyon High School, Rosa's best friends <u>were</u> Toby and Cheryl.

NOUNS AS OBJECT COMPLEMENTS

An object complement follows a direct object and provides additional information that describes or clarifies it. You can find it by asking a question that combines the verb and the direct object with "what?" Look at the following example:

direct object　　　　object complement

She considers her college　*courses*　an excellent　*investment*.

The noun *courses* is the direct object of the verb *considers* ("Considers whom or what?" Answer: courses.) Now if you ask "Considers courses what?" the answer is *investment*—the object complement.

When an object complement appears in a sentence, it always follows the direct object:

direct object　　object complement

We elected　*Vinnie*　*chairperson*.

direct object　　　　object complement

I consider　*Felshia*　my best　*friend*.

EXERCISE 9   *Directions:* Circle the direct objects and the object complements in the sentences below. In each sentence draw an arrow to connect the object to its object complement. The verbs have been underlined for you.

Example:

The class <u>elected</u> Thea president.

1. The team members <u>judged</u> Lori the most improved player.

2. Becky <u>called</u> Norbert her favorite uncle.

3. Sandra <u>found</u> the exercise program an interesting challenge.

4. Houston's opera, ballet, and symphony orchestra <u>make</u> the city an important cultural center.

5. The Acme Company's board of directors <u>named</u> Eileen Mulder vice president in charge of marketing.

6. Stacey <u>considers</u> shopping a waste of time.

7. The organizers of the sales event <u>elected</u> Louis Finney chairperson.

8. Libby <u>named</u> her fish Winifred.

9. Her employees <u>thought</u> Claire a fool.

10. Seventy hours of hard work each week <u>make</u> Alex a successful executive.

Nouns as Appositives

Sometimes a noun or noun phrase immediately follows another noun and renames or identifies the same person or thing. This second noun is an **appositive**. Look at the following example:

noun   appositive
Gordon,   Rick's father, works in a bank.

The noun *Gordon* and the noun phrase *Rick's father* refer to the same person. In fact, this sentence is a shortened version of another sentence:

Gordon, who is Rick's father, works in a bank.

Appositives differ from subject complements and object complements in that appositives can be turned into clauses beginning "who or which is (or are)." An appositive is usually set off from the rest of the sentence by commas, as in the example above. Sometimes, however, a dash or a pair of dashes is used instead, as in this sentence:

My favorite comedians are the Three Stooges—Curly, Moe, and Larry.

When an appositive provides only additional information and is not needed to identify the first noun, it must be marked off from the rest of the sentence either by commas or by dashes. However, sometimes the first noun is unclear without an appositive to help identify the person or thing referred to:

My sister Sharon is the coach.

The noun *Sharon* is an appositive because it helps to identify "My sister" ("My sister who is Sharon"). It is not marked off by commas because without it, it might be impossible to say which of the speaker's sisters is meant.

EXERCISE 10   *Directions:* Circle the complete appositives in the sentences below. Then draw an arrow to connect each appositive to the noun it renames or explains.

Example:

The Zarton telescope, a very expensive instrument, is poorly balanced.

1. The earth, the fifth largest planet, circles the sun at an average distance of 93 million miles.

2. The explosion of the *Hindenburg*, an enormous German dirigible, in 1937 was the first disaster to be documented in photographs.

3. There are more than twenty mountains over 20,000 feet high in the Himalayas, the greatest concentration of high mountains in the world.

4. The geodesic dome, a structure invented by R. Buckminster Fuller, is very light but very strong.

5. Hair conditioners, products intended to make hair easier to manage, work by coating each strand of hair with a thin film.

6. The Holocaust, the destruction of approximately 6 million Jews by the Nazis, lasted from 1933 until 1945.

7. On automobile trips restless children may be interested in Travel Tapes, recordings describing the history and geology of the area through which they are riding.

8. Some people prefer Belgian waffles, big waffles with large, deep indentations, to ordinary waffles.

9. The Armory Show, an art exhibit held in New York in 1913, introduced the people of the United States to modern European art.

10. In 1974 Patricia Hearst, the daughter of publisher Randolph Hearst, was kidnapped by the Symbionese Liberation Army.

FORMING NOUN PLURALS

Nouns can be either singular or plural. That is, they can refer to one thing or to more than one.

Regular Plurals

Changing a noun from its singular form to its plural form is usually simple. The majority of nouns add -*s* to the singular to form the plural, as in the following examples:

boy	boys
table	tables
sorrow	sorrows

Some nouns, however, form the plural by adding -*es* to the singular. Nouns ending in *ch, sh, ss, x,* and *z* form their plurals in this way:

church	churches
dish	dishes
kiss	kisses
box	boxes
waltz	waltzes

EXERCISE 11   *Directions:* Form the plurals of the words below by adding -*s* or   -*es*.

Example: box   *boxes*

1. field
2. tax
3. official
4. princess
5. shoe

6. class
7. topaz
8. newspaper
9. inch
10. crash

An important additional rule concerns nouns ending in *y*. If these nouns end in a consonant followed by a *y*, they form the plural by changing the *y* to *i* and adding -*es*:

company	companies
family	families
story	stories

But if a vowel comes immediately before the final *y*, an *-s* is added, and the *y* is unchanged:

day   days

toy   toys

journey   journeys

EXERCISE 12   *Directions:* Form the plurals of the words below by adding *-s* or by changing *y* to *i* and adding *-es*.
Example: fly *flies*

1. city
2. monkey
3. candy
4. turkey
5. warranty

6. community
7. cherry
8. play
9. destiny
10. ploy

Irregular Plurals

Several categories of nouns have plurals that do not follow these rules. The explanations for irregular plurals are historical: some of the irregular plurals have come down from earlier stages of the English language and others were borrowed from foreign languages. Some nouns, for example, form plurals by changing vowels within the word, as in *foot, feet* and *mouse, mice*. Some make no change at all as in *fish* (singular) and *fish* (plural) or *moose* (singular) and *moose* (plural). Some nouns, such as *scissors* and *trousers*, have no singular forms. Nouns ending in *o* add *-s* or *-es*, as in *solo, solos* but *hero, heroes*.

Nouns borrowed from foreign languages sometimes form regular English plurals, as in *stadium, stadiums*. Some form the same kind of plurals they did in the foreign language, as in *datum, data*. Some nouns have both kinds of plurals; for example, *index* sometimes has its original Latin plural, *indices*, as well as the plural form *indexes*.

Some words that have two acceptable plural forms are listed below:

Words with Two Acceptable Plural Forms

Singular	*Alternative Plurals*
antenna	antennae, antennas
apparatus	apparatus, apparatuses
appendix	appendices, appendixes
beau	beaux, beaus
cargo	cargoes, cargos
criterion	criteria, criterions

curriculum	curricula, curriculums
formula	formulae, formulas
fungus	fungi, funguses
index	indices, indexes
medium	media, mediums
memorandum	memoranda, memorandums
radius	radii, radiuses
scarf	scarfs, scarves
tornado	tornadoes, tornados
vertebra	vertebrae, vertebras
volcano	volcanoes, volcanos
wharf	wharfs, wharves
zero	zeroes, zeros

Occasionally, alternative plural forms of the same word have different meanings. For example, *antennas* are radio and television aerials, but *antennae* are the movable parts found on the heads of insects.

The only sure solution to the problem of forming plurals is to look up doubtful words in the dictionary. However, the following list of common irregular plurals should help:

Common Irregular Plurals

Singular	Plural	Singular	Plural
addendum	addenda	ox	oxen
alumna	alumnae	parenthesis	parentheses
alumnus	alumni	phenomenon	phenomena
analysis	analyses	potato	potatoes
child	children	psychosis	psychoses
crisis	crises	quiz	quizzes
datum	data	self	selves
deer	deer	series	series
elf	elves	sheep	sheep
foot	feet	species	species
goose	geese	stimulus	stimuli
hero	heroes	thief	thieves
leaf	leaves	thesis	theses

life	lives	tomato	tomatoes
loaf	loaves	tooth	teeth
louse	lice	wife	wives
mouse	mice	wolf	wolves
mosquito	mosquitoes	woman	women
oasis	oases	yourself	yourselves

Note that *media* and *data* are both plural forms. *Media* should be used with plural forms of verbs, as in "The mass media have a great deal of influence," but *data* is often treated as a singular noun ("the data is" instead of "the data are").

To form the plural of compound nouns, make the final noun plural unless the first noun is plainly the more important of the two. Here are some examples of plural compound nouns:

> snowballs
>
> handfuls
>
> police officers
>
> insurance policies
>
> *but*
>
> sisters-in-law

EXERCISE 13   Directions: Use a dictionary to find the plurals of the words below.

Example: piano   *pianos*

1. congressman _____
2. nucleus_____
3. cello_____
4. axis_____
5. alga_____

6. cupful _____
7. brother-in-law _____
8. cactus_____
9. bacterium _____
10. sanatorium _____

FORMING POSSESSIVES

The word **case** refers to the forms of nouns and pronouns that indicate their functions in sentences. In English, nouns have only two sets of forms:

one for the **possessive case** and one for all other cases. The possessive case indicates various kinds of possession.

Singular Possessives

Often one noun names a thing that belongs (in some sense) to someone or something. For example, the phrase "the man's hat" is made up of a noun phrase, "the man's," and a noun, *hat*. Here, the hat belongs to the man. Other noun phrases indicating possession follow the same pattern: the second noun belongs to the first one. In these phrases, the first noun is always the one in possessive form—never the second noun. A good way to get this right is to look at the second noun and ask yourself "To whom or what does it belong?" The noun that answers this question must be in the possessive form.

Bear in mind that possession does not necessarily indicate ownership. In "the man's hat" it does. But the noun *man* in "the man's head" is also in possessive form. A man's head belongs to him, of course, but he does not own it in the same way he owns his hat. Or take the phrase "a week's pay." It means "the pay someone earns in a week." Here the pay belongs to the week only in a specialized sense. Other phrases indicating time follow the same pattern:

> this fall's fashions
>
> today's prices
>
> Friday's soccer game

The form of the possessive depends on whether or not the noun naming the possessor ends in *s*. If that noun ends in any letter but *s*, add *'s* to form the possessive:

author	the author's book
city	the city's finances
woman	the woman's job

If the noun already ends in *s*, determine whether it is singular or plural. If a noun that ends in *s* is singular, add *'s*:

James	James's mother
boss	the boss's daughter
class	our class's reunion

Possession can also be indicated by a form using the preposition *of*. The last three possessives above, for example, could be expressed "the mother of James," "the daughter of the boss," and "the reunion of our class." Both ways of expressing the possessive are very common.

EXERCISE 14   *Directions:* Rewrite each phrase below so that it uses an apostrophe to show possession. To change from one form of the possessive to the other, you will need to change the order of the words and to omit some words.

Example: the speed of the printer   *the printer's speed*

1. the preface of the book_____
2. the frame of the mirror _____
3. the hand of Russ _____
4. the wings of the fly _____
5. the depth of the pool _____
6. the hem of the dress _____
7. the capital of Oklahoma _____
8. the beginning of the summer _____
9. the tray of the waitress _____
10. the effects of the sun _____

Plural Possessives

If a noun that ends in *s* is plural, add only an apostrophe to make it possessive.

boys	the boys' books
bosses	the bosses' schedules
ships	the ships' captains

When using a noun that is both plural and possessive, think of the plural form first and the possessive form second. This helps with nouns that end in *y*, such as *company*. Compare these four forms of the word:

the company (singular)

the company's schedule (singular and possessive)

the companies (plural)

the companies' schedule (plural and possessive)

or

the companies' schedules (plural and possessive)

Notice that changing the word *schedule* from singular to plural does not change the form of the possessive. "The companies' schedule" refers to a schedule shared by several companies, but "the companies' schedules" means that the companies have separate schedules.

Remember, only the noun naming the possessor is in the possessive form. To check back, look immediately to the left of the apostrophe—the word to the left of the apostrophe should be the answer to the question "To whom or what does the next noun belong?"

EXERCISE 15   *Directions:* Rewrite each phrase below so that it uses an apostrophe to show possession. To change from one form of the possessive to the other, you will need to change the order of the words and to omit some words.

Example: the length of the skirts   *the skirts' length*

1. the cost of the trucks_____
2. the complaints of the children _____
3. the colors of the carpets _____
4. the salaries of the nurses _____
5. the home of the babies _____
6. the alarm systems of the stores _____
7. the dinners of the mothers-in-law _____
8. the hobbies of the men _____
9. the costumes of the actresses _____
10. the goals of the workers _____

EXERCISE 16   *Directions:* This exercise includes both singular and plural possessives. Rewrite each phrase below so that it uses an apostrophe to show possession. To change from one form of the possessive to the other, you will need to change the order of the words and to omit some words.

   Example: the flavor of the toothpaste   *the toothpaste's flavor*

1. the credit cards of the women _____
2. the birthdays of the girls _____
3. the benefits of the plan _____
4. the backs of the chairs _____
5. the events of the week _____
6. the meetings of the clubs _____
7. the plots of the movies _____
8. the laboratories of the company _____
9. the reunion of the alumni _____
10. the techniques of the managers _____

USING ARTICLES

The words *the* and *a* (with its alternative form *an*) are called **articles**. *The* is the **definite article** and *a* and *an* are the **indefinite articles**. Both kinds of articles introduce nouns, but other words may come between the articles and the nouns they introduce.

Understanding the history of these words can help you decide which article to use. *The* comes from a kind of adjective called a demonstrative, which is used to point things out (*this* and *that* are modern forms of the same word). *A* is related to the number one.

Using the Definite Article

The words *this* and *that* refer to objects that have already been mentioned or that can be pointed to. Similarly, *the* is used when the noun it introduces has already been identified or discussed. *The* is also used to introduce a noun that names something specific. *The* is used in both ways in the following passage:

> When Lucy's parents gave her a new bicycle for her birthday, she seemed very pleased with it. However, an hour later they saw *the* bicycle lying neglected in *the* driveway.

The first *the* refers to the bicycle already mentioned in the previous sentence (and not some other bicycle). The second *the* refers specifically to Lucy's parents' driveway.

Using the Indefinite Article

The indefinite article is related to the number one used in the sense "any one." In other words, *a* or *an* indicates one of a category of things without saying specifically which one. Look at the way *a* is used in the following sentence:

> Lucy's parents saw a bicycle in the driveway.

Here, "a bicycle" refers to any bicycle and is not definite about which one.

A is used before consonant sounds:

> a car
>
> a moose
>
> a zoo

An is used before vowel sounds:

> an apple
> an elephant
> an orator

Use *an* before a word that starts with a vowel sound even though the first letter is a consonant:

> an honest man
> an honor
> an hour

When a word starts with an *h* sound, use *a:*

> a history class.

Use *a*, not *an*, before vowels that sound like consonants:

> a one o'clock appointment (the *o* in *one* sounds like a *w*)
> a university (the *u* in *university* sounds like a *y*)

Making Decisions about Articles

Some general rules can help you choose articles correctly:

A, an, and *the* are used with singular count nouns, such as *answer* and *banana.*

Only *the* can be used with plural count nouns, such as *answers* and *bananas.*

The, but not *a* and *an,* is used with mass nouns: "the air," "the butter."

Normally, no article is used with nouns that refer to all representatives of a class or to ideas expressed in a general way, as in the following examples:

> *People* are funny.

> *Studying* takes *discipline.*

In contrast, when these words refer to specific situations, *the* is used:

> *The people* I work with are funny.

> *The studying* I did last semester took discipline.

While these guidelines should be helpful to you, your greatest aid in determining which article to use is familiarity with the English language. If in doubt, try consulting a large dictionary to see how the articles are used in sample phrases and sentences.

EXERCISE 17   *Directions:* Circle the word that correctly completes each sentence below.

Example:

Clutter can make (a, an) room seem smaller.

1. Beyond the ranch is (a, an) desert that gets only six or seven inches of rain each year.

2. If you're stumped for (a, an) answer in today's crossword puzzle, call 1-800-555-CLUE.

3. A head-on collision between two cars is much less likely to occur than (a, an) off-center collision.

4. Colonel Lurie wore a blue striped shirt and (a, an) yellow polka-dotted tie.

5. By sitting next to (a, an) exit on public transportation, you make it easier for a thief to escape with your belongings.

6. (A, An) kitchen decorated in American Country style is often crowded with baskets, primitive furniture, and other collectibles.

7. Walter stores his extra cash in (a, an) empty cereal box.

8. Sheila always wears (a, an) uniform to work.

9. Each year (a, an) cowbird can lay as many as forty eggs in other birds' nests.

10. It is (a, an) honor to be chosen to attend the convention.

EXERCISE 18   *Directions:* Add *a, an* or *the* where it belongs in each sentence below. Put an X in each space where no article is needed.
Example:

Al is making fifteen dollars _an_ hour at Chambers' Turkey Products.

1. Jill makes it ____ habit to buy clothes on sale.

2. To tell ____ truth, a bank savings account may not be the best place for your money.

3. Helen showed ____ initiative when she decided to start a business of her own.

4. Losing as little as ____ quart of blood can result in shock and unconsciousness.

5. Over____ last 20 years, more than 3 million people have attended the Country Dinner Playhouse.

6. Major changes have taken place in ____ financial services industry.

7. Dr. Richards predicts ____ extinction of the whooping crane.

8. Most people believe that ____ liberty is very precious.

9. Taking a hot bath is____ good way to relax.

10. Lower programming costs raised the net income reported by ____ major television networks this week.

*N*ouns name people, objects, and ideas.

Nouns can be categorized as common nouns, proper nouns, concrete nouns, abstract nouns, count nouns, mass nouns, collective nouns, and compound nouns.

Noun phrases are made up of nouns and the words that describe them.

Noun clauses are groups of words that include subjects and predicates and that function in sentences as nouns.

A sentence's subject can be located by answering a question made up of "Who or what?" with the sentence's verb.

A complete subject consists of a simple subject and its modifiers.

A compound subject includes more than one noun.

Nouns can function as direct objects, indirect objects, and objects of prepositions.

Nouns can also function as subject complements and as object complements.

Appositives are nouns or noun phrases that immediately follow other nouns and rename or identify them.

Most nouns form their plurals by adding -s. The plural of a word ending in ch, sh, ss, x *or* z *is formed by adding -es.*

The plural of a noun ending in y *is formed by changing the* y *to* i *and adding -es unless a vowel precedes the* y, *when only -s is added.*

The possessive of a singular noun is formed by adding an apostrophe and an s; *the possessive of a plural noun is formed by adding an apostrophe except when the plural noun does not end in* s, *when both an apostrophe and an* s *are added.*

The *(the definite article) and* a *and* an *(the indefinite articles) introduce nouns.*

A is used before consonant sounds and an *before vowel sounds.*

3

Pronouns

Most *pronouns replace nouns in sentences. Sometimes pronouns are used instead of nouns to avoid awkward repetition:*

       noun   *pronoun*
    Bullets *are pointed at one end so that* they *can be fired accurately.*

The noun Bullets *and the pronoun* they *refer to the same things. The pronoun is used in this sentence because repeating the noun, as in "Bullets are pointed at one end so that bullets can be fired accurately," would sound clumsy.*

Other pronouns, such as someone *and* anything, *are not used in place of specific nouns. However, they function in sentences in most of the same ways that nouns do — as subjects and objects, for example. Still other pronouns, such as* this *and* that, *point out people, things, and ideas.*

A pronoun often forms part of a **contraction** *(a combination of two words in which an apostrophe marks the place of an omitted letter or letters). "I'll" (I will) and "you're" (you are) are examples of contractions.*

Some pronouns have different forms to indicate differences in person, number, gender, and case:

Person is the distinction between the speaker (first person), the person or people spoken to (second person), and the person or people spoken about (third person). The pronouns *I* and *we* are first person pronouns, the pronoun *you* is a second person pronoun, and the pronouns *he, she, it,* and *they* are third person pronouns.

Number is the classification of words according to whether they refer to one person or thing or to more than one. The pronouns *I, he, she,* and *it* refer only to a single person or thing and are singular. The pronouns *we* and *they* refer only to more than one person or thing and are plural. The pronoun *you* can be either singular or plural.

Gender is the classification of pronouns (and of a few nouns, such as *man* and *woman* or *rooster* and *hen*) according to whether they refer to males or females. The pronoun *he* refers only to a male person or animal, so it is **masculine**. *She* refers only to a female, so it is **feminine**. A few inanimate objects, such as ships, are sometimes regarded as having female gender.

It refers to an inanimate object or to an animal of which the sex is either unknown or is regarded as unimportant. *It* is neuter in gender. A word that is **neuter** is neither masculine nor feminine.

Case is the classification of pronouns and nouns according to whether they are subjects or objects or show possession. For example, *we* is in the **subject case**, meaning it is used as a subject. *Us* is in the **object case**, meaning it is used as the object of a verb or preposition. *Our* is in the **possessive case**, meaning it is used to show possession.

EXERCISE 1   **Directions:** Underline the pronouns in the sentences below. The number of pronouns in each sentence is indicated in parentheses.

Example:

> Some people will not speak up until <u>they</u> are sure of <u>their</u> views. (2)

1. Would you like me to check the expiration date on your last golf magazine? (3)

2. Somebody forgot to tell Sebastian to deflate the hot air balloon at the end of the show. (1)

3. I face Jamie in the tennis match tomorrow, and I am not at all sure I will be able to beat her. (4)

4. Young snakes may shed their skins as many as fourteen times in one year. (1)

5. This is my best friend, Yolanda. (2)

6. I'd like to see the people I used to work with, but I don't really expect anyone at the office to remember me. (5)

7. Because the giraffe's head is shaped like a camel's and its spots resemble a leopard's, it was once known as a camelopard. (2)

8. Although Kit denied being a famous movie actress, nobody believed her. (2)

9. In a desk drawer Duncan found an old photograph of Eddie playing his guitar. (1)

10. Although the woman's skeleton is more than 120 years old, researchers know that she suffered from arthritis. (1)

RECOGNIZING TYPES OF PRONOUNS

Pronouns are classified into six categories. They can be personal, reflexive, relative, interrogative, demonstrative or indefinite.

Personal Pronouns

Personal pronouns refer to specific people or things. They have different forms to indicate differences in person, number, gender, and case, as can be seen in the following list:

Singular Personal Pronouns

	first person	*second person*	*third person*
subject case:	I	you	he (male)
			she (female)
			it (neuter)
object case:	me	you	him (male)
			her (female)
			it (neuter)
possessive case:	my, mine	your, yours	his (male)
			her (female)
			hers (female)
			its (neuter)

Plural Personal Pronouns

	first person	*second person*	*third person*
subject case:	we	you	they
object case:	us	you	them
possessive case:	our, ours	your, yours	their, theirs

EXERCISE 2   **Directions:** Underline the personal pronouns in the sentences below. The number of pronouns in each sentence is indicated in parentheses.
Example:

Maynard resembles <u>his</u> five first cousins on <u>his</u> father's side. (2)

1. A relief pitcher is allowed eight warmup pitches when he enters a game. (1)

2. Bennett wishes his tropical fish were more affectionate toward him. (2)

3. The average wind speed in Great Falls, Montana, is 13.1 miles per hour, making it the windiest city in the United States. (1)

4. Because safes are insulated, they protect valuables from fires as well as from thieves. (1)

5. "Rubber baby buggy bumpers" is my favorite tongue twister. (1)

6. Groucho Marx said, "I never forget a face, but in your case I'll make an exception." (3)

7. Craig's money problems began when he got eight credit cards during his senior year in college. (2)

8. Smiling excitedly, Jane and Alison brought their mother her new kimono. (2)

9. Wilma dislikes realistic movies, preferring fantasies that help her escape from the problems she faces every day. (2)

10. As O. Henry was dying, he said, "Turn up the lights. I don't want to go home in the dark." (2)

Reflexive Pronouns

The following chart lists the **reflexive pronouns**:

	singular	*plural*
first person:	myself	ourselves
second person:	yourself	yourselves
third person:	himself, herself	themselves
	itself, oneself	

This is a complete list; such forms as *hisself, ourself, theirself,* and *theirselves* are not acceptable.

A reflexive pronoun is used when the action of a verb is directed back upon itself. This happens when the same person or thing is both the subject and object of a single verb:

subject   direct object
Marcy hurt *herself* sliding into the pool.

The subject of the verb *hurt* (*Marcy*) and its direct object (*herself*) refer to the same person. *Herself* is a reflexive pronoun. A reflexive pronoun is an object pronoun that reflects the subject just as a mirror reflects a person who looks into it. In other words, a reflexive pronoun is used as an object when the subject both performs the action of the verb and is acted upon.

Reflexive pronouns should not be used as the subjects of sentences:

NOT: Gloria and *myself* enjoy traveling.

Instead, use a personal pronoun in the subject case:

Gloria and *I* enjoy traveling.

REFLEXIVE PRONOUNS IN PREPOSITIONAL PHRASES

A reflexive pronoun can occur in a prepositional phrase when it refers to a person or thing mentioned earlier in the sentence:

The baby walked across the room *by herself*.

Never send Alvaro to buy Christmas gifts because he always buys nicer things *for himself* than for the people on the list.

However, when the pronoun in the prepositional phrase does not refer to a person or thing mentioned earlier, a reflexive pronoun is not acceptable:

NOT: These beach towels are for Carla and *myself*.

Here a personal object pronoun is correct:

These beach towels are for Carla and *me*.

REFLEXIVE PRONOUNS USED AS INTENSIVES

Reflexive pronouns are also used as intensives. An **intensive pronoun** emphasizes or intensifies a noun or pronoun in the same sentence. When reflexive pronouns are used as intensives, they provide no new information; they merely call attention to the noun or pronoun to which they refer. Consider the following sentence:

Mrs. Welch took the curtains down *herself*, but she couldn't see well enough to put them back up again.

The pronoun *herself* refers to Mrs. Welch and stresses the idea that she and no one else took the curtains down. Omitting the reflexive pronoun would not change the meaning of the sentence; it would merely place less emphasis on the idea that Mrs. Welch performed the action without help.

RECIPROCAL PRONOUNS

Closely related to reflexive pronouns are the **reciprocals** *each other* and *one another*. Reciprocals express shared feelings or actions:

Elliott and Olivia love *each other*.

The neighbors depended on *one another* when times were hard.

EXERCISE 3   **Directions:**

1. Identify the underlined words in the sentences below as correct or not correct by using the following code:

C   correct   N   not correct

2. For each incorrect item, write the correct pronoun on the space at the end of the sentence.

Example:

_*N*_   Kelly and <u>myself</u> like the arms and armor collection better than any other part of the museum. ___/___

_____ 1.   The Ivanovs had planned to go to the wedding reception with us, but they ended up going by <u>themself</u>. _____

_____ 2.   William F. Cody called <u>himself</u> Buffalo Bill. _____

_____ 3.   The questionnaires are for Marshall and <u>myself</u>. _____

_____ 4.   Sheila cut <u>herself</u> when she opened the package of brownies. _____

_____ 5.   You advanced students can do the problems <u>yourself</u> and then check the answers in the back of the book. _____

_____ 6.   Steven and Hope blame <u>theirself</u> for causing the fight between their parents. _____

_____ 7.   Doing a job <u>yourself</u> is the only way you can ensure that it gets done right. _____

_____ 8.   Curtis changed the oil <u>hisself</u>. _____

_____ 9.   Sandra and Joan washed <u>themselves</u> thoroughly after coming in from the garden. _____

_____ 10.   The cat lets <u>itself</u> in and out through the little swinging door in the kitchen. _____

Relative Pronouns

A **relative pronoun** incorporates one kind of dependent clause, called a **relative clause**, into a sentence. A relative pronoun always introduces a relative clause. Relative clauses can function in sentences as adjectives or nouns.

If the relative clause functions as an adjective, the relative pronoun links the clause to a noun or pronoun in the main sentence. Look at the relative clause in the following sentence:

relative clause

Four out of five women *who shop for bathing suits* give up without buying a suit.

This complex sentence consists of a main clause, "Four out of five women give up without buying a suit," and a relative clause, "who shop for bathing suits." The pronoun *who* refers to the noun *women* in the main clause. The relative pronoun *who* is also the subject of *shop*, the verb in the relative clause. The entire relative clause functions as an adjective describing *women*.

This is a list of the relative pronouns:

who (whom — object case, whose — possessive case)
whoever (whomever — object case)
that
which
what
whatever
whichever

Who and *whoever* (along with their object and possessive forms *whom, whose*, and *whomever*) refer only to people. *That* is used for both people and things. However, in writing it is almost always better to use *who* for people and *that* for things. A sentence such as "The boy that came in is my brother" is not wrong, but "The boy who came in is my brother" is preferable. *Which* refers to things, not to people. (For information on how to decide between *which* and *that*, see chapter 7.)

What, whatever, and *whichever* also refer to things. When it is used as a relative pronoun, *what* means "that which" ("I got that which I needed out of the deal"):

I got *what* I needed out of the deal.

Whatever means "anything or everything that" ("Let them take anything or everything that they want"):

Let them take *whatever* they want.

Whichever means "any one out of a group that" ("Choose any one out of the group that appeals to you"):

Choose *whichever* appeals to you.

Sometimes a relative pronoun can be omitted without changing the meaning of a sentence:

The car (that) I want to buy is parked out front.

Interrogative Pronouns

Interrogative pronouns are used to ask questions:

Who was that masked man?
What are you looking for?

Which of your new shirts will you wear to the party?

Except for *that*, which is a relative pronoun but not an interrogative one, interrogative pronouns and relative pronouns are identical in form.

Demonstrative Pronouns

There are four **demonstrative pronouns**: *this, that, these,* and *those*. They point out people and things. When people who are talking face-to-face use demonstrative pronouns, they can literally point to the people or things they are talking about:

> *This* is my friend Max.

> I want *that*.

The demonstrative pronouns *this* (singular) and *these* (plural) refer to people and things nearby. The demonstrative pronouns *that* (singular) and *those* (plural) refer to people and things farther away.

In writing, demonstrative pronouns commonly refer to things or ideas mentioned in previous sentences:

> The cat got up on the table and started eating the turkey. *That* [the event mentioned in the previous sentence] made our whole family angry.

Demonstrative pronouns can also appear before things or ideas and help to introduce them:

> *These* are the main things wrong with the house: a leaky roof, a broken staircase, and a flooded basement.

All four of the demonstrative pronouns can also be used as adjectives, as in "these magazines" and "this proposal." *That* can also function as a relative pronoun:

> Mata liked the tie *that* I wore.

Indefinite Pronouns

Indefinite pronouns refer to unspecified people or things. They include words that end in *-body, -one,* and *-thing*:

> Is *anybody* there?

> *Someone* is responsible for this, and I'd like to know who it is.

> Is *everything* all right?

The indefinite pronouns are mostly singular. That is, they are used with singular verbs and are referred to by singular pronouns, as in the following sentence:

> Today, *everyone* pays for his or her own lunch.

Everyone is a singular indefinite pronoun. It is the subject of the verb *pays*, which must be singular to agree with its subject. The pronouns *his* and *her* refer back to *everyone* and must be singular also.

Other examples of indefinite pronouns are *another, each, few,* and *some*. For more information on which indefinite pronouns are singular and which are plural, see "Making Indefinite Pronouns Agree in Number" later in this chapter.

EXERCISE 4   **Directions:** Identify the underlined pronouns in the sentences below by using the following code:

I   interrogative pronoun   IND   indefinite pronoun
D   demonstrative pronoun   R   relative pronoun

Example:

___/___   <u>What</u> is a scrim?

_____ 1.   <u>These</u> are the parts of a dart: the point, the barrel, the shaft, and the flight.

_____ 2.   Many people oppose the new dictator, but <u>some</u> do not.

_____ 3.   <u>Which</u> of the children want to learn to play the kazoo?

_____ 4.   The teeth in the front of your mouth are incisors, and <u>those</u> at the back are sometimes called wisdom teeth.

_____ 5.   Does <u>anybody</u> believe that Marilyn Monroe is still alive?

_____ 6.   Lou Gehrig was the first major league baseball player <u>whose</u> number was retired.

_____ 7.   <u>This</u> is the coldest day of the year so far.

_____ 8.   <u>Who</u> were Pruneface, Mumbles, Itchy, Flattop, and the Rodent?

_____ 9.   Bards, <u>who</u> were poet-minstrels, once had considerable religious and political power in Wales, Scotland, and Ireland.

_____10.   One letter that does not appear on telephone dials in the United States is Q, and <u>another</u> is Z.

UNDERSTANDING PRONOUN CASE

Personal, relative, and interrogative pronouns can be classified as subject, object, and possessive case pronouns.

Choosing between the Subject Case and Object Case

I, you, he, she, it, we, and *they* are the personal pronouns that can be used as the subjects of verbs. They are therefore in the subject case:

He said "Hi" to her. *She* smiled and said, "Hello."

Me, you, him, her, it, us, and *them* are the personal pronouns that can be used as direct and indirect objects of verbs and as objects of prepositions. They are therefore in the object case. In the following sentence, *her* is the direct object of the verb see:

The doctor can *see her* now.

In this sentence, *me* is the indirect object of the verb told:

He *told me* the truth.

And in the sentence below, *us* is the object of the preposition *with*:

The children want to go with *us*.

The pronouns *you* and *it* can be either subjects or objects:

subject
Don't *you* remember me?

object
I remember *you*.

subject
It was clear and cold last night.

object
I lost my wallet, but Hugh found *it* for me.

CHOOSING THE RIGHT CASE FOR RELATIVE PRONOUNS

Who is one of the relative pronouns used as subjects in relative clauses:

The woman *who* was here left a message for Martha.

This sentence consists of a main clause, "The woman left a message for Martha," and a relative clause, "who was here." The pronoun *who* in the relative clause refers to the noun *woman* in the main clause. *Who* is the subject of the verb *was*, so it is in the subject case.

Whoever means "anyone that." Like *who*, it is used when a relative clause begins with its subject:

Please ask *whoever* is in the corridor to come in and help us move this desk.

Note that the case of a relative pronoun is determined by its role in the relative clause. Here, *whoever* is the subject of *is*. The entire relative clause is the object of the verb *ask*. The function of the whole clause in the sentence does not affect the case of the relative pronoun.

Whom is one of the relative pronouns used when relative clauses begin with objects:

The man *whom* I saw didn't leave any messages.

This sentence consists of a main clause, "The man didn't leave any messages," and a relative clause, "whom I saw." The entire relative clause refers to the noun *man*, which is the subject of the main clause. *Whom* is the object of the verb *saw* within the relative clause. (The pronoun *I* is the subject of *saw* — "I saw whom.")

Whom is also used as the object of a preposition:

The man to *whom* I gave the money has disappeared.

Whomever is the object form of *whoever* ("anyone that"). Like *whom*, *whomever* is used when a relative clause begins with an object:

Go into the corridor and ask *whomever* you see to come in and help us move this desk.

The relative pronouns *which, that, what, whichever,* and *whatever* can be either subjects or objects:

subject of a relative clause: The book *which* is on the table is mine.
object of a relative clause: The book *which* you wanted is on the table.

CHOOSING THE RIGHT CASE FOR INTERROGATIVE PRONOUNS

The interrogative pronouns *who* and *whoever* are in the subject case in the following questions because they are the subjects of verbs:

subject
Who wants to come?

subject
Whoever can be telephoning at this time of night?

Whom and *whomever* are used when questions begin with their objects:

object   subject
Whom did *you* see at the meeting last night?

object   subject
Whomever can *he* be telephoning at this time of night?

These interrogative pronouns are also used as objects of prepositions:

To *whom* did you deliver the message?

EXERCISE 5   **Directions:** Circle the word that correctly completes each sentence below.

Example:

The three characters (who, whom) share a hearty breakfast in the first scene of the play are at each other's throats in the last act.

1. (Who, Whom) argues that certain kinds of objects now in European and American museums should be returned to the countries from which they originally came?

2. (Whoever, Whomever) spilled the grape juice on the kitchen floor should clean it up immediately.

3.   The shiny covering of a spacesuit reflects heat away from an astronaut, for (who, whom) intense heat could otherwise be very dangerous.

4.   The note taped to the front door began, "To (whoever, whomever) it may concern."

5.   A person (who, whom) has made many insurance claims is likely to face an increase in his or her insurance rates.

6.   From (who, whom) did you get that impression?

7.   As far as I'm concerned, you can go to the races with (whoever, whomever) you choose.

8.   The people (who, whom) live near the airport have complained for years about the noise and air pollution caused by jets.

9.   (Whoever, Whomever) wants these old magazines can have them.

10. To (who, whom) do you wish to send these roses, sir?

Using the Possessive Case

The personal pronouns *my, mine, your, yours, his, her, hers, its, our, ours, their,* and *theirs* indicate possession. Notice that none of these possessive pronouns includes an apostrophe. They are exceptions to the general rule which requires apostrophes in words that show possession:

This is *Jim's* car.

When a sentence contains a pronoun in the possessive case rather than a noun, no apostrophe is used:

This is *his* car.

Forms such as *your's* or *yours', his', her's* or *hers', our's* or *ours', its'* and *their's* or *theirs'* are not acceptable.

CHOOSING THE RIGHT POSSESSIVE PRONOUN

Whether to use *my* or *mine, your* or *yours, her* or *hers, our* or *ours,* and *their* or *theirs* is determined by whether or not the possessive pronoun is followed by a noun naming the thing possessed. The possessive pronouns *my, your, her, its, our,* and *their* are immediately followed by nouns. The possessive pronouns *mine, yours, hers, ours,* and *theirs* are not followed by nouns. The possessive pronoun *his* is used with or without a following noun. Compare the following sentences:

That's *my* dog.

That dog is *mine*.

In the first sentence, the noun *dog* immediately follows the possessive pronoun. In the second sentence, the pronoun is not followed by a noun but refers to the noun *dog* mentioned earlier in the sentence.

EXERCISE 6   **Directions:**

1. Identify the underlined pronouns in the sentences below as correct or not correct by using the following code:

   C correct   N not correct

2. For each incorrect item write the correct pronoun on the space at the end of the sentence.

Example:

C   Is this clarinet <u>yours</u>? _____

_____1. Mary Lee picked up my briefcase, and now I'm stuck with <u>her's</u>. _____

_____2. Our neighbors' lawns are always better kept than <u>our's</u>. _____

_____3. Gene always has trouble understanding <u>his</u> telephone bill. _____

_____4. I wish I could find dress shoes as attractive and comfortable as <u>your's</u>. _____

_____5. Lauren told me that the idea for the new advertising campaign was <u>hers</u>. _____

_____6. Our telephone is made of white plastic, and <u>theirs'</u> is made of brass and polished wood. _____

_____7. I told the eye doctor that I was seeing lines and spots dancing across <u>my</u> field of vision. _____

_____8. Stuart has spent <u>his'</u> life on the road, moving from city to city. _____

_____9. Because the state faces a huge deficit, programs and jobs may be cut, including <u>ours</u>. _____

_____10. Please tell the people in the copying department that these folders are <u>theirs'</u>, not mine. _____

CHOOSING BETWEEN CONTRACTIONS AND POSSESSIVE PRONOUNS

Whose is a relative pronoun in the possessive case:

The man *whose* cap is on the chair will be back shortly.

This sentence consists of a main clause, "The man will be back shortly," and a relative clause, "whose cap is on the chair." *Whose* refers to the noun *man*, and it also indicates possession. *Cap* is the subject of the verb *is* in the relative clause.

When *whose* is used as an interrogative pronoun, it also indicates possession:

Whose cap is that?

Who's means "who is":

Who's the new bus driver?

A few possessive pronouns resemble contractions of subject pronouns and verbs. The following list compares possessive pronouns in the left-hand column and contractions easily confused with them on the right:

Possessive Pronouns	Contractions
its	it's
their	they're
whose	who's
your	you're

To avoid confusion, remember that contractions are combinations of two words: *it's* stands for *it is*, *they're* for *they are*, *who's* for *who is* or *who has*, and *you're* for *you are*. When in doubt, expand the contraction to see if the sentence makes sense.

Look at the following sentence:

The dog lost (its, it's) bone.

To see which word is correct, try expanding the contraction:

NOT: The dog lost *it is* bone.

If expanding the contraction results in a nonsensical sentence, then the possessive pronoun is correct:

The dog lost *its* bone.

EXERCISE 7

Directions: Circle the word that correctly completes each sentence below.

Example:

I wish (your, you're) kitchen scale were easier to read.

1.   (Whose, Who's) children are playing ball in the street?

2.   I think too many people are talking on car telephones while (their, they're) driving.

3.   (Its, It's) not too late to go out for some fast food hamburgers.

4.   Despite the increasing number of random killings, most murder victims still know (their, they're) attackers.

5. An internal combustion engine derives (its, it's) power from igniting a mixture of air and fuel.

6. Do you know why (your, you're) teeth are so sensitive to heat and cold?

7. Mr. Neft wants to know (whose, who's) car is parked in the vice president's parking space.

8. Skiers must get off chairlifts while (their, they're) still moving.

9. (Whose, Who's) responsible for making our hotel reservations?

10. (Your, You're) one of the best dancers I've ever seen.

Choosing Pronouns Linked by And

Sometimes either a noun and a pronoun or two pronouns are the subjects, objects or complements of the same verb. When this occurs, the pronoun or pronouns must be chosen carefully:

> subjects
>
> Both *he and I* are eligible for the award.

In this sentence, both pronouns are the subjects of the verb *are*, so they are both in the subject case.

> objects
>
> Dad told *Helen and me* to get the fishing tackle.

In this sentence, both the noun *Helen* and the pronoun *me* are objects of the verb *told*. Therefore, the pronoun is in the object case. When a pronoun is the object of a preposition, it is also in the object case:

> preposition   objects of *for*
>
> The new orders were a pleasant surprise *for   Al and me*.

Choosing between We and Us Before Nouns

Sometimes the pronouns *we* and *us* stand immediately before nouns that refer to the same people as the pronouns do. Which pronoun to choose depends on whether it functions in the sentence as a subject or an object:

> subject
>
> *We* youngsters admired our grandmother very much.

In this sentence, the pronoun *we* is immediately followed by the noun *youngsters*, which is an appositive. (An appositive immediately follows a noun or nounlike element and renames or identifies the same person or thing.) *We* is the subject of the verb *admired*, so it is in the subject case.

Us is used when the pronoun is an object of a verb or preposition:

> object
>
> Grandmother told *us* youngsters always to tell the truth.

In this sentence the pronoun *us* is the indirect object of the verb *told* and therefore must be in the object case. You can determine which form of the pronoun to use in this type of sentence by temporarily eliminating the noun:

We ~~youngsters~~ admired our grandmother very much.

Grandmother told us ~~youngsters~~ always to tell the truth.

Choosing Pronouns after Than *or* As

Sometimes a sentence compares one person with another, using the words *than* or *as* to express the comparison. The second of the two people being compared is often referred to by a pronoun. In such sentences, subject pronouns are used when expanding the sentences would make the pronouns subjects:

Shane is taller *than I* (am).

Elizabeth is not as rich *as he* (is).

In some sentences object pronouns are correct after *than* or *as*:

Jane likes Richard more *than me*.

Here the expanded sentence would be "Jane likes Richard more than (she likes) me." However, the subject pronoun would be correct if the writer's meaning is "Jane likes Richard more than I (do)."

EXERCISE 8

Directions: Circle the word that correctly completes each sentence below.

Example:

Eric plays the piano as well as (I), me).

1. "I hope you'll stop in to visit Nancy and (I, me)," said Mr. Berkowitz.

2. Disabled Vietnam veterans spearheaded a drive for equal rights that has benefited all of (us, we) disabled people.

3. Tim says Tiffany is not older than (he, him).

4. (Us, We) baby-sitters can experience baby-sitter burnout after a few years of caring for children.

5. Misty's father asked (her, she) and (I, me) to wait on the steps.

6. Self-portraits by young children can reveal to (us, we) parents emotions that the children may not yet be able to express in any other way.

7. Mrs. Grailish chose Lloyd rather than Martha because she likes Lloyd better than (her, she).

8. (He, Him) and Kathleen are dissatisfied with the way their company evaluates employees' performance.

9. (Us, We) dog lovers were impressed by Jim's willingness to carry his seventy-pound dog up and down the stairs every day.

10. Daniel said his mother sent a box of fudge to Sam and (he, him).

UNDERSTANDING ANTECEDENTS

The word a pronoun refers to is the pronoun's **antecedent**. In the following sentences, the pronouns and their antecedents are italicized.

antecedent   pronoun
Cheryl said   *she* was not responsible for scratching the car.

antecedent   pronoun
The *boys* want to make *their* own breakfast.

Pronouns that have antecedents must agree with them in gender and number. That is, masculine pronouns must refer to nouns naming males, and feminine pronouns must refer to nouns naming females. Likewise, singular pronouns must refer to singular nouns and plural pronouns to plural nouns.

EXERCISE 9   **Directions:** In the sentences below underline the pronouns and circle their antecedents. Then draw an arrow from each pronoun to its antecedent or antecedents.

Example:

Andy and Celeste have spent hundreds of hours restoring their old house.

1. Abrasive cleansers clean well, but they are also likely to scratch the surfaces of pots and pans.

2. Nancy says she plans to spend the whole day reorganizing her closets.

3. The aim of a home fire extinguisher is to cover a burning object with a substance that prevents oxygen from reaching it.

4. Do teenagers want their parents to understand them?

5. Joshua wrote his first autobiography when he was nine years old.

6. Several old friends called Keith to congratulate him after his letter was published in Sunday's newspaper.

7. Claudia uses a rearview mirror clipped onto her bicycle helmet.

8.   Paul thinks the parrot understands what it says to him.

9.   Gwendolyn told Dionysios she disapproved of his working.

10.   Mrs. Wilkowski asked her assistants to present their proposals at the staff meeting Tuesday.

Supplying Missing Antecedents

Sometimes a pronoun appears to have a proper antecedent. However, a closer look reveals that there is really no noun in the sentence to which the pronoun can logically refer. The sentence therefore needs to be revised to provide an antecedent for the pronoun:

NOT: Barbara is interested in geology, but she doesn't

pronoun
want to become *one*.

The antecedent of the pronoun *one* is strongly implied "Barbara doesn't want to become *a geologist*." In conversation, this sentence would probably cause no problem, but in writing, the situation must be clarified. The easiest way to do this is to replace the pronoun with a noun:

Barbara is interested in geology, but she doesn't want

noun
to become a *geologist*.

Making Vague Antecedents Specific

Sometimes a pronoun is used very casually, as if the writer expects his or her readers to decide for themselves what its antecedent might be. The pronoun *they* is often abused in this way:

NOT: If *they* made cashing checks easier for customers at this store, I would shop here more often.

Some person or group of people is responsible for the store's check-cashing policy. However, the pronoun *they* is vague. Replacing it with a specific noun solves the problem:

If *the management* made cashing checks easier for customers at this store, I would shop here more often.

Clarifying Ambiguous and Unclear Antecedents

Occasionally a reader cannot decide which of two or more nouns is a pronoun's antecedent:

pronoun
NOT: Heidi and Sylvia went out to lunch to celebrate *her* promotion.

From this sentence alone, there is no way to tell who was promoted, Heidi or Sylvia. Once again, replacing the pronoun with a noun clarifies the situation:

noun
Heidi and Sylvia went out to lunch to celebrate *Heidi's* promotion.

Sometimes a reader must choose among several possible antecedents of a pronoun. The pronouns *it, they, this, that, these, those,* and *which* are often misused in this way:

> NOT: Some frozen meat pies contain spongy cubes of
> restructured meat, soft vegetables, and too much salt;
> *this* makes them a poor choice for health-conscious buyers.

A reader could probably guess that the pronoun *this* refers to "too much salt" and that the rest of the meat pies' contents are merely unappetizing rather than unhealthy. But rewriting the sentence makes it much clearer:

> Some frozen meat pies contain spongy cubes of restructured meat
> and soft vegetables; in addition, their high salt content makes them
> a poor choice for health-conscious buyers.

Clarifying Remote Pronouns

A pronoun may be so far from its antecedent that the sentence becomes unclear:

> NOT: Corn is one of the crops from which ethanol, a high-octane
> fuel, can be made, *which* is a renewable resource.

The pronoun *which* refers to *Corn*, which is indeed a renewable resource. But the sentence is difficult to read because too many words come between the pronoun and its antecedent. Revision clarifies matters:

> Corn, which is a renewable resource, is one of the crops from which
> ethanol, a high-octane fuel, can be made.

EXERCISE 10

Directions: Identify the sentences below as clear or unclear by using the following code:

C   clear   U   unclear

Example:

U
My cousin, who keeps track of fashion trends, says they are wearing shorter skirts this fall.

_____ 1. As always, if an offer sounds too good to be true, it probably is.

_____ 2. When little Miss Muffet ate her curds, she was eating something similar to cottage cheese.

_____ 3. Maureen uses a memory typewriter-printer, a computer, a laser printer, and a multiple-function telephone, which has created some confusion.

_____ 4. Doreen is using a toothbrush to clean the grout between the bathroom tiles, but it is old.

_____ 5. Bees collect nectar and use it as food.

_____ 6.   Harry and Rich will always remember his birthday celebration.

_____ 7.   If the coiled wire inside a regular light bulb were spread out, it would be about two feet long.

_____ 8.   Victor's mother wants him to go into nursing, but he doesn't want to become one.

_____ 9.   Tailors recommend that suit pants for men be just long enough so that their socks don't show when they walk.

_____ 10.   A quarter-pound burger weighs less than a quarter pound after it has been cooked.

MAKING PRONOUNS AGREE IN NUMBER

If a pronoun's antecedent is singular, the pronoun must be singular as well. If the antecedent is plural, the pronoun must be plural. When pronouns and antecedents correspond in this way, they are said to be in **agreement**.

Making Personal Pronouns Agree in Number

Sometimes a writer is distracted by words that come between a pronoun and its antecedent. The result may be an agreement error, as in the following sentence:

          antecedent   pronoun

NOT: Some American *movies* make more money abroad than *it* does in the United States.

Since the antecedent *movies* is plural, the pronoun must be plural also. When revising to eliminate an error of this sort, be sure to change all the words that need to be changed:

          antecedent   pronoun

Some American *movies* make more money abroad than *they*

verb

do in the United States.

Notice that changing the pronoun to *they* requires a change in the verb from *does* to *do*.

EXERCISE 11   **Directions:**

1. Classify the underlined pronouns in the sentences below as correct or not correct, using the following code:

    C   correct   N   not correct

2. For each incorrect item, write the correct pronoun on the line at the end of the sentence.

Example:

_N_   If blast furnaces are allowed to cool, *it* can crack.__*they*__

_____ 1. Are teenagers less healthy today than *their* parents were as teenagers?_____

_____ 2. A small amount of water in an outboard motor's ignition system can prevent *them* from starting. _____

_____ 3. Many people dislike the Susan B. Anthony dollar because *it* seems too much like a quarter. _____

_____ 4. The tail portion of a plane gives *them* stability. _____

_____ 5. In some African countries the way a woman's hair is braided tells whether or not *she* is married. _____

_____ 6. Tinted car windows reduce sun glare but *it* can decrease visibility at night. _____

_____ 7. Before World War I most Americans did not brush *their* teeth. _____

_____ 8. Air conditioners are useful to allergy sufferers because *it* can remove pollen from the air. _____

_____ 9. If you put mulch around your trees, you don't need to mow as close to *them*. _____

_____10. A horse's fetlock is on the back of *their* leg, above the hoof. _____

Making Indefinite Pronouns Agree in Number

Some indefinite pronouns are always singular. Others are always plural. Still others are sometimes singular and sometimes plural, depending on how they are used. The following sentence contains an agreement error:

NOT: Tell *everybody* not to forget *their* tickets.

A correct version of this sentence is "Tell everybody not to forget his or her ticket." Two pronouns separated by *or* are still singular, so *his* and *her* now agree with their singular antecedent, *everybody*.

If you are unsure of whether a pronoun is singular or plural, check to see whether a singular or plural verb is correct with it. For example, using *everybody* as the subject of a plural verb will convince you that it is a singular pronoun:

NOT: *Everybody agree* that Joseph did the right thing in returning the money.

This sentence should be "Everybody agrees that Joseph did the right thing in returning the money." Like *everybody*, all other pronouns ending in *-body*, *-one* or *-thing* are always singular.

The following chart contains the most common indefinite pronouns and indicates whether they are always singular, always plural or sometimes singular and sometimes plural:

Indefinite Pronouns

always singular

anybody	everybody	nobody	somebody
anyone	everyone	no one	someone
anything	everything	nothing	something
another	each	either	neither
one			

always plural

both	few	many	others
several			

either singular or plural

all	any	more	most
none*	some		

None is occasionally treated as plural, but it is usually regarded as singular.

Compare the following sentences, each of which begins with an indefinite pronoun:

> *Each* of the girls tucked *her* pants into *her* socks to protect against ticks.

> *Both* of the girls tucked *their* pants into *their* socks to protect against ticks.

Notice that all the pronouns in the first sentence are singular but that all the pronouns in the second sentence are plural.

All, any, more, most, and *some* are singular when used with mass nouns and plural when used with count nouns:

mass	singular
noun	verb

All the *sugar*   *is* needed for the cake recipe.

count   plural

noun   verb

All my *friends* *are* going to the movies.

Note that indefinite pronouns that are always plural or sometimes plural can function in sentences as adjectives:

adjective

All the money is in the safe.

adjective

Few people carry large amounts of cash.

These words are pronouns only when they do not immediately precede nouns.

EXERCISE 12   **Directions:** Classify the underlined pronouns in the sentences below by using the following code:

C   correct   N   not correct

Example:

_N_   Luckily, everybody remembered <u>their</u> individual identification number.

_____ 1.   Each of the women will take <u>her</u> own car in to get it inspected.

_____ 2.   Someone left <u>their</u> notebook in the conference room.

_____ 3.   Both of the boys lost <u>his</u> mittens.

_____ 4.   No one has finished <u>his or her</u> holiday shopping yet.

_____ 5.   Both Raymond and Edgar will help with the move, and either of them could drive <u>his</u> own truck.

_____ 6.   When anyone becomes president of the bank, <u>they</u> must promise not to enter politics for at least five years.

_____ 7.   Does anybody have <u>his or her</u> copy of the contract?

_____ 8.   Everyone should floss <u>their</u> teeth for three to five minutes a day.

_____ 9.   Although the party invitation had suggested wearing old clothes, no one wore less than <u>their</u> best.

_____10.   One of the men puts <u>his</u> lunch out on the windowsill every day to keep it cool.

Using Collective Nouns as Antecedents

When the antecedent of a pronoun is a collective noun, the pronoun is usually singular. Collective nouns, such as *audience, class,* and *family,* usually refer to groups as a whole. Using a singular pronoun to refer to a collective noun emphasizes the unity of the group:

collective   pronoun
noun

After three days of deliberation, the *jury* reached *its* verdict.

On the other hand, when a writer wants to emphasize that the people who make up the group are acting individually, a plural pronoun is used:

collective
noun   pronoun

After the trial was over, the *jury* went back to *their* jobs and families.

However, many writers would be more comfortable changing the antecedent to "the members of the jury" to avoid referring to a collective noun by a plural pronoun:

plural
noun

After the trial was over the *members* of the jury went

plural
pronoun

back to *their* jobs and families.

Understanding Antecedents Joined by Or or Nor

When a singular antecedent and a plural antecedent are linked by *or* or *nor,* the pronoun that refers to them should agree with the closer of the two antecedents:

antecedent   antecedent

Today, either the *governor* or *the state senators* will eat

pronoun
their lunches in the cafeteria with the high school students.

The pronoun *their* is plural because the closer of the two antecedents, *senators,* is plural. If the order of the antecedents were reversed, the pronoun would be singular to agree with the nearer antecedent:

antecedent   antecedent

Today, either *the state senators* or the *governor* will eat

pronoun
her lunch in the cafeteria with the high school students.

Since this sounds somewhat awkward, probably most writers would prefer the first version.

A singular pronoun is used when two singular antecedents are linked by *either . . . or* or *neither . . . nor*:

Either Constance or Lucinda left *her* coffee cup in the lounge.

Neither my brother nor my cousin has saved any of *his* old baseball cards.

EXERCISE 13   **Directions:**   Circle the word that correctly completes each sentence below.

Example:

The choir gives (its, their) concert on the third Sunday in May.

1.   The fire company held (its, their) election of officers last week.

2.   Either Jo or Marta gives (her, their) oral report today.

3.   The commission planning the redevelopment of the waterfront presents (its, their) proposal to the mayor next week.

4.   Either the cat or its kittens left (its, their) toy mouse in the middle of the living room.

5.   A group of park workers use (its, their) own cars to patrol the park at night.

6.   The U.S. Army Band presents (its, their) free concert on the lawn of the Whitman Stafford farmhouse Friday at 7:30 p.m.

7.   Neither Rebecca nor Kit will tell us how much (she, they) weighs.

8.   The jazz dance group has (its, their) rehearsal every Thursday.

9.   The afternoon kindergarten class meets (its, their) new teacher for the first time today.

10.   Either Ozzie or Brad left (his, their) gym bag in the locker room.

MAKING PRONOUNS AGREE IN GENDER

Ordinarily, gender agreement causes few problems. Male antecedents are referred to by masculine pronouns, female antecedents by feminine pronouns, and neuter antecedents by neuter pronouns. But using only masculine or only feminine pronouns to refer to antecedents that in real life may be either male or female should be avoided in order not to imply that only men or only women are qualified to do certain jobs or fill certain positions:

> antecedent
>
> NOT: A *doctor* must always put *his* patients' welfare before *his* own convenience.

This sentence implies that only men become doctors.

> antecedent
>
> NOT: Any *president* who wants to be reelected must maintain *his* popularity during *his* first term in office.

This sentence suggests that only men are eligible to be elected president. One way to avoid sexist language is to use two singular pronouns, *he or she, him or her* or *his or hers*, instead of a single masculine pronoun:

> antecedent
>
> A *doctor* must always put *his or her* patients' welfare before *his or her* own convenience.

Because this seems wordy, it is better to rewrite the sentence in the plural:

> antecedent
>
> *Doctors* must always put *their* patients' welfare before *their* own convenience.

When a sentence is rewritten in the plural, not only pronouns and their antecedents but also other words may need to be changed as well:

> *Presidents* who *want* to be reelected must maintain *their* popularity during *their* first *terms* in office.

EXERCISE 14   **Directions:** Eliminate the sexist language from the sentences below by making the singular pronouns plural. Make any other necessary changes in the sentences as well.

Example:

> A builder who includes a daycare center in his commercial development will attract tenants.
>
> *Builders who include daycare centers in*
>
> *their commercial developments will attract tenants.*

1. A hiker should be especially alert when he is in bear country.

_____

_____

2. A district manager should be sure that he is detail oriented and prudent.

_____

_____

3. Self-employment can give a parent some flexibility while she is raising her children.

_____

_____

4. A doctor uses a small hammer to check his patients' reflexes.

_____

_____

5. When a player spikes a volleyball, he hits it sharply downward.

_____

_____

6. A financial planner may earn his living from commissions on the products he sells.

_____

_____

7. With a light meter a photographer can accurately determine the correct setting for his camera.

_____

_____

8. A rider sits more nearly upright on an all-terrain bicycle than he does on an ordinary racing bike.

_____

_____

9. The balloons a cartoonist draws for characters' thoughts differ from those he uses for dialogue.

_____

_____

10. A company director should recognize that free fitness programs can reduce his company's medical costs.

_____

_____

AVOIDING ILLOGICAL PRONOUN SHIFTS

If a writer begins a sentence or a longer passage in the first person, he or she should not switch into the second or third person without a good reason. Similarly, a writer beginning in the second or third person should not suddenly switch into one of the other persons. Switching without a specific purpose can be confusing:

> NOT: When *people* eat lunch with Sally, *you* usually end up talking about sports.

Readers may wonder why the writer begins in the third person with *people* and then switches into the second person by using the pronoun *you*. Revising sentences to eliminate sudden switches in person helps to keep readers' minds where they belong, on what the sentences are communicating:

> antecedent   pronoun
>
> When *people* eat lunch with Sally, *they* usually end up talking about sports.

EXERCISE 15 **Directions:**

1. Classify the sentences below by using the following code:

   C   correct   N   not correct

2. Correct each incorrect sentence on the lines provided. Make all necessary changes in the sentences.

Example:

_N_   If motorists get the results of crash tests before buying new cars, you may be happier with the car you buy.

____ *If motorists get the results of crash tests before buying* ____

____ *new cars, they may be happier with the cars they buy.* ____

____ 1.   To keep your computer running during a blackout, you need a reliable backup power supply.

_____

_____

_____ 2. The stress I feel when I have to fly somewhere on business usually gives me a migraine headache.

_____

_____

_____ 3. If someone is removing an old muffler, you may also have to remove the pipes on either side of it.

_____

_____

_____ 4. A painter should use a tack cloth to clean a surface you are about to paint.

_____

_____

_____ 5. Although you will see moose-crossing signs in Maine, you will not necessarily see any moose.

_____

_____

_____ 6. When people bag grass clippings, your lawn will look better, but there may be no good way to dispose of the clippings.

_____

_____

_____ 7. Muscle cramps, which are sudden, involuntary muscle contractions, can occur while people are exercising or even while they are sleeping.

_____

_____

_____ 8. In a joint checking account, nothing prevents one owner from emptying the account without telling you.

_____

_____

_____ 9.   Some people have to learn to accept responsibility for their mistakes rather than blame other people for them.

_____

_____

_____ 10.   People who maintain proper tire pressure help their tires last longer and improve their cars' fuel economy.

_____

_____

TRY IT OUT

How well do you use pronouns? One way to find out is to analyze some of your writing to see whether you've provided antecedents for the pronouns that need them.

Choose something you have written that is at least one page long. Underline the following pronouns wherever you find them: *he*, *him*, *his*, *she*, *her*, *it*, *they*, *them*, *their*, *this*, *that*, *these*, and *those*. Circle the antecedent of each pronoun, and draw an arrow connecting the pronoun with its antecedent. Check to make sure each pair of words agrees in number and gender. In the sample paragraph that follows, the underlined pronouns agree with their antecedents:

> The air seems to be empty. However, it contains countless molecules of gasses and water vapor along with larger particles, such as pollen grains, ice crystals, dust, and pollutants. The molecules and particles give the sky its color. They intercept and scatter blue light waves from the sun but allow the longer red and yellow waves to pass through the atmosphere. As a result, the sky is blue.

If you find few pronouns in your writing, consider adding some. Using the right pronouns can help you avoid unnecessary repetition of nouns. Pronouns can also provide smooth, logical links between ideas.

Most pronouns replace nouns in sentences.

Some pronouns have different forms to indicate differences in person, number, gender, and case.

Pronouns can be classified as personal, reflexive, relative, interrogative, demonstrative, and indefinite.

Personal pronouns in the subject case are used as subjects, and personal pronouns in the object case are used as objects of verbs and prepositions. Personal pronouns in the possessive case show ownership or some other kind of possession.

Who *and* whoever *are used as subjects, and* whom *and* whomever *are used as objects of verbs and prepositions.*

Personal pronouns do not use apostrophes to show possession.

To choose between a contraction and a pronoun in the possessive case, write out the contraction in full and check to see that it makes sense in your sentence.

The word a pronoun refers to is its antecedent.

Missing antecedents should be provided; vague, ambiguous, unclear, and remote antecedents should be clarified.

Pronouns should agree with their antecedents in number and gender.

Most indefinite pronouns are singular.

Collective nouns are usually referred to by singular pronouns.

When antecedents are joined by or *or* nor, *a pronoun that refers to them agrees with the closer of the two antecedents.*

Sexist pronoun use can be avoided by using paired masculine and feminine singular pronouns or by rewriting whole sentences to make them plural.

Illogical shifts from one person to another should be avoided.

4

Verbs

V*erbs name actions (both physical and mental) and conditions. Verbs that name actions describe how things happen:*

> *The horse* jumps *over the fence.*
> *I* think *about you every day.*

Verbs that name conditions describe how things are or appear to be:

> *Phyllis* is *a police officer.*
> *Owen* seems *intelligent.*

Because many verbs describe actions, the verb is the liveliest of all the parts of speech. Choosing your verbs carefully will help make your writing vivid and energetic.

UNDERSTANDING VERB TENSES

Verbs are listed in dictionaries under **basic forms,** such as *walk*. Changes in the basic forms indicate whether an action or a condition described by a verb occurs in present, past or future time. Most verbs indicate that an action occurred in the past by adding the ending *-ed: walk* (present), *walked* (past). However, many verbs indicate past time by making other changes: *is* (present), *was* (past).

The term **tense** refers to whether a verb is describing an action or a condition in past, present or future time. For example, the verbs *walk* and *is* are in the **present tense**, which means they describe actions or conditions that are taking place now. *Walked* and *was* are in the **past tense**, which means they describe actions or conditions that took place before now.

Many verbs are straightforward. Given the basic forms of these verbs, called **regular verbs,** all the other forms are predictable. For example, the basic form *walk* can be combined with the personal pronouns *I, you* (singular and plural), *we*, and *they* to make statements in the present tense ("I walk," "You walk"). With singular nouns and with the pronouns *he, she*, and *it*, an -*s* is added to the basic form ("The ghost walks," "She walks," "It walks"). To make statements in the past tense, -*ed* is added to a regular verb with any subject ("We walked home from the library yesterday").

Irregular verbs, such as *sing* and *think*, do not follow the standard patterns that regular verbs follow. Irregular verb forms such as *sang, sung*, and *thought* must be memorized.

EXERCISE 1   **Directions:** Identify the tense of the underlined regular verbs in the sentences below. Use the following code:

         PRES   present tense   PAST   past tense

Example:

PRES   The architect's lamp <u>swivels</u> in a 360 degree arc.

_____ 1.   The skydivers <u>joined</u> hands before their parachutes opened.

_____ 2.   Silvio <u>shaves</u> at night in order to save time in the morning before he goes to work.

_____ 3.   Many members of Congress <u>support</u> funding for science but oppose it for the arts.

_____ 4.   The Griffiths family <u>immigrated</u> to the United States from the Netherlands in 1916.

_____ 5.   Hugo often <u>misplaces</u> his portable telephone.

_____ 6.   Our township <u>started</u> a plastics recycling program.

_____ 7.   Flood waters <u>menace</u> the small towns along the Ohio River.

_____ 8.   Kip <u>stopped</u> construction of his new house when Civil War burials were discovered on his property.

_____ 9.   Wally's sunglasses <u>protect</u> his eyes from every angle.

_____10.   Joel <u>attended</u> a soccer camp during the second week of August.

UNDERSTANDING PERSON AND NUMBER

Basic verb forms such as *jump* and *be* do no more than name actions or conditions. Often, however, the basic forms of the verbs are changed to indicate who or what is performing the actions or is being described:

He *jumps*.

The trucks *were* new.

The changes that are made to show who or what is performing an action are matters of person and number.

Person

Person is the term for the distinction between the speaker, the person or people spoken to, and the person or people spoken about. People often speak or write about themselves: "*I eat* cottage cheese for lunch every day." Verbs used with first person pronouns (*I* and *we*) are in the first person. At other times, people speak or write directly to each other: "*You eat* a lot of cottage cheese too, don't you?" Verbs used with second person pronouns (*you*, both singular and plural) are in the second person. People also frequently speak or write about someone else entirely: "*Clara eats* more cottage cheese than the two of us put together." Verbs used with nouns and with third person pronouns (*he, she, it* and *they*) are in the third person.

Number

A verb's subject may name one person or thing *(Clara, the corporation)* or more than one *(friends, skateboards)*. The difference between one and more than one is called **number**. Verbs used with one person or thing are singular in number; those used with more than one are plural. Here is the verb *walk* in the present tense for all three persons, both singular and plural:

	singular	*plural*
first person:	I walk	we walk
second person:	you (singular) walk	you (plural) walk
third person:	he, she or it walks	they walk

EXERCISE 2

Directions: In the columns at the left circle the codes that identify the person and number of the underlined verbs in the sentences below. Use the following code:

1 first person   S singular

2 second person   P plural

3 third person

Example:

1 2 ③ S Ⓟ   Submarines <u>move</u> easily both in and under water.

Person	Number	
1 2 3	S P	1. Whirlpool jets <u>circulate</u> the water in the Boyds' bathtub.
1 2 3	S P	2. We <u>filled</u> the washtub with hot water.
1 2 3	S P	3. Judy <u>spattered</u> paint on her shoes.
1 2 3	S P	4. I <u>dropped</u> the pickle fork down the garbage disposal.
1 2 3	S P	5. You children <u>ate</u> all the Halloween candy.
1 2 3	S P	6. An octopus <u>has</u> three hearts.
1 2 3	S P	7. Sandi, you <u>left</u> your books on the floor.
1 2 3	S P	8. I <u>escaped</u> through the emergency exit at the top of the elevator.
1 2 3	S P	9. Recent design changes at the Belle County Rest Home <u>make</u> life easier for the patients.
1 2 3	S P	10. We <u>wore</u> our matching blue sweaters with the red reindeer on them.

FORMING THE PRINCIPAL PARTS OF VERBS

The **principal parts** of a verb are the basic form, the past tense form, and the past participle. The **past participle** is the form that follows the verb *have* in phrases such as *have walked*. For most verbs, the past participle is identical with the past tense (the basic form plus the ending *-ed*). To test your knowledge of the principal parts of a verb, try filling in the blanks in the following sentences:

I want to _____. (basic form)

Yesterday I _____. (past tense)

I have _____. (past participle)

For *walk*, the correct answers are as follows:

I want to *walk*. (basic form)

Yesterday I *walked*. (past tense)

I have *walked*. (past participle)

Knowing the basic form of a regular verb, such as *walk*, makes it easy to create the past tense (by adding *-ed*) and the past participle (also by adding *-ed*). Most verbs follow the pattern of *walk*. However, English also has well over a hundred common irregular verbs. For irregular verbs, such as *come* and *sing*, knowing the principal parts is essential.

The following chart should help you remember these irregular verbs. By using the chart for a verb such as *arise* you can determine the past tense ("Several unforseen consequences *arose* from the change in the software") and the past participle ("New problems with the software have *arisen* this week").

Common Irregular Verbs

Basic Form	Past Tense	Past Participle
arise	arose	arisen
awake	awoke	awaked or awoken
be	was, were	been
bear	bore	borne or born
beat	beat	beaten or beat
become	became	become
begin	began	begun
bend	bent	bent
bid (command)	bade or bid	bidden or bid
bind	bound	bound
bite	bit	bitten or bit
bleed	bled	bled
blow	blew	blown
break	broke	broken
breed	bred	bred
bring	brought	brought
broadcast	broadcast	broadcast
build	built	built
burn	burned or burnt	burned or burnt
burst	burst	burst
buy	bought	bought
cast	cast	cast
catch	caught	caught
choose	chose	chosen
cling	clung	clung

come	came	come
cost	cost	cost
creep	crept	crept
cut	cut	cut
deal	dealt	dealt
dig	dug	dug
dive	dived or dove	dived
do	did	done
draw	drew	drawn
dream	dreamed or dreamt	dreamed or dreamt
drink	drank	drunk or drank
drive	drove	driven
eat	ate	eaten
fall	fell	fallen
feed	fed	fed
feel	felt	felt
fight	fought	fought
find	found	found
flee	fled	fled
fling	flung	flung
fly	flew	flown
forbid	forbade or forbad	forbidden or forbid
forget	forgot	forgotten or forgot
forgive	forgave	forgiven
freeze	froze	frozen
get	got	gotten or got
give	gave	given
go	went	gone
grind	ground	ground
grow	grew	grown
hang (suspend)	hung	hung

(Note that *hang*, meaning "execute," is regular.)

have	had	had
hear	heard	heard
hide	hid	hidden or hid

hit	hit	hit
hold	held	held
hurt	hurt	hurt
keep	kept	kept
kneel	kneeled or knelt	kneeled or knelt
know	knew	known
lay (put)	laid	laid
lead	led	led
leave	left	left
lend	lent	lent
let	let	let
lie (recline)	lay	lain

(Note that *lie*, meaning "tell an untruth," is regular.)

light	lighted or lit	lighted or lit
lose	lost	lost
make	made	made
mean	meant	meant
meet	met	met
mow	mowed	mowed or mown
pay	paid	paid
prove	proved	proved or proven
quit	quit	quit
read	read	read
rid	rid	rid
ride	rode	ridden
ring	rang	rung
rise	rose	risen
run	ran	run
say	said	said
see	saw	seen
seek	sought	sought
sell	sold	sold
send	sent	sent
set	set	set
shake	shook	shaken

shed	shed	shed
shine (glow)	shone	shone

(Note that *shine*, meaning "polish," is regular.)

shoot	shot	shot
show	showed	shown or showed
shrink	shrank or shrunk	shrunk or shrunken
shut	shut	shut
sing	sang or sung	sung
sink	sank or sunk	sunk
sit	sat	sat
slay	slew	slain
sleep	slept	slept
slide	slid	slid
sling	slung	slung
slink	slunk	slunk
speak	spoke	spoken
spend	spent	spent
spin	spun	spun
spit	spit or spat	spit or spat
split	split	split
spread	spread	spread
spring	sprang or sprung	sprung
stand	stood	stood
steal	stole	stolen
stick	stuck	stuck
sting	stung	stung
stink	stank or stunk	stunk
strike	struck	struck
string	strung	strung
swear	swore	sworn
sweep	swept	swept
swim	swam	swum
swing	swung	swung
take	took	taken
teach	taught	taught

tear	tore	torn
tell	told	told
think	thought	thought
throw	threw	thrown
thrust	thrust	thrust
understand	understood	understood
wake	woke	woken
wear	wore	worn
weave	wove or weaved	woven or weaved
weep	wept	wept
win	won	won
wind	wound	wound
wring	wrung	wrung
write	wrote	written

EXERCISE 3   **Directions:** On the lines at the left write the correct forms of the verbs in parentheses.

Example:

_____*lost*_____   I (lose) another umbrella last week.

_____1.   In 1830 William Huskisson (become) the first person to be run over by a railroad train.

_____2.   All day yesterday Melinda (keep) checking to be sure the pilot light on the stove hadn't gone out.

_____3.   Since Mrs. Weston (get) her food processor, few foods in her kitchen have escaped being sliced, shredded or pureed.

_____4.   After the spider had (spin) a bridge between two supports, it (spin) an orb-shaped web beneath it.

_____5.   Marla (weep) with joy when her son was found.

_____6.   When he was in the sixth grade, Alden (build) a cardboard model of a castle, complete with a moat.

_____7.   Tom and Alexis have (meet) with the judge in his chambers.

_____ 8. While Noel (eat) cotton candy, Jenny (ride) up and down on a pink carousel horse.

_____ 9. Megan had (wear) a green strapless gown to the prom.

_____ 10. Yesterday I (arise) at eight, but my brother had (arise) earlier.

RECOGNIZING TYPES OF VERBS

Verbs can be classified according to the ways they function with subjects, objects, and other verbs. A good dictionary, in addition to providing information about how to spell verbs and about what they mean, also tells whether they are transitive, intransitive, linking or auxiliary verbs. Your dictionary may use abbreviations for this information, such as v.t. to identify a transitive verb.

Transitive Verbs   **Transitive verbs** require direct objects to complete their meanings. They describe actions rather than conditions. If you create a question by adding "Whom?" or "What?" to an action verb and find the answer in the same sentence, the verb is transitive. Take the following sentence, for example:

> verb
> Laura *bought* a thirty-two gallon trash can.

The answer to the question "Bought what?" is "a thirty-two gallon trash can." *Bought* is therefore a transitive verb.

EXERCISE 4   **Directions:** Underline the transitive verbs in the sentences below.

Example:

Rosalee's leather nail bag <u>has</u> eight pockets for tools and nails.

1. Christopher always leaves old newspapers and magazines on the kitchen table.

2. Opossums, Tasmanian devils, bandicoots, and echidnas all have pouches.

3. Amy's three grandchildren visited her last month.

4. Lead poisoning caused the fall of the Roman Empire.

5. Last summer the Animal Rights League rescued a beached whale.

6. More than 700,000 people attend the music festival each year.

7. Mrs. Lang hides her credit cards in a money belt under her clothes.

8. Dennis bought a sheepskin cover for his bicycle seat.

9. The Schaeffers keep a pot of coffee on the stove all day.

10. Charlotte spent $3,000 on new wood floors for her house.

Intransitive Verbs

Intransitive verbs are verbs that describe actions but are not followed by direct objects or complements. The answer to a question created by adding "Whom?" or "What?" to an intransitive verb cannot be found in the same sentence. However, intransitive verbs are often followed by prepositional phrases, as in the following sentence:

> verb
>
> Nat and Lynne *walk* to the office every day, regardless of the weather.

The answer to the question "Walk what?" cannot be found in this sentence. (They may walk two miles to the office every day, but the sentence itself does not provide this information.) The prepositional phrase *to the office* answers the question "Walk where?" which shows it is functioning as an adverb. Remember, direct objects can never be found in prepositional phrases.

Some verbs are always transitive, and some are always intransitive. Many verbs, however, can be either transitive or intransitive, depending on how they are used:

> My grandfather *began* a new life at Ellis Island.

> For my grandfather, a new life *began* at Ellis Island.

The two sentences mean almost the same thing. In the first one, however, the verb *began* is transitive ("Began what?"—"a new life"). In the second *began* is intransitive. "A new life" is the subject of the verb in this sentence, not the direct object. Similarly, in "Nat and Lynne walk to the office every day," *walk* is an intransitive verb. However, in "Nat and Lynne walk the dog every day," *walk* is a transitive verb.

EXERCISE 5   **Directions:** Underline the intransitive verbs in the sentences below.

Example:

Many couples <u>argue</u> about money.

1. The long-time residents of Fox Creek sat on their front steps each evening.

2. Steven retires at the end of this year.

3. Darren and Cynda celebrated until two o'clock in the morning.

4. Ted fell from a fifteen-foot ladder.

5. At the company picnic Niki participated in the egg throw and the water balloon race.

6. Annabel smiled at her twin sons.

7. After a slow first quarter, sales improved gradually.

8. In Sheldon the factory whistle blew each weekday at noon.

9. The delegation from Budapest arrived at nine o'clock.

10. Negotiations with the strikers continued.

Some common irregular verbs may cause special problems. *Lie* is often confused with *lay* and *sit* with *set*. Recognizing which of these verbs are transitive and which are intransitive will help you tell them apart.

AVOIDING MISTAKES WITH *LIE* AND *LAY*

The verb *lie* meaning "tell an untruth" is regular ("Today I lie," "Yesterday I lied," "I have always lied"). When *lie* has this meaning it is intransitive.

The verb *lie* meaning "recline" is intransitive:

Let me *lie* down for a few minutes, and I'll be fine.

The verb *lay* meaning "put down" is transitive:

As soon as I come in the door, I *lay* my keys on the hall table.

Some confusion may result because the past tense of *lie* meaning "recline" is *lay*:

After I *lay* down, I discovered I wasn't sleepy.

The past tense of *lay* (meaning "put down") is *laid*:

I *laid* my keys on the table yesterday evening as usual, but I can't find them now.

The best way to distinguish between the two is to remember that *lie* meaning "recline" is intransitive and *lay* meaning "put" is transitive. The complete principal parts of these verbs are as follows:

basic form	past tense	past participle
lie (tell an untruth)	lied	lied
lie (recline)	lay	lain
lay (put)	laid	laid

AVOIDING MISTAKES WITH *SIT* AND *SET*

The intransitive verb *sit* means "put oneself into a sitting position." It also means "be located":

Sit down, ladies and gentlemen.

The new clock *sits* on the mantlepiece.

The transitive verb *set* means "place":

Set your hats and coats on the empty chairs.

The best way to distinguish between *sit* and *set* is to remember that *sit* is intransitive and *set* is transitive. The principal parts of *sit* and *set* are as follows:

basic form	past tense	past participle
sit	sat	sat
set	set	set

EXERCISE 6   **Directions:** Circle the word that correctly completes each sentence below.

Example:

Floyd (lay, laid) in the hammock while Sandy washed her new car.

1. When she gets a headache, Deirdre (lies, lays) down in a dark room for several hours.

2. Ryan (sat, set) his Swiss Army knife on the bedside table next to his wallet and keys.

3. Bill (lain, laid) his hammer on the bench and began looking for longer nails.

4. Norman and Lynn spread an old tablecloth on the ground and (sat, set) in the grass to eat their picnic supper.

5. If you feel your hair standing on end during a thunderstorm, (lie, lay) down quickly to avoid being hit by lightning.

6. Joan and Kate (sat, set) so close to the front of the theater that they had to lean back to see the movie.

7. The new trophy (sat, set) on the bookcase.

8. Jean had (lain, laid) in the sun so long that her skin was bright pink.

9. Jack always (sits, sets) down one cup of coffee, forgets about it, and pours another.

10. Mayor Johansson helped (lie, lay) the cornerstone for the new municipal building.

Linking Verbs

Linking verbs are followed not by objects but by subject complements—words, phrases or clauses that rename or describe subjects. Linking verbs describe conditions, not actions. The verb *be* in its various forms (*am, is, are, was,* and *were*) is the most common linking verb. Consider the following sentence:

linking
verb

The control panel on our toaster oven *is* hard to read.

"Hard to read" describes the control panel, and the verb *is* links the first part of the sentence with the second.

Some other common linking verbs are *appear, become,* and *seem.* Verbs such as *feel* and *look* can be linking verbs or not, depending on how they are used. For example, in the sentence "Jack felt ashamed," *felt* is a linking verb. However, in the sentence "Jack felt the heat of the fire," *felt* is a transitive verb.

EXERCISE 7 **Directions:** Underline the linking verbs in the sentences below.

Example:

Tile floors <u>are</u> easy to clean.

1. The sound of the wind chimes always seems soothing.

2. Elyse looks wonderful in her polka-dotted tennis dress.

3. My favorite snack is oatmeal cookies with walnuts and chocolate chips.

4. Jane's steering wheel feels hot.

5. None of the clocks in the house was right.

6. Julia Child was the host of the first how-to show on television.

7. Very low-calorie diets seem risky.

8. Thomas appeared tired after the debate.

9. Which breakfast cereals are most nutritious?

10. A hummingbird's nest is slightly larger than a bottle cap.

Auxiliary Verbs

Some verbs, called **auxiliary** or **helping verbs**, do not appear alone in sentences but always accompany one or more other verbs. Some examples of auxiliary verbs are *have, be, do, can, might,* and *would*. (Some of these verbs do sometimes appear alone in sentences but when they appear alone they are not considered to be auxiliary verbs. *Be*, for example, is also a common linking verb.)

Two or more verbs can be combined to create verb phrases. **Verb phrases** are closely related groups of verbs that function in sentences the same way single verbs would. The following sentences contain verb phrases:

The horse *was jumping* over the fence.

Phyllis *will become* a police officer.

Owen *had seemed* intelligent.

Auxiliary verbs combine with basic forms of verbs, present participles and past participles (the third principal parts of verbs) to make verb phrases. **Present participles** are basic forms of verbs plus the ending *-ing*, such as *walking, locating,* and *remembering*. Past participles of regular verbs, such as *walked, located,* and *remembered*, end in *-ed*.

Often one or more modifiers, such as adverbs, appear between an auxiliary verb and the rest of a verb phrase. These modifiers are not considered part of the verb phrase. For example, in the sentence "Claudio has always liked music," *always* is an adverb and "has liked" is the complete verb phrase.

A **finite verb** is any verb that can function as the main verb of a sentence. Verb forms such as present participles (*walking*, for example) or past participles (such as *written*) are not finite verbs.

Finite verbs always come first in verb phrases, followed by one or more nonfinite verbs. Only one finite verb can occur in a verb phrase. In "I *have been walking*," for example, only *have* is a finite verb. *Been* is a past participle, and *walking* is a present participle.

EXERCISE 8

Directions: Identify the underlined verbs in the sentences below by using the following code:

    F   finite verb   N   nonfinite verb

Example:

  N   Beth was <u>adjusting</u> the thread tension guide on the sewing machine.

_____ 1.   Two-year-old Graham Gasta <u>won</u> first prize in last Sunday's Tiny Tots Parade.

_____ 2.   Fifteen million refugees are <u>awaiting</u> asylum.

_____ 3. The hypermarket <u>contains</u> one long aisle just for cat food.

_____ 4. Demand for tickets at Riverfront Stadium in Cincinnati has <u>been</u> so high that scalpers have been getting $35 a ticket.

_____ 5. A lowland gorilla <u>ripped</u> a drinking fountain from the wall of his cage.

_____ 6. Three hundred thousand motorcyclists <u>gathered</u> this week in Sturgis, South Dakota, for the Black Hills Motor Classic.

_____ 7. In Saudi Arabia, Donald Duck is called Batut, and in Finland he is <u>known</u> as Aku Ankka.

_____ 8. Lava from a volcano <u>closed</u> the last road out of Kalapana Tuesday.

_____ 9. At 208 feet, the Cape Hatteras Lighthouse in North Carolina <u>is</u> the tallest lighthouse in the country.

_____ 10. Someone has <u>cooked</u> cabbage in this building almost every day this week.

HAVE

Forms of the verb *have* combine with the past participle to create verb phrases. Sometimes the verb *will* is also used.

> I *have* walked
>
> You *had* walked
>
> He will *have* walked

BE

The verb *be* is very irregular. This means you need to memorize all its forms:

present tense

	singular	*plural*
first person:	I am	we are
second person:	you are	you are
third person:	he, she, it is	they are

past tense

first person:	I was	we were
second person:	you were	you were

third person: he, she, it was they were

The auxiliary verb *be* combines with present participles to create verb phrases. Sometimes the verbs *have* and *will* are also included:

I *am* walking.

You *were* walking.

She will *be* walking.

We have *been* walking.

You had *been* walking.

They will have *been* walking.

In these sentences, *be* is used as an auxiliary verb. In a sentence such as "I am tired," however, *be* functions as a linking verb.

Do

The auxiliary verb *do* has several uses:
To help make other verbs negative:

I *do*n't go there anymore.

In negative statements, the verb *do* comes first, followed by the adverb *not* (often contracted to *n't*), followed by the basic form of the main verb.
To create questions:

Does your mother know?

In this kind of question, a form of the verb *do* appears first, followed by the subject and then by the basic form of the main verb.
To substitute for other verbs:

Does your mother know? She *does*.

Here the verb *does* appears instead of the verb *knows*. ("She knows" would also be correct.)
To make other verbs emphatic:

She *does* know.

"She does know" means "She knows, even if you think she doesn't" or "She knows, even though it may surprise you." Here *does* is included for emphasis.

MODAL AUXILIARIES

Other auxiliary verbs are called **modal auxiliaries**. Some common modal auxiliaries are *can, could, may, might, must, ought, shall, should, will,* and *would*. They are used with the basic forms of verbs to express writers' attitudes toward what they are writing. They express a wide range of meanings. For example, *can* indicates ability, *must* indicates necessity, and *will* indicates future time (that is, it indicates either the intention that something will happen or the expectation that it will).

Each modal auxiliary has only one form. In other words, modal auxiliaries have no present participles or past participles. Unlike most verbs, modal auxiliaries do not have third person singular forms created by adding *-s*. They are always followed in verb phrases by basic forms of verbs:

I *can* go.	I *may* stay.	I *must* decide.
You *can* go.	You *may* stay.	You *must* decide.
She *can* go.	She *may* stay.	She *must* decide.
We *can* go.	We *may* stay.	We *must* decide.
They *can* go.	They *may* stay.	They *must* decide.

EXERCISE 9

Directions: Underline the auxiliary verbs in the sentences below.

Example:

> Annetta <u>might</u> produce a movie about her home town, Bisbee, Arizona.

1. I am crocheting a jacket for the baby.

2. You should visit the Inner Harbor when you go to Baltimore.

3. Melanie's health insurance did not cover the cost of her baby's birth.

4. Three people can sit comfortably in the cab of a large pickup truck.

5. Experts predict that oil prices will rise.

6. Lean beef may contain up to twenty-two and a half percent fat.

7. Cherry pie filling, tapioca, and tomato sauce had been spilled inside the oven.

8. I would like to concentrate on the things I do best, such as napping.

9. Allison can already tell time on a digital clock, but she has not learned to read a clock with hands.

10. Saralynn is reading a book in the shower.

EXERCISE 10

Directions: Identify the type of verb underlined in each sentence below. Use the following code:

T	transitive	L	linking
I	intransitive	A	auxiliary

Example:

T   I <u>want</u> a pizza with pepperoni, sausage, ham, and bacon on it.

_____ 1.   Our shower massage <u>is</u> very relaxing.

_____ 2.   Cyanide <u>causes</u> death by blocking the absorption of oxygen.

_____ 3.   Molly <u>was</u> late for work again today.

_____ 4.   You <u>would</u> probably pack your belongings more carefully than a professional mover would.

_____ 5.   Suzanne <u>has</u> a billfold made of eel skin.

_____ 6.   Child-safe rear door locks <u>should</u> be a standard feature on a family sedan.

_____ 7.   Montezuma's successor, Chitlahua, <u>died</u> of smallpox after a reign of only four months.

_____ 8.   Some woolen clothing <u>can</u> be washed in home washing machines if a delicate cycle is selected.

_____ 9.   Maggie quickly <u>recovered</u> from her broken heart.

_____ 10.   More than 20,000 plants <u>belong</u> to the daisy family.

CREATING VERB TENSES

Once you have mastered the principal parts of a verb (the basic form, the past tense, and the past participle), creating the tenses is relatively simple. Verbs change their forms or combine with other verbs to express tense. Verb **tenses** indicate when actions take place, either in general or in relation to other actions. They also describe whether an action takes place only once or over a period of time. There are six tenses: the present, the past, the future, the present perfect, the past perfect, and the future perfect. In addition, each of these tenses also occurs in the progressive.

The Present Tense

The basic form of the verb is used for the entire present tense of regular verbs except for the third person singular, which ends in -*s*. Because the same form occurs in most of the present tense, pronouns are often needed to clarify a present tense verb's person and number:

	singular	plural
first person:	I walk	we walk
second person:	you walk	you walk
third person:	he, she, it *walks*	they walk

Verbs in the **present tense** describe actions that take place at the same time as they are being described:

I *see* a herd of deer in the meadow.

In addition, the present tense has the following uses:
To indicate a time in the future:

I *leave* for Chicago tomorrow.

To describe habitual actions:

Sarah *visits* her mother on Saturdays.

To tell general truths:

Everyone *wants* to be happy.

To write about books, movies, and other narratives:

In the play *Peter Pan*, Peter *is* a boy who never *grows* up.

To tell stories more vividly:

I *ask* the police officer if he is going to give me a ticket and he *answers*, "Do birds fly?" (This use of the present tense is considered informal.)

EXERCISE 11   **Directions:** Underline each of the present tense verbs in the sentences below.

Example:

Today the average pig <u>has</u> an inch of fat on its back compared to two inches in 1970.

1. At the end of *Casablanca* the police chief orders his men to round up the usual suspects.

2. Larry hates to make decisions.

3. The tongue of a Parson's chameleon is one and a half times longer than its body.

4. Because of a feud among the members of the ambulance squad, emergency services for Ghost Lake residents end this week.

5. Iced tea sometimes turns cloudy in the refrigerator.

6. A woman is twice as likely as a man to die from her first heart attack.

7. Judith rarely takes her food processor out of the kitchen cabinet.

8. Complete strangers compliment Lu on her hairstyle.

9. My doctor emphasizes the prevention of disease.

10. The governor hopes to force retailers to cut milk prices.

The Past Tense

Verbs in the **past tense** describe actions or conditions that took place at a time before they are described:

Albert Einstein needed twelve hours of sleep a night.

A regular verb indicates the past tense by adding *-ed* to the basic form for all persons and both numbers. Because the same form is used throughout the past tense, pronouns are often needed to clarify a past tense verb's person and number:

	singular	plural
first person:	I walked	we walked
second person:	you walked	you walked
third person:	he, she, it walked	they walked

If the basic form of a verb ends in *e*, only *-d* is added in the past tense (as in *stared*). If the basic form ends in *y* preceded by a consonant, the *y* is changed to *i* and *-ed* is added (as in *studied*). In words of one syllable ending in a single consonant preceded by a single vowel, the final consonant is doubled before *-ed* (as in *patted*). In longer words, the final consonant is doubled before *-ed* when the stress falls on the last syllable. For example, in *occurred* the *r* is doubled because the last syllable is stressed. In *listened* the first syllable, not the last, is stressed, so the *n* is not doubled.

To find the past tense of an irregular verb, you can refer to the chart of common irregular verbs earlier in this chapter. You can also use a dictionary to find the spelling of the past tense of an irregular verb.

EXERCISE 12

Directions: Change the present tense verbs in the sentences below to the past tense. Write the verbs on the lines at the left.

Example:

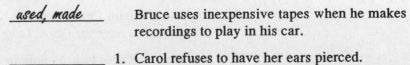

used, made   Bruce uses inexpensive tapes when he makes recordings to play in his car.

_____ 1. Carol refuses to have her ears pierced.

_____ 2. Our ceiling is so high that we have a remote control for our ceiling fan.

_____ 3. Rita wants you to buy two cans of tuna and some iced tea mix.

_____ 4. The Dunns discuss every major purchase before they make it.

_____ 5. When he has a cold, Dad puts a dish towel over his head and inhales steam from a pan of hot water.

_____ 6. The review board accepts every nominee.

_____ 7. Gerald lights the candles and carries the cake into the family room.

_____ 8. Mrs. Lopez uses a wheelchair lift to get to the second story of her house.

_____ 9. Lucy plans every detail of her vacations, but Paul likes more spontaneous trips.

_____ 10. Salvador's ice cream stand resembles a gigantic milk can.

The Future Tense

Verbs in the **future tense** describe actions that will take place after they are described:

Toru *will make* a chocolate-peanut butter ice cream pie for Nolan's birthday party.

The future tense is created by adding *will* to the basic form of the main verb:

	singular	plural
first person:	I will walk	we will walk
second person:	you will walk	you will walk
third person:	he, she, it will walk	they will walk

The future tense, like the present tense, can be used to express general truths:

Wealth alone *will* not *bring* happiness.

EXERCISE 13   **Directions:** Change the present tense verbs in the sentences below to the future tense. Write the verbs on the lines at the left.

Example:

will prevent   Overcrowded airwaves sometimes prevent fire fighters' beepers from receiving emergency signals.

_____   1. The Pine Valley Memorial Games benefit the families of police officers.

_____   2. In swamps, shallow wells bring up bad water.

_____   3. A knee injury keeps Ron from playing football this fall.

_____   4. The Powells hold a garage sale every spring.

_____   5. Lilacs bloom poorly in inadequate light.

_____   6. Jessica is a pediatric nurse practitioner.

_____   7. Stretching muscles before exercising helps athletes avoid sprains and strains.

_____   8. "You and no other" is engraved on Michelle's wedding ring.

_____   9. Linda's minestrone contains corn, carrots, zucchini, celery, yellow squash, broccoli, tomatoes, and green beans.

_____   10. Climbing stairs causes a rapid increase in heart rates.

The Perfect Tenses

There are three **perfect tenses**: the present perfect, the past perfect, and the future perfect. The perfect tenses are used to describe how an event in the present, past or future continues to be relevant at a later time. The following sentence is in the past tense:

past: Mario *arrived* home.

This sentence describes an event in the past but says nothing about the present. Mario may still be home, or perhaps he has gone out again; the sentence reports nothing beyond his arrival at some time in the past. Here is a similar sentence in the present perfect:

present perfect: Mario *has arrived* home.

This sentence both reports Mario's arrival and also suggests that he is still at home.

The present perfect is also used to describe events that started in the past and continue into the present:

present perfect: Leontyne *has shopped* at that store since she was a child.

This sentence suggests that Leontyne still shops at the same store.

The perfect tenses combine the past participles of verbs with one or more auxiliary verbs. For the present perfect the auxiliary verb *have* is combined with the past participle of the main verb:

present perfect: I *have walked* downtown every day for a year.

Notice that for the third person singular, *has,* not *have*, is used in the present perfect:

	singular	plural
first person:	I have walked	we have walked
second person:	you have walked	you have walked
third person:	he, she, it *has* walked	they have walked

The past perfect describes an event in the past and shows that it was still relevant at a later time. Consider the following sentence:

past perfect: Mario *had* already *arrived* home when his mother walked in.

This sentence relates an earlier past event, Mario's arrival home, to a second past event, his mother's walking in.

In the past perfect tense *had* is used with the past participle of the main verb:

	singular	plural
first person:	I had walked	we had walked
second person:	you had walked	you had walked
third person:	he, she, it had walked	they had walked

The future perfect describes an event in the future and shows its relevance to another event in the future:

future perfect: Mario *will have arrived* home by the time his mother walks in.

The future perfect describes actions that will take place before some specified or predictable time:

future perfect: I *will have returned* home by eleven o'clock.

The future perfect combines the auxiliary verbs *will* and *have* with the past participle of the main verb:

	singular	plural
first person:	I will have walked	we will have walked
second person:	you will have walked	you will have walked
third person:	he, she, it will have walked	they will have walked

EXERCISE 14   **Directions:** On each line at the left write the form of the verb specified in parentheses.

Example:

had bought   Before Mr. Kaufman's fourth child was born he (buy/past perfect) a heavy-duty clothes washer.

_____ 1. Unfortunately, Adam (forget/past perfect) to attend his memory skills seminar.

_____ 2. By this time tomorrow, Tim (drive/future perfect) across four states.

_____ 3. In order to kiss the Blarney Stone in County Cork, Ireland, Padgett (climb/past perfect) 127 steps at Blarney Castle.

_____ 4. Ira showed me the rubber snake he (win/past perfect) at the state fair.

_____ 5. Scientists (measure/present perfect) winds of more than 150 miles an hour during severe thunderstorms.

_____ 6. Over the summer Ronnie (learn/past perfect) to dance the rhumba, the tango, and the lambada.

_____ 7. By Tuesday I (spend/future perfect) my whole paycheck.

_____ 8. Arthur (take/present perfect) four days off this week in order to participate in a croquet tournament.

_____ 9. By next year Eloise and Isaac (build/future perfect) their own log cabin.

_____ 10. Carmel's mathematics professor (inspire/present perfect) her to become a math major.

The Progressive Forms

All six tenses also have progressive forms. Progressive forms combine the auxiliary verbs *be, have,* and *will* with the present participle (which ends in *-ing*). The **progressive** emphasizes that the event being described is in progress. In other words, it is continuing, was continuing or will continue (depending upon the tense). Consider the following sentence:

past progressive

While I *was walking* home, I met my friend Al.

The past progressive "was walking" describes an action continuing over a period of time in the past. While it was going on, a second action, described by "I met," took place. The walking began before the meeting with Al and continued after it was over.

The progressive also indicates habitual actions, as in the following sentence:

present progressive

I *am walking* a lot more now.

The use of the progressive in this sentence indicates that the walking has become a habit.

Compare the simple tenses with their progressive forms in the chart below:

	simple tense	progressive
present:	I walk	I am walking
past:	I walked	I was walking
future:	I will walk	I will be walking
present perfect:	I have walked	I have been walking
past perfect:	I had walked	I had been walking
future perfect:	I will have walked	I will have been walking

The progressive is illustrated more fully at the end of this chapter.

EXERCISE 15   **Directions:** On each line at the left, write the form of the verb specified in parentheses.

Example:

will be waiting   I (wait/future progressive) in the car while you get your teeth cleaned.

_____   1. Miss Moreau (look/present progressive) for a name for the men's fragrance she will be marketing in the fall.

_____ 2. By the end of September, Ginny (care/future perfect progressive) for her mother for seven years.

_____ 3. Animal rights activists (protest/present perfect progressive) against the greased pig chase.

_____ 4. Dad (ride/present progressive) the twelve-speed bike he bought for Joshua.

_____ 5. Rob (leave/future progressive) the wheelchair at the door of the airplane.

_____ 6. Mandy knew that Marcus (collect/past perfect progressive) miniature elephants since he was a teenager.

_____ 7. In the Diaper Derby, babies (crawl/past progressive) toward plastic buckets filled with dollar bills.

_____ 8. I (look/past perfect progressive) forward to my high school reunion until I found out that my best friend could not attend.

_____ 9. The store managers (work/past progressive) with marketing and production personnel as part of an interdependent team.

_____ 10. Buyers today (refuse/present perfect progressive) to pay for features they do not need.

UNDERSTANDING SEQUENCE OF TENSES

The term **sequence of tenses** refers to time relationships between verbs. When the actions described by the verbs in a sentence take place at approximately the same time, the verbs should be in the same tense:

present   present

Weak batteries *are* the main reason cars *do* not *start* in cold weather.

Often the verbs in sentences should be in different tenses. However, you should be careful not to shift tenses unless you have a reason for doing so:

present   past

NOT: When Alice Walker *is* a little girl, she *was* shot in the eye with a BB gun.

An improved version of this sentence is "When Alice Walker was a little girl, she was shot in the eye with a BB gun." In this sentence the condition and action described by the verbs clearly belong in the same tense.

When two or more verbs occur in the same sentence, their tenses should be consistent with the times of the actions they describe. Consider the following sentence:

NOT: As soon as I *finish* this, I *left*.

The first action ("I finish") will take place before the second action ("I left"). Therefore, if the first action will take place in the near future, the second one must take place further on in the future, not in the past. The logical sequence is to describe the first event in the present tense to indicate future time, and the second event in the future tense:

present   future
As soon as I *finish* this, I *will leave*.

Another way to make the sentence consistent is to put both verbs into the past tense:

As soon as I *finished* this, I *left*.

When describing a sequence of actions, consider the order in which the actions take place and choose tenses which convey a sense of this order to your readers. Note that shifting from one tense to another is fine as long as the time relationships between the events you describe are clear:

Freezer burn *is* the dehydration of frozen foods that *have been wrapped* improperly or *stored* too long.

The first verb, *is*, expresses a general truth; it is therefore in the present tense. The verbs *have been wrapped* and *stored* are in the present perfect tense because they describe events that occur before freezer burn develops.

EXERCISE 16   **Directions:** Correct the sequence of tenses in the sentences below by correcting the underlined verbs on the lines at the left.

Example:

bought   Abigail went into the furniture store and <u>buys</u> a mahogany chest for her bedroom.

_____ 1. After Sally chose the puppy, she <u>takes</u> it home in a doll's baby buggy.

_____ 2. Tricia's new lipstick <u>lasts</u> for nine hours, but it smelled and tasted like turpentine.

_____ 3. Regina never feels satisfied with what she does
and <u>wanted</u> a better life for herself.

_____ 4. When Manny was in college, he <u>wins</u> his first
orchid contest.

_____ 5. Luella will decide to drink bottled water after
she <u>tasted</u> the tap water here.

_____ 6. After Maureen <u>writes</u> in her diary, she hid it in
the secret drawer of her roll-top desk.

_____ 7. When Vicky retired, she <u>starts</u> belly dancing
lessons.

_____ 8. Brad can never remember telephone messages,
but he <u>had</u> memorized hundreds of sports statistics.

_____ 9. The goliath beetle we caught was more than
four inches long and <u>weighs</u> three-and-a half
ounces.

_____ 10. Marlon's lawn mower does not start on cold
days unless he <u>put</u> it in a sunny spot for at least
half an hour.

USING THE INTERROGATIVE

Interrogative sentences ask questions. They can be created in several
ways:
  With auxiliary verbs:

  Do you want to go to the movies?

  Can you water ski?

  In this kind of question the auxiliary verb comes first, followed by a
subject, followed by a main verb.
  With verbs followed by subjects:

  Is this your book?

  The declarative sentence "This is your book" is in the usual order:
subject-verb. Reversing the order of the subject and verb (and changing the
end mark to a question mark) makes the sentence a question.

With question words:

Who called?

What is a kob?

When did that package arrive?

Where is my paycheck?

Why shouldn't I go?

How do you play bingo?

Note that a sentence beginning with a question word may include an auxiliary verb as well, as in "When *did* that package arrive?" or "Where *has* my paycheck been?"

With a question mark:

You're twenty-one years old?

Ending a declarative sentence with a question mark is enough to turn it into a question. Usually, the question mark signals that the speaker does not believe the information provided by the declarative sentence or is guessing.

EXERCISE 17   **Directions:** Turn the declarative sentences below into questions by following the directions given in parentheses.

Example:

Claudia's sofa disappeared from her office just before she was fired. (Start with *Did*.)

Did Claudia's sofa disappear from her office

just before she was fired?

1. The indentation below the nose is known as the philtrum. (Use the question mark only.)

_____

_____

2. Robot arms assemble products such as automobiles and television sets. (Start with *How*.)

_____

_____

3. Lightning causes millions of dollars in home and property damage each year. (Start with *Does*.)

_____

_____

4. Nero, the Roman emperor, was only 31 when he died. (Start with the verb.)

_____

_____

5. Maria has read all thirty-eight of Shakespeare's plays. (Start with *Has*.)

_____

_____

6. Taking aspirin can reduce the chances of heart attacks in men over fifty. (Start with *Can*.)

_____

_____

7. Emily's television set receives 105 channels. (Use only the question mark.)

_____

_____

8. The covering on the end of a shoelace is called an aglet. (Start with *Is*.)

_____

_____

9. Janet was reading the advertising panels on the walls of the subway car. (Start with *Why*.)

_____

_____

10. Martin is one of the students watching the Senate debate from the galleries. (Start with the verb.)

_____

_____

MAINTAINING AGREEMENT BETWEEN SUBJECTS AND VERBS

Subjects and verbs must correspond in person and number. Words corresponding in this way are in **agreement**. In order to agree, singular subjects require singular verbs, and plural subjects require plural verbs. These two sentences illustrate this rule:

> subject   verb
> The *girl*   *plays* in the back yard after school.

> subject   verb
> The *girls*   *play* in the back yard after school.

Notice that each subject-verb pair has one *-s* ending. In the present tense, when both nouns and verbs are regular, the verbs end in *-s* in the singular and the nouns end in *-s* in the plural.

Some situations pose problems, however. Sometimes the structure of a sentence obscures the connection between its subject and verb. At other times, it is difficult to be sure whether subjects are singular or plural.

Avoiding Errors When Words Come between Subjects and Verbs

When verbs immediately follow subjects in sentences, few problems arise. Often, however, modifiers come between subjects and verbs. Take the following sentence, for example:

> subject   verb
> The *baby-sitter* for the DeVries children *braids* Patti's
>
> object
> *hair* each time she comes.

The basic structure of this sentence is "The baby-sitter braids Patti's hair" (S-V-O). With most of the modifiers removed from the sentence, it is easy to see that *The baby-sitter* is a singular subject and that the verb *braids* must be third person singular. The DeVries children mentioned in the prepositional phrase do not perform the action of the verb *braids* and therefore do not influence whether the verb is singular or plural.

When words come between subjects and verbs, it is useful to remember that subjects never occur in prepositional phrases. Crossing out prepositional phrases should help you analyze sentences for their basic structures:

> subject   verb
> The *baby-sitter* ~~for the Devries children~~ *braids* Patti's
>
> object
> *hair* each time she comes.

Dependent clauses can also come between subjects and verbs, and they do not affect subject-verb agreement either.

EXERCISE 18   **Directions:** Circle the word that correctly completes each sentence below.

Example:

The lights on the dashboard (warn, warns) of possible mal-functions.

1. Meat from sheep more than eighteen months old (is, are) mutton.

2. Gas ranges with electric ignitions (use, uses) less gas than those with pilot lights.

3. A cargo ship that does not have fixed routes (is, are) known as a tramp.

4. Ambrosia, the food of the gods according to Greek myths, (give, gives) those who eat it eternal youth and beauty.

5. Narrow fingers of land extending into a body of water (is, are) called spits.

6. Ray, along with two of his friends, (plans, plan) to visit Miami.

7. The planes on the runway (follows, follow) the taxiway to the terminal.

8. The leaves of the cherry tree (is, are) poisonous.

9. Exact locations on the earth's surface (is, are) pinpointed on photographs taken from space.

10. The compressed air tanks under the cab of the truck (causes, cause) Arturo extra worry on a long trip.

Avoiding Errors in Sentences with More than One Subject

Verbs with compound subjects are usually plural:

      subject   verb
Tom and Edward *are* best friends.

The only exception occurs when the compound subject refers to a single idea:

      subject   verb
Ham and eggs *is* Jenny's favorite breakfast.

When compound subjects are joined by *or, either . . . or* or *neither . . . nor*, the verb agrees with the part of the subject that is closer to it in the sentence:

        subject   subject verb
Either *Tom's sisters* or *Edward knows* where Tom is now.

The verb *knows* is singular because *Edward*, the part of the compound subject closer to the verb, is singular. If a sentence of this kind seems awkward to you, you can always rewrite it to put the other subject first. Reverse the order and the situation changes:

Either Edward or Tom's sisters *know* where Tom is now.

EXERCISE 19   **Directions:** Circle the word that correctly completes each sentence below.

Example:

Neither Chrissy nor her friends (wears, wear) ankle bracelets anymore.

1.   At the bank Stephen and Guy always (asks, ask) for two dollar bills.

2.   Either the librarian or his assistant (pastes, paste) the call number onto the spine of a new book.

3.   Liquid bleach and heavy-duty detergent usually (does, do) a good job of cleaning Sid's dirty work clothes.

4.   Sod or branches covered with mud (is, are) used to make a hogan.

5.   Neither the lion tamer nor the three lions (seems, seem) to interest Nelson's son.

6.   Being tired or feeling bored (causes, cause) people to blink more often.

7.   Flavio and Connie (is, are) learning Morse code in Scouts.

8.   Either Elliott or Olivia (takes, take) Elliott's baby brother to the park every day.

9.   Neither Chris nor Channing (checks, check) the oil regularly.

10.   Mata and Wayne (do, does) not have credit cards.

Avoiding Errors When Verbs Follow Subjects

In some sentences the usual word order is reversed. In sentences beginning with *Here, There* or *Where* followed by forms of the verb *be*, the subject follows the verb:

            verb   subject
There *were* too many *people* at the pool today.

Sometimes a writer reverses the subject and the verb to achieve a surprising or dramatic effect:

                                                              verb
We were all ready to leave for the theater when in *came*

subject
Shirley, wearing a yellow bikini.

Reversing the order of the subject and the verb does not alter the need for agreement between them. The person or thing performing the action of the verb is still the subject.

EXERCISE 20   **Directions:** Circle the word that correctly completes each sentence below.

Example:

There (was, (were)) open-top cars, boxcars, and flatcars on the freight train.

1. In the basement of the White House (is, are) bombproof rooms containing an emergency command post.

2. Where (is, are) the baggage compartment on this bus?

3. Among the space junk orbiting the earth (is, are) discarded bolts, springs, and cables.

4. Here (is, are) the washers and slugs that people tried to use in Rock Valley's parking meters.

5. At the top of the list of the most commonly used words in the English language (is, are) the word *the*.

6. Outside Terry's back door (is, are) a narrow slab of concrete she calls her patio.

7. Among the most commonly treated phobias (is, are) agoraphobia, the fear of open or public places.

8. On the ocean liner (is, are) a theater and lecture hall, a jogging track, a miniature golf course, and a shopping arcade.

9. There (is, are) no proof that vitamins help prevent colds.

10. In Christine's wallet (is, are) pictures of her two children and her sister's dog.

Avoiding Errors with Subject Complements

Linking verbs agree with their subjects, just as other verbs do. However, since both subjects and subject complements name or describe the same people or things, a writer is sometimes tempted to make verbs agree with complements rather than with subjects. Consider the following sentence:

subject
subject   verb   complement
The best *part* of a trip to Egypt *is* the *pyramids.*

The subject of the verb *is* in this sentence is *part* (singular), not *pyramids* (plural), so this sentence is correct.

EXERCISE 21   **Directions:** Circle the word that correctly completes each sentence below.

Example:

Our main concern (is) are) increased salaries and benefits.

1. The first thing Mom saw when she came in (was, were) dirty clothes all over the floor.

2. The largest unanticipated expense (was, were) between-meal snacks.

3. Zoning laws (is, are) our committee's first target.

4. My favorite meal (is, are) hot dogs with sauerkraut.

5. His business (is, are) computers.

6. During the storm our entertainment (was, were) videotaped movies.

7. The surprises (was, were) a burgundy felt hat and a silver bracelet.

8. The problem (is, are) long waves without crests known as swells.

9. The cause of Alice's car trouble (was, were) defective inflation valves on the tires.

10. Wiley's main interest (is, are) scale models of Corvettes.

Avoiding Errors with Indefinite Pronouns

Most indefinite pronouns are always singular. *Anybody, each, everybody,* and *somebody* are among the indefinite pronouns that take singular verbs:

verb pronoun
Is   anybody here?

pronoun verb
Each   was the best of its kind.

Other indefinite pronouns, such as *both, few, many,* and *several* are always plural:

pronoun   verb   pronoun   verb
Many of my friends *have* good jobs, but *few   are willing* to lend me money.

Still other indefinite pronouns, such as *all, any, most,* and *some,* are sometimes singular and sometimes plural. When these pronouns refer to mass nouns, they are singular. When they refer to count nouns, they are plural:

pronoun   verb
Most of Jan's enthusiasm *was* gone.

In this sentence, the pronoun *Most* refers to the mass noun *enthusiasm*. The verb is therefore singular.

> pronoun   verb
> *Most* of my clothes *were destroyed* in the fire.

In this sentence, however, the pronoun *Most* refers to the count noun *clothes*. The verb is therefore plural.

EXERCISE 22   **Directions:** Circle the word that correctly completes each sentence below.

Example:

> Everyone (complains, complain) when gas prices go up.

1. Most of Benito's shirts (has, have) at least one pocket.

2. Somebody (is, are) addressing all the wedding invitations with a fountain pen.

3. Everyone in the Hundley family (buys, buy) a new toothbrush twice a year.

4. Few of my friends (dislikes, dislike) both crunchy peanut butter and the smooth variety.

5. Each of the messages on the answering machine (is, are) for Dody.

6. Everybody (benefits, benefit) from getting a flu shot.

7. Nobody (remembers, remember) that the space between the thumb and the first finger is called the purlicue.

8. Some of the children (stops, stop) at the ice cream shop every day.

9. Nothing (ends, end) the baby's crying except being rocked in the rocking chair.

10. All of the workers who enter by the main gate (passes, pass) through a metal detector.

Avoiding Errors with Collective Subjects

Although collective nouns refer to groups, they usually take singular verbs:

> subject verb
> Our *team* *is* the best in the conference.

On rare occasions, writers may want to emphasize that a group is made up of individuals. To do so, they may choose a plural verb:

> subject   verb
> After graduation, the *team* *are* going their separate ways.

Many writers would change this sentence to "After graduation, the members of the team are going their separate ways," but treating *team* as a plural subject is also acceptable.

The collective noun *number* is singular when it occurs in the phrase *the number* but plural when it occurs in the phrase *a number*:

> subject   verb
> *The number* of people who want to buy widgets *is* very small.

> subject   verb
> *A number* of people *are* in the store trying to buy widgets.

Titles of poems, stories, books, and movies take singular verbs even when they appear to be plural:

> subject   verb
> *Breathing Lessons   is* a novel by Anne Tyler.

Titles of organizations take singular verbs even though they may end in *-s*:

> subject   verb
> *Apex Associates   is* going out of business.

A quantity regarded as a whole takes a singular verb:

> subject   verb
> *Ninety-five dollars   is* too much to pay for a radio.

EXERCISE 23 **Directions:** Complete each sentence below by circling the correct word in parentheses.

Example:

> A number of parents (objects, (object)) to the proposed longer school year.

1. Healthcare Associates (is, are) the firm that recently rented new office space on Springdale Road.

2. The team (accepts, accept) its plaque at a pep rally today.

3. IBM (is, are) marketing computers for home buyers.

4. Our group (remains, remain) united in its support of equal pay for equal work.

5. *The Grapes of Wrath* (is, are) one of my favorite books.

6. The number of people who apply fake beauty marks (is, are) surprising.

7. Two years (was, were) a long engagement.

8. Ten dollars an hour (is, are) a good salary for someone who has just completed training.

9.   The faculty (is, are) leaving their seats and beginning to congratulate the graduates.

10.   Eight hundred dollars (is, are) a good price for that car.

Avoiding Errors with Nouns Singular in Meaning but Plural in Form

Some nouns, such as *economics*, look plural because they end in -*s* but are singular in meaning. They take singular verbs:

     subject   verb

Economics was my favorite subject in college.

Single objects that appear to have two parts take plural verbs:

      subject   verb

My *eyeglasses are* missing.

      subject   verb

Joey's *pants were* too long, so he had them altered.

EXERCISE 24   **Directions:** Circle the word that correctly completes each sentence below.

Example:

Physics (is, are) my favorite subject this semester.

1.   The good news (is, are) that Rental World reports a profit of $42 million this year.

2.   Electronics (interests, interest) Elena.

3.   Kim's jeans (is, are) in the wash.

4.   Scissors used for a variety of tasks quickly (becomes, become) dull.

5.   The binoculars I would like to buy (costs, cost) more than forty dollars.

6.   Fish Springs, Utah, (is, are) sometimes so quiet that fish can be heard spitting at passing insects to bring them down into the water.

7.   Your glasses (is, are) on the kitchen counter.

8.   Linguistics (is, are) the major Gary has chosen.

9.   Red trousers (is, are) part of the butchers' uniforms at Trim Right Meats.

10.   Mathematics (is, are) easy for Kerry.

UNDERSTANDING VOICE

In most sentences, the subjects perform actions. In passive sentences, however, the subjects are acted upon. Whether a subject is acting or acted upon is a matter of **voice**.

Identifying the Active Voice and the Passive Voice

The following sentence is in the active voice:

The Americans defeated the British at Yorktown in 1781.

This sentence describes an action the Americans performed. A sentence in which the performer of the action is the subject of the verb is in the **active voice**.

A sentence in which the target of the action is the subject of the verb is in the passive voice. The following sentence is in the **passive voice**:

The British were defeated by the Americans at Yorktown in 1781.

This sentence describes the same event as the first one does, but it focuses on the British, who were defeated, rather than on the Americans, who defeated them. To reflect this change of focus, the direct object in the first sentence *(the British)* becomes the subject of the second sentence. The subject of the first sentence *(The Americans)* has been moved to a prepositional phrase in the second sentence.

To change a sentence from the active voice into the passive voice, turn the direct object of the active sentence into the subject of the passive one. (Only sentences with direct objects—that is, sentences with transitive verbs—can be changed into passive sentences.) To make the verb in an active sentence passive, choose a third person form of the verb *be* in the same tense as the verb in the active sentence. If the new subject is singular, make the verb singular. If it is plural, make the verb plural. Then add the past participle of the main verb in the active sentence. For example, the active sentence "Rahman found a twenty dollar bill" can be transformed into the passive sentence "A twenty dollar bill was found by Rahman." The direct object of the active sentence ("twenty dollar bill") becomes the subject of the passive sentence.

The performer of an action often appears in the passive sentence in a phrase beginning with the preposition *by*. However, some passive sentences focus only on the person or thing being acted upon, and the subject is not considered important enough to mention. Look at the following example:

Astronauts are considered poor insurance risks.

Obviously, astronauts are considered poor risks by *someone*—by people in insurance companies called actuaries whose task it is to calculate the risks involved in various kinds of jobs. But the focus is presently on the astronauts, not the actuaries. In fact, for the writer's purpose, the people who perform the action are unimportant.

The passive voice is also used when the performer of an action is unknown:

Footprints *were left* in the wet concrete.

Sometimes writers want to avoid mentioning someone who has performed a negative or controversial action. Consider the following two sentences:

passive voice: The money was stolen.

active voice: The cashier stole the money.

The first sentence simply reports the theft, while the second sentence places the blame. The first sentence might be used by someone who does not want to mention the cashier's guilt.

The following diagram shows the relationship between the parts of active and passive sentences:

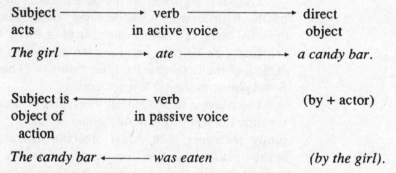

EXERCISE 25   **Directions:** Indicate whether the verbs in the sentences below are in the active voice or the passive voice by using the following code:

A   active voice   P   passive voice

Example:

<u>*A*</u>   Two inmates punched their way out through the walls of the jail.

_____ 1.   The Bowie knife was named after Jim Bowie, the hero of the Alamo.

_____ 2.   George took twenty-four pictures of his new sports car.

_____ 3.   Influenza and famine killed 20 million Russians between 1914 and 1924.

_____ 4.   The music industry's platinum records are usually made of nickel and are covered with foil or paint, not platinum.

_____ 5. The ginkgo tree dates back to the time of the dinosaurs.

_____ 6. The slash mark used in fractions is known as a virgule.

_____ 7. Woodrow Wilson is pictured on the $100,000 bill.

_____ 8. A group of lions is called a pride, and a flock of larks is called an exaltation.

_____ 9. Some plants contain chemicals that interfere with the digestion of plant-eating animals.

_____10. *Murmuring*, *mist*, and *chimes* are considered to be among the most beautiful words in the English language.

Avoiding Overuse of the Passive Voice

The passive voice is very useful to writers who want to focus attention on the target of an action rather than on the performer. However, some writers use the passive voice too much.

Writing is more effective and interesting when most sentences are in the active voice. Active sentences are shorter and more vivid. Whenever you use the passive voice, ask yourself why you are doing so. If you can think of an answer such as "to focus attention on the target of the action," let the passive voice stand. Otherwise, change passive sentences into active ones.

EXERCISE 26 **Directions:** Rewrite the sentences below to convert them from the passive voice to the active voice. Make all necessary changes without altering the meanings of the original sentences.

Example:

The dust from Cooper's power sander is collected by a suction hose.

A suction hose collects the dust from Cooper's power sander.

1. Commercially baked bread is lifted gently from its baking pan by vacuum cups.

_____

_____

2. A cookbook was compiled by the band parents' organization to sell as a fund raiser.

_____

_____

3. A piece of rock from the moon is contained in one of the windows in Washington National Cathedral.

    _____

    _____

4. Bradley's clowning skills were perfected by him at Clown Camp in La Crosse, Wisconsin.

    _____

    _____

5. Boiled hard-shell crabs were ordered by Cathleen.

    _____

    _____

6. Every suggestion made by me is criticized by Russell.

    _____

    _____

7. If boots are worn by you for hiking, break them in before taking a long hike.

    _____

    _____

8. The Laytons' house was painted, inside and out, by the Laytons every other year.

    _____

    _____

9. A stroller, a crib, a playpen, a bassinet, and a high chair were bought by Gwen and Bradford.

    _____

    _____

10. Safety violations had been reported by me as early as June 1990.

    _____

    _____

TRY IT OUT

Do you overuse the passive voice? Analyze your own writing to find out. Choose a sample of your writing, preferably something formal such as an assignment you wrote for a college course. Underline each verb and label it as either active voice or passive voice. Then for each verb in the passive voice, consider whether you had a good reason for using the passive.

Unless you had a good reason for using the passive, your sentences would probably be more effective in the active voice, so you should transform any remaining passive sentences into active ones. Suppose you find a sentence in the passive voice such as this one:

> Four tons of plastic are discharged into the ocean by American warships each day.

This sentence would be more vivid and memorable in the active voice:

> American warships discharge four tons of plastic into the ocean each day.

Note that the active sentence is shorter and easier to understand than the passive sentence.

UNDERSTANDING MOOD

Mood is the use of verbs to indicate a person's attitude toward what he or she is saying or writing. There are three moods: the indicative, the imperative, and the subjunctive.

Identifying the Indicative Mood

In the **indicative mood**, verbs state facts or ask questions about them. Therefore, by using the indicative mood, writers suggest that their statements are (probably) true. People who ask questions in the indicative mood expect factual answers:

> What *is* a nightmare?

> A nightmare *is* a dream in which someone *feels* helpless, powerless or threatened by violence.

The vast majority of sentences are in the indicative mood.

Identifying the Imperative Mood

The **imperative mood** is used for requests and commands. Imperatives exist only for the second person (you). The basic form of the verb is used for both singular and plural:

Johnny, please *stay* out of there.

Children, *keep* off the grass!

Negative imperatives combine the auxiliary verb *do* and the adverb *not* (often contracted to *n't*):

Johnny, *don*'t *trample* the flowers.

Children, *don*'t *fight*.

Identifying the Subjunctive Mood

By using verbs in the subjunctive mood, writers suggest that their statements are not true although they may wish that they were. Verbs in the **subjunctive mood** express desires, requests or suggestions. They also indicate imaginary or hypothetical conditions (sometimes called conditions contrary to fact):

    subjunctive
If I *were* rich, I would live in Hawaii.

Similar ideas can be expressed with the auxiliary verbs *could, might, ought, should,* and *would*:

I *would* like to be rich so I *could* live in Hawaii.

The auxiliary verbs *would* and *could* are known as **conditional** forms. They tell what would be true in imagined situations. In some sentences both the conditional and the subjunctive are used:

conditional   subjunctive
I *would* live in Hawaii if I *had* a job there.

                        subjunctive   conditional
If just wishing something *made* it come true, I *would* be in Hawaii now.

If the condition that is described is likely to happen rather than merely hypothetical, the indicative mood is used:

indicative   indicative
I *will* live in Hawaii when I *retire*.

Certain expressions, such as *as if* and *as though*, introduce verbs in the subjunctive mood:

The Brownes spend money <u>as if</u> they *were* millionaires, but they're just as poor as we are.

Sheila talks about Brendan <u>as though</u> they *were* already married, and they aren't even engaged yet.

Verbs that express commands or requests in the indicative mood are often followed by verbs in the subjunctive. Among them are *ask, demand, insist, recommend, request,* and *require*:

indicative   subjunctive

The gas station attendant *asked* that Ronald *pull* up a little closer to the pump.

indicative   subjunctive

The man *insists* that he *be* excused from jury duty.

indicative   subjunctive

The doctor *recommended* that Paula *go* on a strict diet.

EXERCISE 27   **Directions:** Identify the mood of the verb underlined in each sentence below by using the following code:

S   subjunctive   IMP   imperative   I   indicative

Example:

___*S*___   If a flea market <u>were</u> held at the drive-in during the day, Mr. Eddins could probably afford to continue showing movies at night.

_____ 1.   Caked ash that remains in the bowl of a pipe after it has been smoked <u>is</u> known as dottle.

_____ 2.   President Downing insists that the demonstration <u>be</u> ended.

_____ 3.   The show would be better if the cast <u>were</u> more familiar with the new format.

_____ 4.   Do<u>n't</u> <u>forget</u> to water the lawn while we're gone.

_____ 5.   Requests that Yosemite <u>become</u> a national park were granted in 1890.

_____ 6.   When Silvio was ready to leave the restaurant, his new trench coat <u>was</u> missing, and someone else's old coat hung in its place.

_____ 7.   <u>Vote</u> for Indira for class president.

_____ 8.   Josh felt as if he <u>were</u> not treated fairly.

_____ 9.   The mayor <u>urged</u> the graduates not to forget their urban roots.

_____10.   <u>Buy</u> chowder and clam cakes at the Golden Bucket in Seekonk, Massachusetts.

Forming the Subjunctive

In the present subjunctive, verbs appear in their basic forms:

I suggest that every applicant *fill* (not *fills*) out the form carefully.

In the past subjunctive, the verbs are identical with those in the past indicative. The past subjunctive is used for imaginary or hypothetical situations:

Annie wishes she *knew* (not *knows*) how to dance.

The verb *be* has two subjunctive forms: *be* (the present subjunctive) and *were* (the past subjunctive). *Be* is used for suggestions and requirements:

Alec's boss insists that he *be* (not *is*) on time for work every day from now on.

Were is used for desires and for imaginary or hypothetical situations:

If I *were* (not *was*) Alec, I'd do what Gilda wants.

EXERCISE 28   **Directions:** Circle the word that correctly completes each sentence below.

Example:

Mr. Waldman recommends that Dorinda (be) is) promoted.

1. Even though the election isn't until next week, Junella acts as if she (was, were) already elected homecoming queen.

2. I insist that Marc (stop, stops) coming to class in that gorilla suit.

3. Miss Lincoln demands that James (prepare, prepares) carefully for each case.

4. If I (was, were) you, I would never give up that apartment.

5. We demand that a new counselor (be, is) hired.

6. I wish the wallpaper (was, were) lighter since the room is so small.

7. Mrs. McKellop requests that Vivette (come, comes) to her office at once.

8. I move that nominations (be, are) closed.

9. Park rules require that each person (leaves, leave) by midnight.

10. I wish I (own, owned) a new car.

Tenses and Moods of a Regular Verb

Indicative Mood

<u>The Present Tense:</u> Active Voice

	singular	plural
first person	I love	we love
second person	you love	you love
third person	he, she, it loves	they love

<u>The Present Tense:</u> Passive Voice

	singular	plural
first person	I am loved	we are loved
second person	you are loved	you are loved
third person	he, she, it is loved	they are loved

<u>The Past Tense:</u>   Active Voice

	singular	plural
first person	I loved	we loved
second person	you loved	you loved
third person	he, she, it loved	they loved

<u>The Past Tense:</u>   Passive Voice

	singular	plural
first person	I was loved	we were loved
second person	you were loved	you were loved
third person	he, she, it was loved	they were loved

<u>The Future Tense:</u> Active Voice

	singular	plural
first person	I will love	we will love
second person	you will love	you will love
third person	he, she, it will love	they will love

The Future Tense: Passive Voice

	singular	plural
first person	I will be loved	we will be loved
second person	you will be loved	you will be loved
third person	he, she, it will be loved	they will be loved

The Present Perfect Tense: Active Voice

	singular	plural
first person	I have loved	we have loved
second person	you have loved	you have loved
third person	he, she, it has loved	they have loved

The Present Perfect Tense: Passive Voice

	singular	plural
first person	I have been loved	we have been loved
second person	you have been loved	you have been loved
third person	he, she, it has been loved	they have been loved

The Past Perfect Tense: Active Voice

	singular	plural
first person	I had loved	we had loved
second person	you had loved	you had loved
third person	he, she, it had loved	they had loved

The Past Perfect Tense: Passive Voice

	singular	plural
first person	I had been loved	we had been loved
second person	you had been loved	you had been loved
third person	he, she, it had been loved	they had been loved

The Future Perfect Tense: Active Voice

	singular	plural
first person	I will have loved	we will have loved
second person	you will have loved	you will have loved
third person	he, she, it will have loved	they will have loved

The Future Perfect Tense: Passive Voice

	singular	plural
first person	I will have been loved	we will have been loved
second person	you will have been loved	you will have been loved
third person	he, she, it will have been loved	they will have been loved

The Present Progressive: Active Voice

	singular	plural
first person	I am loving	we are loving
second person	you are loving	you are loving
third person	he, she, it is loving	they are loving

The Present Progressive: Passive Voice

	singular	plural
first person	I am being loved	we are being loved
second person	you are being loved	you are being loved
third person	he, she, it is being loved	they are being loved

The Past Progressive: Active Voice

	singular	plural
first person	I was loving	we were loving
second person	you were loving	you were loving
third person	he, she, it was loving	they were loving

The Past Progressive: Passive Voice

	singular	plural
first person	I was being loved	we were being loved
second person	you were being loved	you were being loved
third person	he, she, it was being loved	they were being loved

The Future Progressive: Active Voice

	singular	plural
first person	I will be loving	we will be loving
second person	you will be loving	you will be loving
third person	he, she, it will be loving	they will be loving

The Future Progressive: Passive Voice

	singular	plural
first person	I will be being loved	we will be being loved
second person	you will be being loved	you will be being loved
third person	he, she, it will be being loved	they will be being loved

The Present Perfect Progressive: Active Voice

	singular	plural
first person	I have been loving	we have been loving
second person	you have been loving	you have been loving
third person	he, she, it has been loving	they have been loving

The Present Perfect Progressive: Passive Voice

	singular	plural
first person	I have been being loved	we have been being loved
second person	you have been being loved	you have been being loved
third person	he, she, it has been loved	they have been being loved

The Past Perfect Progressive: Active Voice

	singular	plural
first person	I had been loving	we had been loving
second person	you had been loving	you had been loving
third person	he, she, it had been being loving	they had been loving

The Past Perfect Progressive: Passive Voice

	singular	plural
first person	I had been being loved	we had been being loved
second person	you had been being loved	you had been being loved
third person	he, she, it had been being loved	they had been being loved

The Future Perfect Progressive: Active Voice

	singular	plural
first person	I will have been loving	we will have been loving
second person	you will have been loving	you will have been loving
third person	he, she, it will have been loving	they will have been loving

The Future Perfect Progressive: Passive Voice

	singular	plural
first person	I will have been being loved	we will have been being loved
second person	you will have been being loved	you will have been being loved
third person	he, she, it will have been being loved	they will have been being loved

The Subjunctive Mood

The Present Subjunctive: Active Voice

	singular	plural
first person	(he, she insists) I love	(he, she insists) we love
second person	(he, she insists) you love	(he, she insists) you love
third person	(he, she insists) he, she, it love	(he, she insists) they love

The Present Subjunctive: Passive Voice

	singular	plural
first person	(he, she insists) I be loved	(he, she insists) we be loved
second person	(he, she insists) you be loved	(he, she insists) you be loved
third person	(he, she insists) he, she, it be loved	(he, she insists) they be loved

The Past Subjunctive: Active Voice

	singular	plural
first person	(if) I loved	(if) we loved
second person	(if) you loved	(if) you loved
third person	(if) he, she, it loved	(if) they loved

The Past Subjunctive: Passive Voice

	singular	plural
first person	(if) I were loved	(if) we were loved
second person	(if) you were loved	(if) you were loved
third person	(if) he, she, it were loved	(if) they were loved

The Imperative Mood

	singular	plural
second person	love	love

EXERCISE 29   **Directions:** Write out a complete set of tenses and moods for the verbs *hunt* (a regular verb) and *see* (an irregular verb).

*V*erbs name actions and conditions.

Regular verbs follow predictable patterns, but irregular verbs do not.

Verbs may be in the first person, the second person or the third person.

Verbs may be singular or plural.

The principal parts of a verb are the basic form, the past tense form, and the past participle.

Transitive verbs describe actions and require direct objects to complete their meanings.

Intransitive verbs describe actions but are not followed by direct objects or complements.

Linking verbs are followed not by objects but by subject complements.

Auxiliary (or helping) verbs, such as have, be, *and* do, *always appear with other verbs.*

Verb phrases are closely related groups of verbs that function in sentences the same way single verbs do.

Present participles are basic forms of verbs plus the ending -ing.

Finite verbs can function as main verbs in sentences, but nonfinite verbs, such as present participles, cannot.

A modal auxiliary verb, such as can, could, *and* may, *has only one form.*

The present tense describes actions or conditions that are taking place while they are being described.

The past tense describes actions or conditions that took place before they are described.

The future tense describes actions or conditions that will take place after they are described.

The perfect tenses indicate how an event or condition in the present, past or future continues to be relevant at a later time.

The progressive emphasizes that an event or condition being described is in progress.

The sequence of verb tenses within a sentence must be consistent with the times when the actions or conditions described by the verbs take place.

Interrogative sentences ask questions.

When subjects and verbs correspond in person and number, they are said to be in agreement.

Words that come between subjects and verbs do not affect the number or person of the verbs.

Verbs with compound subjects are usually plural, but when subjects are joined by or *the verb agrees with the subject closer to it.*

Reversing the order of a subject and verb does not alter the need for agreement between them.

Verbs agree with their subjects, not with their subject complements.

Most indefinite pronouns take singular verbs.

Collective nouns are usually singular.

Nouns can be singular in meaning but plural in form.

A sentence in which the performer of an action is the subject of the verb is in the active voice, but a sentence in which the target of the action is the subject of the verb is in the passive voice.

Factual sentences are in the indicative mood.

Requests and commands are in the imperative mood.

Verbs in the subjunctive mood express desires, conditions contrary to fact, and some requests.

Verbs in the present subjunctive appear in their basic forms, and verbs in the past subjunctive are identical with those in the past indicative.

5

Verbals

Verbals *are closely related to verbs. However, they function in sentences not as verbs but as nouns, adjectives, and adverbs. The difference between a verb and a verbal can be seen in the following examples:*

Ahmed reads *the book.*

Reading *is fun for Ahmed.*

In the first sentence, the word reads *describes an action. It is a verb, and its subject is the noun* Ahmed. *In the second sentence, however, the word* reading *names an action. It is a verbal and functions in this sentence as the subject of the verb* is.

There are three kinds of verbals: infinitives, participles, and gerunds. Infinitives, such as to run *and* to become, *function in sentences as nouns, adjectives, and adverbs. Participles, such as smiling in "a smiling face" and written in "a written apology," function as adjectives. Gerunds, such as* Smoking *in "Smoking can endanger your health" and* Flying *in "Flying is expensive," function as nouns.*

By using verbals correctly, you can add interest and variety to your writing. For example, in the following sentence, the participle barking *describes the noun* dogs *and makes the sentence more vivid:*

The barking *dogs frightened the children.*

IDENTIFYING INFINITIVES

Infinitives are basic forms of verbs preceded by the word *to*. For example, the infinitive of the verb *walk* is *to walk*.

Infinitives share some of the characteristics of verbs. Like verbs, they can have subjects and objects, and they can be modified by adverbs. Infinitives function in sentences as nouns, adjectives or adverbs:

noun

I love *to eat* breakfast in bed.

adjective

Our plan *to visit* Omaha was changed.

adverb

Your telephone number is easy *to remember*.

The word *to* is usually a preposition. Directly preceding the basic form of a verb, however, *to* is regarded as a marker (a sign of the infinitive) rather than a preposition. Following a few verbs (*hear, help, let, make, see,* and *watch* are the most common) the marker *to* is omitted:

We heard her *sing* (not *to sing*).

The whole family watched Amanda's ship *sail* (not *to sail*) away from the dock.

The word *to* can also be omitted from all except the first infinitive when infinitives appear in a series:

Elliott asked a waiter *to slip* the diamond ring on the stem of a rose, *(to) place* it on a silver tray, and *(to) deliver* it to Olivia.

Including *to* with each infinitive would make the sentence more formal.

EXERCISE 1   **Directions:** Underline the infinitives in the sentences below.

Example:

I want <u>to improve</u> my volleyball game before coed volleyball begins in October.

1. Julie spent thirty dollars to get her nails sculpted.

2. When Barry was transferred to Kansas City, his company helped his wife to find a job there.

3. Lourdes refuses to iron anything until she can find a good cordless iron.

4. We plan to finish our Thanksgiving dinner before the football games begin.

5. Oil tankers can be redesigned to reduce the chances of oil spills.

6. The tipover switch was supposed to turn off the electric heater as soon as it was knocked over.

7. Cornelia had hoped to learn Italian before she visited Rome.

8. Few people eat diets so unbalanced that they need to take vitamin supplements.

9. Are law enforcement officials likely to overreact if there is another crisis?

10. Two-door coupes continue to sell well.

Choosing among the Forms of the Infinitive

The standard form of the infinitive *(to call)* is known as the present infinitive. The present participle of a verb *(calling)* and the past participle *(called)* can be combined with *to be* and *to have* to create other kinds of present infinitives *(to be calling* and *to be called)* as well as perfect infinitives *(to have called, to have been calling,* and *to have been called)*.

Whether to use a present infinitive or a perfect infinitive depends on the time relationship between the infinitive and the main verb in a sentence. The tense of the main verb establishes the time frame of the sentence; a present infinitive describes an action occurring either at the same time or later. Compare the tenses in these sentences:

present tense: Ronald *wants* to find a new apartment.

past tense: Ronald *wanted* to find a new apartment.

past perfect tense: Ronald *had wanted* to find a new apartment.

In each of these sentences, the main verb *(wants, wanted, had wanted)* establishes the time of the action. Then the present infinitive *(to find)* describes an action occurring at the same time as or later than the action described by the main verb.

Perfect infinitives, on the other hand, describe actions that occurred before the action described by the main verb:

perfect infinitive
Jill is sorry *to have spoken* to Rick that way.

Jill is sorry now, but the act she regrets occurred in the past. (Notice that in this sentence the word *to* in "to Rick" is a preposition, not the marker of an infinitive.)

Understanding Infinitive Phrases

Infinitives can also be accompanied by subjects, objects, and modifiers. A group of words consisting of an infinitive and any other words needed to complete its meaning is called an infinitive phrase. Consider the following sentence:

subject   verb
To do a difficult job well <u>can be</u> very rewarding.

Here, the words "To do a difficult job well" function together as the subject of the verb. Infinitive phrases function in sentences just as unaccompanied infinitives do—as nouns, adjectives or adverbs.

EXERCISE 2   **Directions:** Underline the infinitive phrases in the sentences below.
Example:

Corrinne loves <u>to ride the moving sidewalks at the airport</u>.

1. Gayle uses chisels, a hammer, and a splitting tool to make her
    stone sculptures.

2. People seem to be drawing remarkably different conclusions
    from the same data.

3. Many zoo animals can learn to adjust to unfamiliar foods, but
    koalas eat only eucalyptus leaves.

4. An employee known to have been embittered against the com-
    pany left several abusive messages on the voice mail system.

5. The best time to watch for meteors is between midnight and
    sunrise.

6. Some corruption is too extensive to be comprehended easily by
    the general public.

7. Whenever they stand in line at the supermarket, the Wilsons like
    to read the headlines of the tabloids to each other.

8. Spaghetti tongs are used to lift cooked spaghetti from boiling
    water.

9. The first comic strip to appear in print was "The Yellow Kid."

10. Phil was rumored to have been looking for another job long
    before he found one.

**Using
Infinitives as
Nouns,
Adjectives, and
Adverbs**

Infinitives and infinitive phrases function in sentences in the same ways
that nouns, adjectives, and adverbs do.

INFINITIVES AS NOUNS

When infinitives function in sentences as nouns, they can be subjects,
objects, and subject complements, just as other nouns can:

As a subject: *To dance* is an enjoyable experience.

As an object: Ronald wanted *to leave*.

As a subject complement: Lucy's aim is *to finish*.

Infinitive phrases such as "To dance the rhumba," "to leave immediately," and "to finish college" could fulfill the same roles in these
sentences as the infinitives do.

INFINITIVES AS ADJECTIVES

Adjectives describe or limit nouns or pronouns. That is, they help distinguish the specific person, place or thing a noun or pronoun refers to from others of the same type. (For more on adjectives, see chapter 6.) Unlike most other adjectives, which usually precede the nouns they describe, infinitives and infinitive phrases functioning as adjectives follow nouns:

                                        adjective noun

Regina told Harry that *Dress for Success* was a *good* `book`

infinitive

to read   before he started his new job.

In this sentence both *good* and the infinitive *to read* describe the noun *book*, so both of them function as adjectives.

INFINITIVES AS ADVERBS

Infinitives and infinitive phrases can also function as adverbs. Adverbs describe or limit verbs, adjectives, other adverbs, verbals, and whole sentences. They answer a variety of questions about the words they modify, such as "Where?" "Why?" "When?" and "How?" (For more on adverbs, see chapter 6.) Look at the following sentence:

       verb   infinitive phrase

Alice spoke   *to set the record straight.*

In this sentence the infinitive phrase *to set the record straight* acts as an adverb modifying the verb *spoke*, answering the question "Why?" ("Why did Alice speak?" "She spoke to set the record straight.")

EXERCISE 3   **Directions:** Circle the abbreviations that identify the ways the underlined infinitive phrases function in the sentences below. Use the following code:

       N   noun   ADV   adverb   ADJ   adjective

Example:

  (N)   ADJ   Whenever Rachel isn't watching him, Buddy likes to slide down the bannister.

   N   ADV   1.   The manager of a convenience store in Canada piped Muzak into the store's parking lot <u>to discourage teenagers from loitering</u>.

   N   ADJ   2.   Cavities can begin <u>to develop</u> as soon as baby teeth appear in a child's mouth.

   N   ADV   3.   Solar collectors use reflecting surfaces <u>to direct sunlight onto collection panels</u>.

ADJ	ADV	4. Just as your mother always told you, the best type of bread <u>to eat</u> is dark bread, not white bread.
ADJ	ADV	5. Rory bought a computer so that he could take work home from the office, but he uses it mostly <u>to play games</u>.
ADJ	ADV	6. Doug has never been one <u>to complain about his sports injuries</u>.
N	ADJ	7. The best time <u>to shop for air conditioners</u> is during cool weather.
N	ADJ	8. The concave bottom of a water ski helps <u>to increase stability</u>.
N	ADJ	9. Installing smoke detectors is a good way <u>to save lives</u>.
N	ADV	10. Mei needed extra-strong tissues <u>to remove the clown make-up from her face and hands</u>.

Using Pronouns with Infinitives

When pronouns are the objects of infinitives, they are in the objective case:

Because Ron said he had seen the movie, Joan decided *to ask him* whether or not she should go.

Here the pronoun *him* is in the objective case because it is the object of the infinitive *to ask*.

When pronouns are the subjects of infinitives, they are also in the objective case:

Ron told Joan the movie was excellent and advised *her* (not *she*) *to go* see it as soon as she could.

Avoiding Split Infinitives

In an infinitive the word *to* and the basic verb that follows it form a close-knit unit. Placing words between *to* and the verb often seems awkward:

NOT: Although an earthquake temporarily interrupted the 1989 World Series, the A's and Giants arranged *to*, a week later, *resume* play.

An infinitive in which *to* and the verb are divided by one or more other words is called a **split infinitive**. Bringing the two parts of the infinitive together results in a more natural-sounding sentence:

Although an earthquake temporarily interrupted the 1989 World Series, the A's and Giants arranged *to resume* play a week later.

Some writers prefer never to split infinitives. However, while closely related words should not be separated without a good reason, sometimes words do seem to fit naturally between *to* and the verb:

> Mark's generosity in this crisis seems *to* more than *make* up for his earlier stinginess.

In this sentence, *not* splitting the infinitive would seem awkward to many writers, but others would still prefer to write "seems more than to make up for his earlier stinginess" to avoid splitting the infinitive. Since opinions differ on splitting infinitives, you may want to play it safe by keeping the two parts of infinitives together.

EXERCISE 4   **Directions:** Underline the words that split the infinitives in the sentences below. Then draw an arrow to show one place to which the underlined word could be moved.

Example:

> Insect repellents discourage insects, but they're not able to actually kill them.

1. Good soup does not need to necessarily be expensive.

2. Antonina hopes to definitely take advantage of the ten dollar discount offered at Hair You Are this week.

3. When Kay went to finally get her pendant appraised, she found out that it was worth only fifteen dollars.

4. To safely roller skate, a skater should wear knee pads, elbow pads, and a helmet.

5. Luis plans to immediately fly to Puerto Rico after final exams are over.

6. The new management's main policies are to severely cut salaries of middle managers and to take more marketing risks.

7. A housefly is able to sometimes live for seventy-six days.

8. An eighteen-wheeler truck is mounted on a fuel tower to dramatically advertise Eddie's Quick Stop Truckers' Heaven.

9. Several new magazines are designed to directly appeal to African-American readers.

10. Legal ethics require a lawyer to immediately report the unethical actions of another lawyer.

IDENTIFYING PARTICIPLES

In addition to their uses in verb phrases, both **present participles** (verb forms ending in *-ing*) and **past participles** (verb forms ending in *-d* or *-ed* in regular verbs) function as adjectives. In the following sentence, the present participle *growing* functions as an adjective to describe the noun *child*:

<blockquote>

participle   noun

A *growing*   child needs a good night's sleep.
</blockquote>

In the next sentence, the past participle *buried* describes the noun *treasure*:

<blockquote>

participle   noun

The beachcombers discovered *buried*   treasure.
</blockquote>

Adjectives usually appear in sentences directly in front of the nouns they describe. When participles are used as adjectives, they can appear in sentences in the same positions as other adjectives, but they can also follow the words they describe. In the following sentence, the past participle *broken* comes immediately in front of the noun:

<blockquote>

participle   noun

That *broken*   chair belongs in the trash.
</blockquote>

In the next sentence, the past participle comes after the noun:

<blockquote>

noun   participle

That chair *broken*   by Uncle Leo belongs in the trash.
</blockquote>

EXERCISE 5   **Directions:** Underline the participles in the sentences below. Each sentence contains one participle.

Example:

Clark's drum major uniform includes <u>tasseled</u> boots, breeches, a jacket with epaulets, and a hat with a plume.

1. The proposed bicycle routes would follow toll roads through several states.

2. Holograms, images created by laser light, appear to be three dimensional.

3. The egret, its head tilted to one side, prepared to spear its prey.

4. Annie soldered the colored pieces of glass together.

5. Many unaccompanied children regularly fly across the country.

6. In the nineteenth century mews were stables or carriage houses grouped around courtyards.

7. Briggs named his car Whistler because of the hissing sounds it makes.

8. Scuba divers breathe compressed air from tanks with mouthpieces.

9. New Yorkers assume that a flashing "Don't Walk" sign actually means "Run."

10. Pictures taken by Viking I and Viking II show that the surface of Mars looks much like the American Southwest.

Using Participial Phrases in Sentences

Participial phrases consist of participles and any other words needed to complete their meanings. In the following sentence, the participial phrase "Smiling at the children" consists of a present participle, *smiling*, and a prepositional phrase, *at the children*:

participial phrase
Smiling at the children, their father reached for the cookie jar.

Here the participial phrase functions as an adjective to describe the noun *father*.

Participial phrases always function as adjectives describing nouns or pronouns. In the following sentence, a participial phrase consisting of a past participle *(torn)* and a prepositional phrase *(by the strong winds)* describes the noun *sail*:

Torn by the strong winds, the sail flapped uselessly against the mast.

In the next sentence the participial phrase is made up of a present participle *(lying)* and a prepositional phrase *(on the kitchen floor)*. "Lying on the kitchen floor" describes the noun *newspapers*:

She was annoyed by the crumpled newspapers *lying on the kitchen floor*.

Participial phrases can include objects as well as prepositional phrases, as in the following sentence:

present   prepositional
participle   object   phrase
Spending   an hour   in the beauty salon, Melissa got a facial with a steam mist.

Here the participial phrase consists of a present participle *(Spending)*, the object of the participle *(an hour)*, and a prepositional phrase *(in the beauty salon)*. The whole participial phrase describes the noun *Melissa*.

EXERCISE 6   **Directions:** Underline the participial phrases in the sentences below.
Example:

Helen collects sunglasses <u>made in the fifties and sixties</u>.

1. A hovercraft crosses a body of water on a cushion of air blown through jets in the underside of its hull.

2. Chip describes himself as an innocent guppy swimming among the sharks.

3. Laurel came to work wearing shorts, a blouse, a tailored jacket, sheer hose, and flat shoes.

4. Heather wears adhesive bandages decorated with cartoon characters.

5. The floor plan of the new house includes one room labeled as an atrium and another called a mud room.

6. A barometer measures the weight of the air covering the earth's surface.

7. El Dorado was the fabled city of gold sought by early Spanish explorers in the New World.

8. Isobars are lines on maps connecting points with equal barometric pressure.

9. Greatcoats were the heavy overcoats worn by soldiers in the Revolutionary War.

10. Because lasers can be focused accurately, they are used in communication devices transmitting messages as far away as the moon.

Using Absolute Phrases in Sentences

An **absolute phrase** modifies an entire sentence rather than any specific word in the sentence. It consists of a noun or pronoun, a present participle or a past participle, and the words that modify them. An absolute phrase usually comes at the beginning or end of a sentence and is set off by a comma. In the following sentence, the absolute phrase "The milk having soured" modifies the whole main clause, "Martha drank her coffee black":

absolute phrase
The milk having soured, Martha drank her coffee black.

Sentences with absolute phrases tend to be a little awkward. You can usually improve them by changing the absolute phrases into subordinate clauses:

subordinate clause
Because the milk had soured, Martha drank her coffee black.

EXERCISE 7   **Directions:**
1. Underline the absolute phrases in the sentences below.
2. On the lines beneath the sentences, rewrite the sentences using the absolute phrases as subordinate clauses.
Example:

The thunderstorm being over, Oscar finally stopped barking.

When the thunderstorm was over,

Oscar finally stopped barking.

1. Time having been called, Marcella flipped through her program to find the names of the players.

_____

_____

2. The monkeys making their distinctive alarm calls, the leopard moved silently through the grass.

_____

_____

3. The litter having been removed from the roadside, the Scouts returned to their bus.

_____

_____

4. The electricity having gone off, we went to bed.

_____

_____

5. The weather being good, the picture will be taken outdoors.

_____

_____

6. The luncheon having ended, everyone began to leave the conference.

_____

_____

7. All things considered, the bake sale was a success.

_____

_____

8. Jeff absent-mindedly watched the traffic pass, the gas over
flowing from the car's tank.

_____

_____

9. The fireworks exploding overhead, I watched the
celebration from my rented house on the hillside.

_____

_____

10. The times being bad, we should save more money.

_____

_____

Avoiding Misplaced Participial Phrases

When a participial phrase is not an absolute phrase, it modifies the nearest noun or pronoun, just as an adjective would. In the following sentence, the participial phrase "Laughing at Bret's joke" describes the noun *Cynthia*:

> participial phrase   noun
> *Laughing at Bret's joke*, Cynthia spilled some of her soft drink on the new rug.

Sometimes, however, a writer intends a participial phrase to describe not the nearest noun or pronoun but one occurring later in the sentence. The result can be unintentionally humorous:

> NOT: Wearing a billowing white veil, the groom watched the bride walk down the aisle.

The writer obviously intended the participial phrase "Wearing a billowing white veil" to describe the bride; unfortunately, as the sentence is written, it describes the groom instead. The following sentence expresses what the writer intended:

> The groom watched the bride, wearing a billowing white veil, walk down the aisle.

You can avoid misplacing modifiers if you remember that participial phrases should always be as close as possible to the nouns or pronouns they describe.

EXERCISE 8

Directions: Rewrite the sentences below to correct the misplaced participial phrases. Also make any other changes you think are necessary.

Example:

Claiming she never wins anything, the lottery ticket was thrown away by Zoraida.

Claiming she never wins anything,

Zoraida threw away the lottery ticket.

1. Containing a bullet pouch, mace holder, pen holder, and handcuff case, a policeman wears a belt that stores much more than a gun.

   _____

   _____

2. Putting in many extra hours at the supermarket, the fire company is no longer Gary's first priority.

   _____

   _____

3. Changing the designs of U.S. coins, millions of dollars would probably be raised through sales to coin collectors by the government.

   _____

   _____

4. Now believed to be Iceland, the Romans called a land north of Britain Ultima Thule.

   _____

   _____

5. Spreading drops of honey through the hive and fanning them with their wings, the amount of water in nectar is reduced by bees.

   _____

   _____

6. Considering the Bacharach's property too small for the number of donkeys they have, a protest was filed at city hall by the neighbors.

_____

_____

7. Using the computerized sewing machine, elaborate lettering and decorative patterns were sewn by Johanna.

_____

_____

8. Running to my car, a ring was found by me.

_____

_____

9. Wearing a morning coat and striped trousers, tea was brought in on a silver tray by the butler.

_____

_____

10. Using a metal detector, the lost class ring was searched for by May and Frederick.

_____

_____

Avoiding Dangling Participial Phrases

A participial phrase must describe or modify something. If it is an absolute phrase, it modifies the entire sentence. If not, it describes a noun or pronoun in the main part of the sentence. Participial phrases modifying words that do not appear in a sentence are called **dangling participial phrases**. Like misplaced participial phrases, they are sometimes unintentionally humorous:

NOT: Taking the ferry across the harbor, the Statue of Liberty came into view.

Revising the sentence clarifies the writer's intention:

Taking the ferry across the harbor, I saw the Statue of Liberty come into view.

EXERCISE 9   **Directions:** Indicate whether or not the sentences below contain dangling participial phrases by using the following code:

C   correct   I   incorrect

Example:

__/__   Believing the ten-year-old clothes in the back of her closet will someday come back into fashion, none of them have been thrown away.

_____ 1.   Containing tennis courts and pools, some marinas are more like resorts than boat garages.

_____ 2.   Having watched the movie closely, the ending was confusing.

_____ 3.   Viewing alcohol as a beverage, it is often not considered a drug.

_____ 4.   Scrubbers are small chemical plants reducing the amount of sulfur emitted by burning coal.

_____ 5.   Judging subliminal messages to be ineffective, such advertisements were abandoned in the 1950s.

_____ 6.   Trying to decide whether to buy a mask of Woody Allen or of Frankenstein, Joey lingered thoughtfully by the drugstore display.

_____ 7.   Imagining that life exists on Titan, one of Saturn's moons, many science fiction stories have been written.

_____ 8.   Remarking that too many Americans have forgotten what Memorial Day means, the parade attracted a very small crowd.

_____ 9.   Having been laid off from his job in an aircraft factory, Virgil became a detective in order to pay his mortgage bills.

_____ 10.   Riding on a rubber raft, Leslie and Colleen traveled down the Snake River.

TRY IT OUT

Starting every sentence you write with its subject might make your life easier, but it could become tedious for your readers. To keep readers interested, you can vary the way you begin some of your sentences. Infinitive and participial phrases make good beginnings because they allow you to suggest complicated relationships between your ideas. Suppose you had written the following sentence:

> The librarian told stories about the first day of school.

This sentence would be more interesting and informative if it began with an infinitive phrase or a participial phrase:

> To allay children's fears of kindergarten, the librarian told stories about the first day of school.

> *or*

> Allaying children's fears of kindergarten, the librarian told stories about the first day of school.

Try adding your own introductory infinitive phrases or participial phrases to the sentences below:

1. Hope made a telephone call.
2. The group began to sing.
3. Olivia agreed to marry Elliott.
4. Charlie bought the car.
5. Kristie wore a bullet-proof vest.

AVOIDING SENTENCE FRAGMENTS CONTAINING VERBALS BUT NOT COMPLETE VERBS

Infinitives and participles cannot function as main verbs. In other words, they can never be the only verbs in sentences or clauses. A group of words that contains an infinitive or a participle rather than a main verb is a sentence fragment:

> NOT: Lois to eat chili.

> NOT: Lois eating chili.

You can correct fragments containing only infinitives and participles by adding a verb:

> Lois *likes* to eat chili.

> Lois *likes* eating chili.

EXERCISE 10   **Directions:** Identify the items below by using the following code:

F   sentence fragment   C   complete sentence

Example:

_C_   Cirrus clouds are high, wispy clouds containing a large number of tiny ice crystals.

_____ 1.   In 1787 Delaware becoming the first state to ratify the Constitution.

_____ 2.   Big Bertha was a huge cannon used by the Germans in World War I.

_____ 3.   A flock of starlings known as a murmuration.

_____ 4.   Benjamin Franklin invented bifocal glasses.

_____ 5.   Like Washington, DC, Brasilia, Brazil, is a planned community.

_____ 6.   How to spell *embarrass* and *ukulele*.

_____ 7.   A ten-gallon hat actually holds less than one gallon.

_____ 8.   About one out of every three new houses to have a garage with an automatic door opener.

_____ 9.   A van carrying seven or eight people and a great deal of luggage.

_____ 10.   The Environmental Protection Agency recently reporting a decline in toxic pollution.

IDENTIFYING GERUNDS

When verb forms ending in *-ing* are used as nouns, they are called **gerunds.** Like verbs, gerunds name actions or conditions:

Mary's *complaining* gives me a headache.

Believing Don's stories is often impossible.

Like other nouns, gerunds can function in sentences as subjects, objects, subject complements, and objects of prepositions:

As a subject: *Smoking* can ruin your health.

As an object: The fire code prohibited *smoking*.

As a subject complement: His worst habit was *smoking*.

As an object of a preposition: Howard was fined for *smoking* in the subway.

EXERCISE 11   **Directions:** Underline the gerunds in the sentences below.

Example:

<u>Tripping</u> the main circuit breaker turned off all the lights.

1. Packing small items in stuffsacks is a good way to organize a suitcase.

2. Mrs. Hagan attended a seminar yesterday on trends in accounting.

3. A bank or department store must give a reason for refusing to give someone a credit card.

4. Automatically accepting someone else's advice is almost always a mistake.

5. Mr. Fanning was arguing that company managers should understand the practical, though challenging, aspects of manufacturing.

6. Eating skunks does not seem to bother great horned owls.

7. Naomi criticized Eugenia for choosing a yellow bedspread, yellow curtains, and a ruffled yellow tablecloth.

8. Zoe accidentally ended the telephone call by bumping the cutoff button on the receiver.

9. World War I demonstrated the need for standardizing manufactured items such as screws.

10. Rhea is making baby food by pureeing fruits and vegetables in her blender.

Distinguishing Gerunds from Participles

Gerunds can be distinguished from present participles only because they function in sentences as nouns rather than adjectives. In the following sentence, *reading* is a gerund because it functions as a noun (the subject of the verb *is*):

gerund

College-level *reading* is often difficult.

But in this sentence, *reading* is a participle describing the noun *skills*:

participle

Good *reading* skills are needed for success in college.

EXERCISE 12   **Directions:** Identify the underlined words in the sentences below as gerunds or participles by using the following code:

G   gerund   P   participle

Example:

_P_   A <u>tilting</u> floor might be a sign that a building has a serious structural problem.

_____ 1.   Lawrence keeps his brother awake by <u>snoring</u> all night.

_____ 2.   The sequoias of central California are the largest <u>living</u> things on earth.

_____ 3.   A <u>cooking</u> fire should be made in a safe place, such as on a flat rock.

_____ 4.   <u>Diving</u> should be forbidden in above-ground pools, which are only about four feet deep.

_____ 5.   Leaving the <u>starting</u> line of a drag race too soon is called red-lighting.

_____ 6.   Our videotape on <u>burglar-proofing</u> our home was stolen, along with our video recorder and television set.

_____ 7.   At the aquarium Katie likes <u>watching</u> the whale shark.

_____ 8.   Thanks for the tips on <u>negotiating</u> a better salary.

_____ 9.   A pontoon bridge rests on <u>floating</u> piers.

_____ 10.   "Madam, I'm Adam" is a palindrome, a sentence <u>reading</u> the same forward and backward.

Using Gerund Phrases in Sentences

Gerunds are often modified by adverbs and introduced by definite or indefinite articles:

gerund   adverb
Practicing constantly improved Mika's skating.

article   gerund
The   practicing was time consuming but not difficult.

Gerund phrases consist of gerunds and any other words needed to complete their meanings. They function in sentences in the same ways one-word gerunds do:

As a subject: *Smoking cigarettes* can ruin your health.

As an object: The fire code prohibited *smoking anywhere in the building*.

As a subject complement: His worst habit was *smoking cigars*.

As an object of a preposition: By *smoking heavily* Cami endangered the health of her unborn child.

Sometimes infinitives functioning in sentences as nouns are interchangeable with gerunds. Changing from one to the other does not alter the meaning of a sentence. For example, the sentence "To remember the birthdays of all my cousins is impossible" can be changed to "Remembering the birthdays of all my cousins is impossible."

EXERCISE 13   **Directions:** Underline the infinitive phrases in the sentences below. Then change the infinitives to gerunds and write them on the lines at the left.

Example:

Sucking   To suck on plain hard candies can relieve a cough due to a cold.

_____ 1. To blend two words results in an entirely new word, such as *chortle*, a blend of *chuckle* and *snort*.

_____ 2. Jani's three-month old baby loves to look into the safety mirror above his crib.

_____ 3. Peanut butter will keep for several weeks at room temperature, but to refrigerate it extends its shelf life.

_____ 4. According to my doctor, to descend even 1,000 feet can help relieve altitude sickness.

_____ 5. To advertise job openings is relatively inexpensive, but advertisements are seldom seen by people who are not actively looking for jobs.

_____ 6. Many people believe that to be shy is a charming quality.

_____ 7. To play the national anthem before sporting events is traditional in the United States.

_____ 8. Ernie kept telling me that to install a prefabricated disappearing attic staircase was a reasonable task for two people working together.

_____ 9. To move a camera from side to side is called panning.

_____ 10. To get ahead in business is the main goal of the networking organization Robin attends.

Using Possessives with Gerunds

Nouns or pronouns preceding gerunds are in the possessive case:

> gerund
>
> *The star's singing* left much to be desired.

> gerund
>
> *His acting*, however, was first rate.

Sometimes an adjective comes between the noun or pronoun and the gerund. When this happens, the noun or pronoun should still be in the possessive case:

> gerund
>
> *Doug's* constant *chattering* makes him unpopular at work.

EXERCISE 14   **Directions:** Circle the word that correctly completes each sentence below.

Example:

> Jim supports (our, us) launching solar-powered satellites that would beam electricity down to the earth.

1. (Marcy, Marcy's) getting elected was mostly a matter of luck.

2. Sean and Joe say that (their, them) buying special spiked boots was necessary for ice climbing.

3. (You, Your) wearing camouflage pants all the time actually makes you stand out in a crowd.

4. (Jessie, Jessie's) wearing a black dress for her wedding caused several arguments in our family.

5. The worst mistake was (me, my) buying platinum from a telephone salesperson.

6. (Clay, Clay's) acting calmly helped me to calm down.

7. My (dentist, dentist's) leaving the television set on all the time distracts me while I am having my teeth filled.

8. Buzz knew that (him, his) parallel parking might cause him to fail his driver's test.

9. (Lucy, Lucy's) carrying a set of skeleton keys in her purse worried her friends.

10. Everyone in Leah's house woke up because of (her, she) dropping the fishing tackle on the kitchen floor.

KEEPING VERBALS PARALLEL

Many sentences provide lists of two, three or more words, phrases or clauses separated by commas. Such lists should be parallel. Items in a list are **parallel** when they are in the same grammatical form. The following sentence contains a series of three verbals, only two of which are infinitives:

> NOT: Antoine uses the attachments on his Swiss Army knife *to magnify small items, filing his nails*, and *to measure insects he finds.*

To be parallel, all three items should be in the same grammatical form:

> Antoine uses the attachments on his Swiss Army knife *to magnify small items, to file his nails*, and *to measure insects he finds.*

In a sentence like this one, you can use *to* in each of the parts (to magnify, to file, and to measure) or in only the first one (to magnify, file, and measure). However, using *to* in two parts of the sentence is not acceptable (NOT: to magnify, file, and to measure.)

This sentence could also be rewritten using gerunds rather than infinitives:

> Antoine uses the attachments on his Swiss Army knife *for magnifying small items, filing his nails*, and *measuring insects he finds.*

The rule for repeating *for* in this sentence is the same as the rule for using *to* in the previous example: *For* can be used with all three gerunds (for magnifying, for filing, and for measuring) or only with the first one, (for magnifying, filing, and measuring), but it cannot be used with two of the three (NOT: for magnifying, filing, and for measuring).

EXERCISE 15   **Directions:** Rewrite the underlined sections of the sentences below to make them parallel. Follow the directions in parentheses after each item.

Example:

> This summer the Sioux Center Recreation Department will sponsor classes <u>in swimming and to lift weights</u>. (Use gerunds.)

> *in swimming and in lifting weights*

1. Propylene glycol is a colorless ingredient used in foods <u>to thicken them, helping their ingredients combine smoothly, and preserving them</u>. (Use infinitives.)

_____

_____

2. A bulldozer is used <u>for pushing earth and to grade it</u>. (Use infinitives.)

_____

_____

3. In ancient Rome people used perfume <u>for bathing, to soak their clothing, and even to give their horses a more pleasant odor</u>. (Use gerunds.)

_____

_____

4. Humid air is responsible <u>for encouraging mildew, to warp wood, and to rust metal</u>. (Use gerunds.)

_____

_____

5. Among the warning signs of possible arson are the insured person <u>not being at home during the fire and to have removed valued belongings before the fire</u>. (Use gerunds.)

_____

_____

6. The bridge girders are equipped with detectors <u>to gauge stress and alerting a computer</u> when repairs are needed. (Use infinitives.)

_____

_____

7. <u>Removing the front door and to carry the four-poster bed upstairs</u> were the hardest parts of the move. (Use gerunds.)

_____

_____

8. Service robots work closely with humans to do repetitive tasks such as <u>making french fries and to clean washrooms</u>. (Use gerunds.)

_____

_____

9. <u>Increasing dietary intake of calcium and to exercise regularly</u> are ways to prevent osteoporosis. (Use gerunds.)

_____

_____

10. Gerald was annoyed at himself <u>for taping his traveler's checks to the back of the mirror in his motel room and then to forget to take them with him the next day</u>. (Use gerunds.)

_____

_____

Verbals are closely related to verbs, but they function in sentences as nouns, adjectives, and adverbs.

Infinitives are basic forms of verbs preceded by the word to.

Infinitive phrases consist of infinitives and any other words needed to complete their meanings.

Infinitives can be used as nouns, adjectives, and adverbs.

Pronouns used as subjects or objects of infinitives should be in the objective case.

Some writers prefer never to split the two parts of an infinitive.

Present participles are verb forms ending in -ing which sometimes function as adjectives.

Past participles are verb forms ending in -ed which sometimes function as adjectives.

Participial phrases, which consist of participles and other words needed to complete their meanings, function as adjectives.

An absolute phrase consists of a noun or pronoun, a present participle or a past participle, and the words that modify them. An absolute phrase modifies an entire sentence.

Participial phrases should be located as close as possible to the words they modify.

The words modified by dangling participial phrases do not appear in the sentences in which the participial phrases appear.

Infinitives and participles cannot function in sentences as main verbs.

Gerunds are verb forms ending in -ing which function in sentences as nouns.

Gerund phrases consist of gerunds and any other words needed to complete their meanings. They function as nouns in sentences.

Nouns or pronouns preceding gerunds should be in the possessive case.

Verbals that appear in lists of two or more words or phrases should be parallel, which means they should be in the same grammatical form.

6

Adjectives and Adverbs

*A*djectives and adverbs are **modifiers**. *Modifiers make words more specific by describing or limiting them in some way. Some writers overuse modifiers, hoping an abundance of adjectives and adverbs will make up for an imprecise choice of nouns and verbs. However, carefully selected adjectives or adverbs can make writing more interesting and memorable.*

ADJECTIVES

Adjectives modify nouns and pronouns:

      adjectives
An *old brown* shoe was lying on the floor of the closet.

The adjectives *old* and *brown* in this sentence describe this particular shoe and help distinguish it from other shoes.

Many adjectives answer the question "What kind of?" about the words they modify. ("What kind of shoe was it?" "An *old brown* shoe.") Other adjectives answer the questions "How many?" and "Which one?":

There are *500 sheets* of paper in a ream.

A sirocco is a *hot Saharan* wind.

Identifying Adjectives

Often you will be able to recognize adjectives by their positions immediately before nouns:

Rowena's calculator has *large* keys.

Despite the *heavy* snow, *many* people were not wearing boots.

Yuri Gagarin was the *first* man to travel into *outer* space.

Adjectives are also often found in predicates after linking verbs:

Mariela feels *lonely*.

Computer images can be *beautiful*.

Psychiatrists must be *licensed*.

Sometimes you can identify adjectives by their endings. Many (though not all) adjectives are formed from nouns and other parts of speech. The chart below illustrates endings that are commonly used to change nouns into adjectives:

Nouns	Endings	Adjectives
reason	-able	reasonable
person	-al	personal
wood	-en	wooden
hope	-ful	hopeful
magnet	-ic	magnetic
girl	-ish	girlish
excess	-ive	excessive
care	-less	careless
coward	-ly	cowardly
poison	-ous	poisonous
stone	-y	stony

Short adjectives change their endings to compare people, things or ideas:

Clem's *older* boy started school yesterday.

I own the *oldest* house on the block.

Longer adjectives add *more* and *most*:

My cat is *more* intelligent than Cindy's dog.

My niece is the *most* interesting five-year-old child I've ever met.

Numbers are often used as adjectives:

There were *300* cars parked on the lawn in front of the church.

In this sentence, the number *300* answers the question "How many?" Numbers functioning as adjectives that answer the question "How many?" are called **cardinal numbers**.

A number such as *first*, on the other hand, answers the question "Which one?" in the following sentence:

The *first* one to arrive should turn on the lights.

Numbers functioning as adjectives that answer the question "Which one?" are called **ordinal numbers.**

EXERCISE 1 **Directions:** Underline the adjectives in the sentences below. The number of adjectives in each sentence is indicated in parentheses.

Example:

A <u>severe</u> thunderstorm can produce tornados. (1)

1. *Gone with the Wind* is the only book that Margaret Mitchell ever wrote. (1)

2. Adrienne thinks good manners are the basis for good personal relationships. (3)

3. Americans spend more time on the telephone today than they did in 1980. (1)

4. The compulsive gambler bets in an attempt to relieve psychic pain. (2)

5. Life Savers are formed by shaping a sugary mixture around a rod. (1)

6. At the Ritz the same movie has been playing at midnight for six months. (2)

7. Mistletoe is a parasitic shrub. (1)

8. A universal wrench works with nuts and bolts of various sizes. (2)

9. A trigamist has three husbands or wives. (1)

10. Gemma's top priority in a car is a big trunk. (2)

Understanding Adjective Patterns

Adjectives can precede the words they describe, follow them or appear after linking verbs in predicates to describe the subjects of sentences.

THE ADJECTIVE-NOUN PATTERN

Most adjectives appear in sentences immediately before the nouns they describe:

                                 adjective   noun

I like fireworks that end in a burst of   *red*   stars.

When a noun is preceded by an article (*a, an* or *the*), the usual order is article-adjective-noun:

article   adjective   noun

 An   *immature*   sloth clings to its mother for the first year of its life.

THE NOUN-ADJECTIVE PATTERN

Adjectives occasionally follow the nouns they describe:

At that moment a woman, *tall and stately*, entered the room.

Here the adjectives *tall* and *stately* describe the noun *woman*.

Adjectives used as object complements also follow the nouns they describe:

direct   object
object   complement

Ronnie called his brother   *stupid*.

Here the adjective *stupid* completes the meaning of the noun *brother*. (**Object complements** follow direct objects and provide additional information that describes or clarifies them. Object complements can be either nouns or adjectives. For more information on nouns as object complements, see chapter 2.)

THE SUBJECT-LINKING VERB-ADJECTIVE PATTERN

Adjectives often follow linking verbs. These adjectives describe the subjects of the linking verbs, so they are called subject complements. (**Subject complements** follow linking verbs and rename or describe the subjects of the verbs. They can be either nouns or adjectives. For more information on nouns as subject complements, see chapter 2.) Another name for a subject complement that is an adjective is a **predicate adjective**:

predicate
subject   adjective

That restaurant is *expensive*.

Here the adjective *expensive* describes the noun *restaurant*.

EXERCISE 2   **Directions:** Identify the underlined adjectives in the sentences below as object complements or predicate adjectives. Use the following code:

OC   object complement   PA   predicate adjective

Example:

OC   Mrs. Burke called my proposal <u>foolish</u>.

_____ 1.   Apartments are rarely <u>cheaper</u> than dorm rooms.

_____ 2.   Elliott's flattering comments made Olivia very <u>happy</u>.

_____ 3.   Grass roots grow about as far down as the grass is <u>high</u>.

_____ 4.   Rachel dyed her shoes <u>mauve</u>.

_____ 5.   Canned tuna should be <u>moist</u>, <u>firm</u>, and moderately <u>salty</u>.

_____ 6.   Helen Keller was <u>blind</u> and <u>deaf</u> from the age of two.

_____ 7.   I always find Andy's jokes very <u>funny</u>.

_____ 8.   Will what seems profound today appear <u>trivial</u> in ten years?

_____ 9.   Your mistake made the ice cream too <u>salty</u>.

_____ 10.   The office workers who were eating snacks in the lounge seemed <u>relaxed</u> and <u>cheerful</u>.

TRY IT OUT

Would you like your writing to be more interesting and memorable? One way to achieve this goal is to be more specific. Active verbs and well-chosen nouns play a part in bringing your writing to life. However, distinctive adjectives can also help make writing more vivid. For example, a sentence such as "A girl watched a movie in the house" is less interesting than "A frightened girl watched a terrifying horror movie in the dark, lonely house." The difference between these two sentences is that adjectives have been added to the second sentence.

Another idea to try is using words that appeal to the five senses: sight, hearing, taste, smell, and touch. The sentence "A car distracted Jeremy from his work" does not appeal to the senses. By providing some specific sensory detail, the following sentence gives a more complete picture: "An old Ford backfiring outside the warm office distracted Jeremy from his monthly budget projections."

Try adding adjectives to the sentences below to make them more interesting. If you wish, make other changes in the sentences as well. Feel free to invent details.

1. An article in a magazine gave a woman an idea.

2. The team won the game.

3. I removed some things from the desk top and spread out a map.

4. A man prepared and ate a meal.

5. Yasmin bought a car and took a trip.

Using Participles, Nouns, Phrases, and Clauses as Adjectives

Present and past participles can function in sentences as adjectives, and even nouns are sometimes used to modify other nouns or pronouns. In addition, entire phrases and clauses can be used as adjectives.

USING PARTICIPLES AS ADJECTIVES

Both present and past participles can function as adjectives:

> present
> participle
> The *jumping* horses were beautiful to watch.

In this sentence the present participle *jumping* functions as an adjective to modify *horses*.

> past
> participle
> When I was young, we taped up our *broken* baseball bats and used them for softball.

Here, the past participle *broken* functions as an adjective to modify *bats*.

USING NOUNS AS ADJECTIVES

Nouns can function as adjectives that describe other nouns or pronouns:
> A *copper* pan is hard to clean.

Here *copper*, which is usually a noun, functions as an adjective, answering the question "What kind of?" about the noun *pan*.

Often the only way to tell whether a word is a noun or an adjective is to see how it functions in a sentence:

> noun
> Justin took a *matchbook* from the Candlelight Restaurant even though he doesn't smoke.

In the first sentence *matchbook* is a noun, the direct object of the verb *took*.

> adjective
> Justin collects *matchbook* covers that feature advertisements for restaurants.

In the second sentence, however, *matchbook* is an adjective. It describes the noun *covers*.

EXERCISE 3

Directions:

1. Identify the underlined words in the sentences below as nouns or adjectives. Use the following code:

> N   noun   ADJ   adjective

2. For each noun used as an adjective, write the noun it describes on the line at the end of the sentence.

Example:

ADJ   We finally found the cat in the <u>bedroom</u> closet.
         closet

_____ 1.   More than 60 percent of accidents in nuclear plants take place during <u>night</u> shifts. _____

_____ 2.   A crib mattress should fit a <u>crib</u> snugly without any gaps between the edge of the mattress and the bars.
         _____

_____ 3.   The queen of one kind of <u>army</u> ant can produce 3 million offspring in its lifetime. _____

_____ 4.   Islands tend to have fewer species of animals than are found on the <u>mainland</u>. _____

_____ 5.   When Eli's car was stolen, he called the thieves on his <u>car</u> telephone and negotiated with them for the car's return.
         _____

_____ 6.   Industries in federal prisons manufacture everything from electrical cables to Smokey Bear fire <u>safety</u> signs.
         _____

_____ 7.   Painted wooden <u>fish</u> are used as decoys in ice fishing.
         _____

_____ 8.   Radio telescopes produce images derived from <u>radio</u> waves emitted by celestial objects. _____

_____ 9.   So many of my friends have moved recently that I started using a pencil to write in my <u>address</u> book. _____

_____ 10.   When soap is used in hard water, it can leave a dull <u>film</u> on hair. _____

USING PHRASES AND CLAUSES AS ADJECTIVES

Sometimes phrases and clauses function as adjectives:

```
              adjective
     noun    phrase
The glass in the sink is cracked.
```

Here the prepositional phrase "in the sink" answers the question "Which one?" about the noun *glass*. It therefore functions as an adjective.

```
     noun        adjective clause
The house that my grandfather built has been sold.
```

In this sentence the relative clause "that my grandfather built" functions as an adjective. It answers the question "Which one?" about the noun *house*.

Most phrases and clauses used as adjectives follow the words they describe:

A room *with such small windows* should be painted white.

In this sentence the prepositional phrase "with such small windows" describes the noun *room*.

People *who leave their shopping carts in supermarket parking spaces reserved for the handicapped* ought to be ashamed of themselves.

In this sentence the relative clause "who leave their shopping carts in supermarket parking spaces reserved for the handicapped" modifies the noun *People*.

EXERCISE 4 **Directions:**

1. A prepositional phrase functioning as an adjective or a clause functioning as an adjective has been underlined in each sentence below. Identify it by using the following code:

  P   prepositional phrase   C   clause

2. Write the noun described by the phrase or clause on the line at the end of the sentence.

Example:

___*C*___ The young woman <u>whose car was being towed away</u> cried uncontrollably. ___*woman*___

_____ 1. An avocet is a graceful, long-legged bird <u>with a thin, curved bill</u>. _____

_____ 2. Some small animals may die in a forest fire, but animals <u>that survive</u> quickly return to repopulate burned-out areas. _____

_____ 3. Almost everything Amy owned was stolen from the locked trunk <u>of her car</u>. _____

_____ 4. A bagpipe's melody is played on the eight open holes <u>in the chanter</u>. _____

_____ 5. A coin dropped in a vending machine trips a delicately balanced lever <u>that releases the product selected</u>. _____

_____ 6. Tanning, which became fashionable in the 1920s, is actually the body's defense <u>against ultraviolet rays</u>. _____

_____ 7. Getting the car tuned up ruined Carol's budget <u>for this week</u>.
_____

_____ 8. Timothy wanted to know the truth <u>about his sleepwalking</u>.
_____

_____ 9. The girl <u>whom I met at the softball game</u> lives in Detroit.
_____

_____ 10. Todd's children attend school in the building <u>where he works</u>.
_____

Coordinate Adjectives

When two or more adjectives in a row describe the same word, and the adjectives can appear in whatever order the writer chooses, they are **coordinate adjectives**:

> A *competent, enthusiastic* staff is the main thing parents should look for when choosing a daycare center.

In this sentence the adjectives *competent* and *enthusiastic* both describe the noun *staff.* If the adjectives were reversed, the sentence would still have the same meaning:

> An *enthusiastic, competent* staff is the main thing parents should look for when choosing a daycare center.

However, some pairs of adjectives can appear in only one order:

> Bob bought a suit and *several silk* ties before he started his new job.

Here the adjectives *several* and *silk* both describe *ties.* Notice that the adjective *several* must appear in the sentence before the adjective *silk*; "silk several ties" does not sound natural. Thus, *several* and *silk* are not coordinate adjectives.

Now look at the following sentence and decide whether the adjectives describing *balloons* are coordinate or not:

> Edward bought *bright, colorful* balloons to celebrate the first day of summer.

Both *bright* and *colorful* describe *balloons*, but this time reversing them works smoothly: "colorful, bright balloons" sounds as natural as "bright, colorful balloons." They are therefore coordinate.

Another test for coordinate adjectives is to put *and* between them. The words "bright and colorful balloons" sound natural, so *bright* and *colorful* are coordinate. "Several and silk ties" does not sound natural, so the adjectives *several* and *silk* are not coordinate. Coordinate adjectives require a comma between them; adjectives that are not coordinate do not require commas.

EXERCISE 5   **Directions:**

1. Identify the underlined adjectives as coordinate or not coordinate by using the following code:

   C   coordinate   NC   not coordinate

2. Insert commas between the coordinate adjectives. Do not punctuate adjectives that are not coordinate.

Example:

_**C**_   A <u>wary</u> , <u>anxious</u> police officer watched the angry crowd.

_____ 1.   Galileo's telescope was a <u>simple</u> <u>lead</u> tube with two lenses.

_____ 2.   <u>Our</u> <u>school</u> lunch will be cheese pizza, mixed vegetables, and chilled peaches.

_____ 3.   Balsa is a <u>soft</u> <u>light</u> wood.

_____ 4.   The <u>largest</u> <u>tabletop</u> television sets require sturdy tables.

_____ 5.   Unnecessary bleaching will lead to <u>faded</u> <u>deteriorating</u> fabric.

_____ 6.   Shampoo advertisements promise <u>shiny</u> <u>silky</u> hair.

_____ 7.   My mother taught in a <u>little</u> <u>red</u> schoolhouse.

_____ 8.   Before the 1890s, toothpaste was marketed in porcelain jars, not in <u>soft</u> <u>metal</u> tubes.

_____ 9.   The cello has a <u>deep</u> <u>rich</u> tone.

_____10.   Are there <u>safe</u> <u>inexpensive</u> allergy medications?

Compound Adjectives

Sometimes a group of two or more words forms a unit that describes one noun or pronoun. This kind of group is called a **compound adjective**. The individual words in the group may belong to any of the parts of speech.

When a compound adjective appears before the word it describes, hyphens are usually used between the words of the compound:

> We now have a *clear-cut* objective: to sell as many raffle tickets as we can.

In this sentence, the compound adjective *clear-cut* describes *objective*, just as a one-word adjective would.

However, when a compound adjective follows the word it describes, no hyphens are used:

> Our objective is *clear cut* : to sell as many raffle tickets as we can.

Sometimes adverbs appear in compound adjectives, as in "a *well*-conceived plan." However, when adverbs that end in *-ly*, such as *easily* and *suddenly*, form part of a compound, no hyphen is used between them and other words in the group:

> Busy people need a list of *easily prepared* meals to make when they don't have time to cook.

The adverb *very* is not hyphenated when it is part of a compound adjective. Sometimes common compound adjectives are also not hyphenated.

EXERCISE 6   **Directions:**

1. Underline the compound adjectives in the sentences below.
2. Hyphenate the compound adjectives that precede nouns.

Example:

> Bottle- nosed dolphins rolled to the surface of the shallow water for breaths of air.

1. The first all talking movie, *Light of New York*, appeared in 1928.

2. The name Netherlands literally means "lands that are low lying."

3. Caroline's favorite kind of tea has a baked apple aroma and a spicy taste.

4. On the two mile trail through Mississippi's Bienville National Forest, the most common trees are loblolly, shortleaf, and longleaf pine.

5. Shirley's prize winning tomato weighed more than four pounds.

6. Of all games Monopoly is the largest selling.

7. Fiber optic wires carry far more data than ordinary cables.

8. Jeannette has a battery powered sweeper that very easily removes crumbs from the dinner table.

9. A hand is a four inch unit of measurement used to determine the height of horses.

10. Billions of calls are made to toll free numbers each year.

Proper Adjectives

Proper adjectives are adjectives formed from proper nouns:

> proper
> adjective
> The *American* dollar is accepted in many countries other than the United States.

The proper adjective *American*, which describes dollar, is formed from the proper noun *America*.

proper
adjective

The town of Cape Coral contains many beautiful *Victorian* houses.

The proper adjective *Victorian* comes from Victoria, the queen of England from 1837 to 1901. Victorian is a style of architecture that became popular in her time and is named after her.

Like proper nouns, proper adjectives are capitalized. However, a few of them have become so familiar that they have become ordinary adjectives. In the following sentence the proper adjective *French*, formed from the proper noun *France*, is capitalized:

Linda bought her mother a bottle of *French* perfume for her birthday.

In this sentence, however, the adjective *french* is not capitalized:

Linda bought a hamburger and *french* fries for lunch.

People no longer associate this kind of fried potato with France. As a result, they treat *french* as an ordinary adjective rather than a proper adjective. However, writing *French fries* is not wrong.

EXERCISE 7   **Directions:** Capitalize the proper adjectives in the sentences below. Each sentence contains one proper adjective.

Example:

A salary was originally a sum of money given to *R*oman soldiers to buy salt.

1. About ninety percent of all known plant varieties are african plants.

2. Three of the asian girls who have become friends speak to each other in English because their native languages are different.

3. The ancient egyptian people knew that eating sweets led to tooth decay.

4. The first english possession outside Europe was Newfoundland.

5. The word *khaki* comes from the hindi term for dust colored.

6. Don and Trevor drove from British Columbia to Alaska on the alcan Highway.

7. Scientists report that brazilian wildlife includes a large number of sloths, anteaters, and armadillos, along with a wide variety of multicolored birds and a great many insects.

8. Unlike Europeans, american shoppers do not buy foods such as cream cheese and chocolate syrup in metal or plastic tubes.

9. Thomas Jefferson planted poplars along pennsylvania Avenue in Washington, DC.

10. I wish I could afford to go to more broadway plays.

ADVERBS

Adverbs modify words that cannot be modified by adjectives. Adverbs modify verbs, adjectives, other adverbs, verbals, and whole sentences. In the following sentence the adverb *quickly* modifies the verb *run*:

　　　　　　　　　　　　　　　　　　verb　　adverb

As we turned the corner, we saw a rabbit run　*quickly* back into the bushes.

Here the adverb *especially* modifies the adjective *glad*:

　　　　　　adverb　　　adjective

Michelle was *especially*　glad she had remembered her parents' anniversary.

In this sentence the adverb *very* modifies the adverb *soundly* (*soundly* modifies the verb *slept*):

　　　　　　　　　　　　adverb　　adverb

He fell onto the bed and slept *very*　soundly for ten hours.

Here the adverb *clearly* modifies the gerund *writing*:

　　　　　　　　　　gerund　　adverb

Helen was praised for writing　*clearly*.

Gerunds are verbals that function as nouns. Because they are closely related to verbs, they can be modified by adverbs just as verbs can. In the next example, the adverb *Surely* modifies the whole sentence:

Surely the train will be late.

EXERCISE 8　　　**Directions:**

1. An adverb is underlined in each of the sentences below. Circle the word the adverb modifies.

2. Identify the part of speech of the word the adverb modifies by using the following code:

　　　V　verb　　　　ADJ　adjective　　　　ADV　adverb

Example:

_____✓_____   Some used car dealers <u>always</u> (provide) warranties.

_____ 1.   We <u>recently</u> cleaned our windows with a combination of ammonia, rubbing alcohol, liquid dishwashing detergent, and water.

_____ 2.   The amount of pollution caused by a product is becoming <u>increasingly</u> important to consumers.

_____ 3.   Microwaved cakes bake <u>quickly</u>, but they do not necessarily look good.

_____ 4.   His family calls Mr. Baugh a workaholic because they're convinced that he works <u>too</u> hard.

_____ 5.   Holly seemed to make money <u>almost</u> effortlessly as long as the stock market continued to rise.

_____ 6.   Lack of exercise <u>frequently</u> causes back pain.

_____ 7.   A sloop has <u>only</u> one mast.

_____ 8.   The word *abracadabra* was <u>once</u> considered capable of curing a fever.

_____ 9.   An X inside a circle is a hobo's sign that a householder is <u>very</u> generous.

_____10.   I decided that learning to play Go was <u>much</u> too difficult.

Recognizing Adverbs

Many adverbs end in *-ly*:

Jon sang *sweetly*.

Caleb was *extremely* angry.

Annie spoke *truthfully*.

Adding the ending *-ly* to many adjectives turns them into adverbs:

Adjectives	Adverbs
sweet	sweetly
extreme	extremely
truthful	truthfully

A few adjectives, such as *true* (adverb: *truly*) and *due* (adverb: *duly*), drop the final *e* before adding *-ly*, but most adverbs do not drop the *e* before *-ly*.

Many adverbs are not formed from adjectives and do not end in *-ly*:

She ran *fast*.

Mel was *too* busy to go to the party.

Perhaps I spoke out of turn.

In addition, some common adjectives, such as *friendly* and *lovely*, end in *-ly*. Therefore, it is not possible to identify a word as an adverb based on its ending alone.

Adverbs answer a variety of questions about the words they modify. The left-hand column of the following list contains some questions answered by adverbs. The right-hand column contains an example of an adverb that answers each question:

Questions	Examples
How?	The men worked *slowly*.
How often?	I visited my aunt *frequently*.
To what degree?	Sue finds math *very* easy.
When?	Come here — *now*!
Where?	You left your glasses *there*, on the sofa.

Clauses and phrases acting as adverbs also answer these questions. Look at the following sentence, for example:

As soon as my brother comes back, we will go *to get a pizza*.

The dependent clause "As soon as my brother comes back" acts as an adverb modifying the verb *will go*. It answers the question "When?" The infinitive phrase "to get a pizza" acts as an adverb modifying *will go* and answers the question "Why?"

In the sentence "You left your glasses there, on the sofa," "on the sofa" is a prepositional phrase that functions as an adverb. It answers the question "Where?" with the verb *left*.

EXERCISE 9   **Directions:** Underline the one-word adverbs in the sentences below. Each sentence contains a single one-word adverb.

Example:

> Janeen's driver-training teacher <u>calmly</u> asked her to move to the right side of the road.

1. Millions of bison formerly roamed the American plains.

2. Gray snakes can quickly climb trees.

3. Mysteries by and about women are selling well.

4. Someone allergic to one drug can have the same reaction to a chemically similar medication.

5. A koala spends most of its time resting and sleeping because its metabolism is extremely slow.

6. Hydrogen peroxide is a very weak antiseptic.

7. Janet and Fred are painting the basement floor today.

8. The newspaper headline is only one word: "Champions!"

9. The United States Senate has been called the most exclusive club in the world.

10. In the 1950s high school graduates could earn reasonably good salaries.

Putting Modifiers Where They Belong

Modifiers should appear in sentences as close as possible to the words they describe. Placing them elsewhere sometimes leads to confusion. Notice the location of *only* in the following sentences:

> I love *only* you.

This means "I love you, and you alone," which is perhaps what the object of someone's affections longs to hear. ("I love you only" means about the same thing.) But placing *only* elsewhere in the sentence could lead to a misunderstanding:

> I *only* love you.

This could mean "The only emotion I feel for you is love (but not friendship or respect)." Moving the modifier still further away changes the meaning again:

> *Only* I love you.

This sentence means "I'm the only one who loves you."

Sometimes a modifier placed between two words might be modifying either of them:

> NOT: The person summoned *urgently* hoped he had been chosen for the promotion.

Was the person summoned urgently or was he hoping urgently? The way the sentence is written, there is no way to tell. Rewriting it clarifies its meaning:

> The person *urgently* summoned hoped he had been chosen for the promotion.

> *or*

> The person summoned hoped *urgently* that he had been chosen for the promotion.

Choosing the Right Modifiers

Adjectives and adverbs are both modifiers. However, an adjective should not be used where an adverb is required:

NOT: I did *good* on yesterday's English test.

Good is an adjective, so it can modify only a noun or pronoun. Using it to modify a verb *(did)* is not acceptable. The adverb needed here is *well*:

I did *well* on yesterday's English test.

Using an adverb where an adjective is needed is also an error:

NOT: The kitchen smelled *badly* before Sherm cleaned it up.

Smelled is sometimes a linking verb, as it is in this sentence. Therefore, the word following it should be a subject complement. Adverbs are never subject complements, and *badly* is an adverb, so the adjective *bad* is required instead:

adjective

The kitchen smelled *bad* before Sherm cleaned it up.

When *smelled* is not a linking verb, it can be modified by an adverb:

After having his nose broken five times, the ex-fighter

adverb

smelled *badly*.

This sentence means that the ex-fighter's sense of smell was no longer working properly. In "The ex-fighter smelled bad," the adjective "bad" describes the fighter.

A few common compound words, such as *already* and *everyday*, are modifiers. When the two words making up the compounds appear in separated form (as in *all ready* and *every day*) they have different meanings than the compounds do. Here the adverb *already* means "before now:"

I *already* cashed my paycheck.

In this sentence *already* is an adverb modifying *cashed*.
However, in this sentence *all ready* means "completely prepared:"

I was *all ready* to leave when the telephone rang.

Here, *all* is an adverb modifying the adjective *ready*.

In the following sentence, because *everyday* is an adjective modifying *occurrences*, it should be written as one word:

Mistakes are *everyday* occurrences around here.

However, *every day* is not an adjective in the following sentence, so it is written as two separate words:

We go through this routine *every day*.

Here *every* is an adjective modifying *day*.

EXERCISE 10 **Directions:** Underline the errors in the sentences below and correct them on the lines at the left.

Example:

awfully A barracuda's teeth are <u>awful</u> large and knifelike.

_____ 1. When baskets are caulked with resin or clay, they can be real useful for cooking or carrying water.

_____ 2. This fall's television shows are sure interesting.

_____ 3. Jefferson did good in the state-wide art contest held last spring.

_____ 4. John's every day shirts are all white, ivory or light blue, but his ties are always colorful.

_____ 5. I ran bad in my first race, but in the second race I did much better.

_____ 6. The children are already for the picnic.

_____ 7. The dead skunk under the foundation of the house continued to smell badly for weeks.

_____ 8. The ginger ice cream tasted well.

_____ 9. Letters publicizing the reunion celebration for the class of 1985 have all ready been mailed.

_____ 10. Daphne scored perfect on the mathematics section of her college entrance examination.

Understanding Negatives

Negatives are words such as — *no, not, neither, nor, never, none, no one,* and *nothing.* Other words — *barely, hardly,* and *scarcely,* for example — are also classified as negatives. They suggest ideas that are almost, but not quite, completely negative.

USING NEGATIVES IN SENTENCES

Not is an adverb that is often used to make sentences negative. In such sentences *not* can immediately follow forms of the verb *be*:

I am *not* ready to go yet.

You were *not* here to help me plan my trip.

Making sentences negative often means adding auxiliary verbs:

auxiliary
verb
I *do* <u>not</u> know when the train leaves.

auxiliary
verb
I *have* <u>not</u> packed yet.

Notice that in sentences like these *not* immediately follows the auxiliary verb and precedes the remainder of the verb phrase.

Not often combines with auxiliary verbs to form contractions, which are combinations of words in which apostrophes mark the places where letters were omitted:

I *don't* want to see you again.

Never is an adverb that usually appears immediately before verbs and makes sentences strongly negative:

I *never* want to see you again.

Unlike *not* and *never*, other common words expressing negative ideas are not adverbs. *No*, for example, is usually an adjective; it modifies nouns (as in "We have *no* bananas"). *None, no one,* and *nothing* are pronouns that can function as subjects or objects and convey negative ideas at the same time:

We have *none* left.

No one Ellie knew was there.

Nothing you can say will make any difference.

The contraction *ain't* is on everyone's short list of grammatical errors. It should never be used in formal writing, and most people consider it a mistake even in informal writing or speech.

EXERCISE 11   **Directions:** Make the sentences below negative by adding negative words where they belong and making any other necessary changes. There is more than one way to transform each sentence.
Example:

never
Consumers / need to pay for unsolicited merchandise.

1.   I can afford a new dishwasher this year.

2.   Brent believes that nausea and lightheadedness are good reasons to stop an exercise workout.

3.   A local check will clear this bank in three days.

4.   A smoke detector can determine whether smoke is coming from frying food or from a house fire.

5. Mr. Gowers's children gave him flowers for Father's Day.

6. The temperature falls below zero in Hawaii.

7. A flea market is held every Saturday and Sunday at the Englewood Farmers' Market.

8. Professor Furness studies seabirds.

9. I want to visit Pamplona to see the running of the bulls through the streets of the town.

10. Lee plans to enter the watermelon-seed-spitting contest in Paul's Valley, Oklahoma.

AVOIDING DOUBLE NEGATIVES

One negative word is enough to make an entire sentence negative. Adding a second negative word is not only unnecessary but also unacceptable:

NOT: I did*n't* do *nothing*.

Here, the contracted form of *not* is sufficient to make the entire sentence negative. The addition of a second negative word, *nothing*, does not help. The following version of the sentence is negative enough:

I did*n't* do anything.

A **double negative** is the use of two negative words when one of them is unnecessary.

Barely, hardly, and *scarcely* are also sufficient by themselves to make sentences negative. Adding an additional negative word to a sentence already containing one of these words is an error:

NOT: I've had *hardly no* rest since school started.

In this revised version, the word *hardly* by itself is enough to suggest the negative idea:

I've had *hardly* any rest since school started.

EXERCISE 12   **Directions:**

1. Identify the sentences below by using the following code:

  C   correct   I   incorrect

2. Correct the incorrect items on the lines provided.

Example:

___*I*___   There isn't no muscle in the body stronger than the tongue.

_____*There isn't any muscle in the body*_____

_____*stronger than the tongue.*_____

_____ 1.   No insects have lungs.

_____

_____

_____ 2.   Scarcely no train stations are larger than Grand Central Station in New York City.

_____

_____

_____ 3.   I don't have nothing in my purse, so I don't care if it's stolen.

_____

_____

_____ 4.   Plate armor could not be penetrated easily because its smooth surfaces deflected blows.

_____

_____

_____ 5.   Jerry never visited no place he liked better than home, so he finally started staying home most of the time.

_____

_____

_____ 6.   I don't think I should be expected to see a dog in a constellation made up of only two stars.

_____

_____

_____ 7.   Exercise helps dieters lose fat, not muscle.

_____

_____

_____ 8.   We will never accept no new production standards.

_____

_____

_____ 9.   Manx cats have hardly no tails.

_____

_____

_____ 10.   Vultures do not make no noises except for occasional hisses.

_____

_____

FORMING COMPARATIVES AND SUPERLATIVES OF ADJECTIVES AND ADVERBS

Many adjectives and adverbs are descriptive words, identifying the words they modify as having particular qualities. A sentence reporting that one person or thing has more of some quality than another requires a **comparative** form of an adjective or adverb, such as *larger* or *more easily*. When one person or thing has more of some quality than two or more others, a **superlative** form, such as *largest* or *most easily*, is needed.

Adjectives and adverbs form comparatives and superlatives in one of two ways. Endings may be added (*-er* for comparatives and *-est* for superlatives). Or *more* (for comparatives) and *most* (for superlatives) can be placed immediately before the adjectives or adverbs. Some adverbs, such as *very* and *perhaps*, do not form comparatives and superlatives.

Forming Comparatives and Superlatives of Adjectives

Which comparative or superlative form of an adjective to use is usually determined by how many syllables the adjective has. Most adjectives with one syllable form the comparative by adding the ending *-er*. The ending *-est* is added to most one-syllable adjectives to form the superlative:

<blockquote>Sun is a tall boy for his age.</blockquote>

Comparative: Jin is *taller* than Sun.

Superlative: Hwa, however, is *tallest*.

Some adjectives with two syllables form their comparatives and superlatives with *more* and *most*, such as *modest (more modest, most modest)* and *varied (more varied, most varied)*. Others can form them both ways, such as *friendly (friendlier* or *more friendly, friendliest* or *most friendly)* and *happy (happier* or *more happy, happiest* or *most happy)*. When in doubt, consult a dictionary to find the correct comparative and superlative forms.

More and *most* are used to form comparatives and superlatives of adjectives containing three or more syllables:

Meg is a successful investor.

Comparative: Beth is *more successful* than Meg.

Superlative: Amy, however, is *most successful*.

A comparative or superlative form of an adjective can be placed between a noun and its article, just as other adjectives can. Sometimes, however, *a, an* or *the* is used with a comparative or superlative form that is not followed by a noun. In such a construction the comparative or superlative adjective modifies an unexpressed word, *one*:

Beth is the *more successful (one) of the two.*

Hwa is the *tallest (one) of the three.*

EXERCISE 13   **Directions:** Underline the comparatives and superlatives in the sentences below.

Example:

Children often prefer <u>blander</u> foods than adults do.

1. Quasars, pulsars, and black holes are the most mysterious phenomena in the universe.

2. Alexander Graham Bell's patent for the invention of the telephone was the most valuable ever issued.

3. Would you be willing to pay higher taxes if they paid for a reduction in air pollution?

4. Jo's strongest epithets are "gadzooks" and "shucks."

5. The dik-dik is one of the smallest members of the antelope family.

6. Traditional architecture helps people see which parts of a building are most important.

7. White popcorn is more crunchy than yellow popcorn.

8. On an electric blanket higher settings turn on greater numbers of wires.

9. The Alaskan moose is the world's largest species of deer.

10. Libby is willing to buy anything she thinks will help her become more organized.

Forming Comparatives and Superlatives of Adverbs

Like most one-syllable adjectives, most adverbs with one syllable form their comparatives and superlatives with the endings *-er* and *-est*:

My horse ran fast.

Comparative: Your horse ran *faster*.

Superlative: His horse ran *fastest*.

Most adverbs have two or more syllables. These adverbs form their comparatives and superlatives with *more* and *most*:

Alfred did his work quickly.

Comparative: Bob did his work *more quickly* than Alfred.

Superlative: Of the three, Cal did his work *most quickly*.

For most adjectives and adverbs, *less* and *least* are the forms used in negative comparisons:

Aaron is *less intelligent* than Claudia.

Of all the workers, George did the project *least efficiently*.

However, *fewer* is used rather than *less* with count nouns:

count
noun

There are *fewer people* here today than there were yesterday.

Mass nouns, on the other hand, form negative comparisons with less.

mass
noun

There is *less sugar* in this recipe than in the other one.

EXERCISE 14 Directions: Fill in the comparative and superlative forms of the adverbs listed below.

Example:	Comparatives	Superlatives
easily	*more easily*	*most easily*

1. carelessly _____

2. fast _____

3. quickly _____

4. adequately _____

5. hard _____

6. obviously _____

7. quietly _____

8. consistently _____

9. soon _____

10. neatly _____

Recognizing Irregular Comparatives and Superlatives

The adjectives and adverbs in the list below have irregular comparative and superlative forms:

Irregular Comparatives and Superlatives

	comparatives	superlatives
bad	worse	worst
badly	worse	worst
far	farther	farthest
	further	furthest
good	better	best
little	less	least
many	more	most
much	more	most
old	older	oldest
	elder	eldest
well	better	best

Avoiding Misuse of Comparatives and Superlatives

Most comparative and superlative forms are easy to use. However, being aware of a few common errors will help you avoid misusing them.

AVOIDING -ER AND -EST WITH LONG ADJECTIVES AND ADVERBS

The endings *-er* and *-est* are used only with one- or two-syllable adjectives and with one-syllable adverbs. Using these endings with longer adjectives or adverbs is not acceptable:

NOT: This picture is *beautifuler* than that one.

Beautiful is a three-syllable adjective, so its correct comparative form is *more beautiful*:

This picture is *more beautiful* than that one.

AVOIDING DOUBLE COMPARATIVES AND SUPERLATIVES

To form comparatives and superlatives of adjectives and adverbs, either add endings or use *more* and *most*. Using both at the same time is not acceptable:

NOT: My mother worked the most hardest of any person I ever knew.

Hard is a one-syllable adverb, so adding the ending *-est* is correct:

My mother worked the *hardest* of any person I ever knew.

AVOIDING SUPERLATIVE FORMS FOR COMPARATIVE FORMS

When only two people or things are being compared, it is a mistake to use a superlative form:

NOT: Greg is the *kindest* of the two brothers.

Since only Greg and his brother are being compared, the comparative form *kinder* is correct:

Greg is the *kinder* of the two brothers.

AVOIDING COMPARISONS WITH WORDS THAT CANNOT BE COMPARED

Some adjectives and adverbs name qualities that a person or thing either possesses or does not possess. These adjectives and adverbs cannot be compared because there is no way to possess more or less of the qualities they name. When George Orwell writes in his satire *Animal Farm* that "All animals are equal, but some animals are more equal than others," his satiric point depends on the fact that two people, animals or things are either equal or they are not. *Unique* is another adjective that should never be compared: it means "the only one of its kind," so one thing cannot be *more unique* than another.

EXERCISE 15   **Directions:**

1. Identify the sentences below by using the following code:
   C   correct   I   incorrect
2. Correct the incorrect items on the lines provided.

Example:

___/___   Worsted fabrics are more smoother than ordinary wool cloth.

_____*Worsted fabrics are smoother than*_____

_____*ordinary wool cloth.*_____

_____ 1.   The best surfing beaches face west.

_____

_____

_____ 2.   Please take the biggest of these two pieces of pie.

_____

_____

_____ 3.   Our representative made the list of the ten most obscure members of Congress.

_____

_____

_____ 4.   Hydrogen is the most abundant of all the elements in the sun.

_____

_____

_____ 5.   Of all the written records people have made, the earlier are accounts of financial transactions.

_____

_____

_____ 6.   Michael and Ralph both talk a great deal, but Ralph is the most talkative of the two.

_____

_____

_____ 7.   Nanette is the most unique person I have ever known.

_____

_____

_____ 8.   Margot and Keith both did well on the driving test, but Keith got the higher score.

_____

_____

_____ 9.   In this suit I feel as if I could win an award for worse-dressed person of the year.

_____

_____

_____ 10. Of the twins, Len weighs most and is tallest.

_____

_____

RECOGNIZING CONJUNCTIVE ADVERBS

Good writers often indicate transitions between one idea and the next so that readers can follow their thoughts. **Conjunctive adverbs**, such as *first, however, likewise,* and *finally*, act as signposts to help guide readers easily from idea to idea. These adverbs modify whole sentences.

Below is a chart showing the most common conjunctive adverbs. The words grouped together on the chart are related in meaning.

Common Conjunctive Adverbs

addition

also	besides	furthermore	moreover

contrast

conversely	however	instead	nevertheless
nonetheless	otherwise	still	

emphasis

certainly	indeed	surely

time

finally	later	meanwhile	next
subsequently	then	first	second
third (and so on)			

comparison

likewise	similarly

consequence

accordingly	consequently	hence

summary

therefore	thus

In addition to the one-word conjunctive adverbs on this list, phrases such as *for example, on the other hand, as a result,* and *for instance* also provide smooth transitions between ideas.

Using Conjunctive Adverbs in Sentences

Conjunctive adverbs indicate the relationship between one idea and the next. Consider these two sentences, for example:

Anything can be counterfeited.

Shoppers should be wary of goods sold at unusually low prices.

The second of these sentences mentions one consequence of the idea expressed in the first sentence. A writer wishing to clarify the relationship between the two ideas could use a conjunctive adverb that suggests this relationship:

Anything can be counterfeited; accordingly, shoppers should be wary of goods sold at unusually low prices.

Conjunctive adverbs need not appear at the beginnings of sentences and clauses. Like many adverbs, they can be placed in different positions without changing the meanings of sentences:

People from New York are New Yorkers, and people from Philadelphia are Philadelphians. *However*, people from Sioux Falls are called people from Sioux Falls.

The conjunctive adverb *however* could be moved to a different position with no effect on the meaning of the sentence:

People from Sioux Falls, *however*, are called people from Sioux Falls.

Where writers put conjunctive adverbs depends on how they want to pace a sentence and what they want to emphasize.

EXERCISE 16   **Directions:** Circle the conjunctive adverbs that fit best in the sentences below.

Example:

Peat cutters who found the well-preserved body of the Lindow Man thought he was a recent murder victim. (However,) Likewise), he had died more than two thousand years before.

1. A bestiary is a collection of fanciful moral tales about imaginary animals such as unicorns; bestiaries (also, hence) credit real animals with improbable behavior, such as an adder's putting a stone in one ear and its tail in the other to deafen itself.

2   Fish from Lake Malawi are famous for their variety; (likewise, subsequently), they are known for their interesting behavior.

3. Birds sometimes drop banyan seeds into the crowns of palm trees. The seeds can (instead, subsequently) germinate and send down roots that smother and kill the trees.

4. Malcolm spends every weekend working on his model train layouts. (Furthermore, Conversely), he bought a new house because it has a basement large enough for the layouts.

5. Bluebeard forbids his wife to enter one room of his castle; (nevertheless, thus), she enters the room, where she finds the dead bodies of Bluebeard's former wives.

6. Satellites were originally intended to monitor weather; (consequently, however), today they are used for such tasks as tracking whales and checking on irrigation systems.

7. Enrico tried repeatedly to start his car; (finally, meanwhile), he gave up and took the bus home.

8. Most fish have organs in their skins that sense the movement of other fish; (hence, otherwise), they can coordinate their movements with those of other fish in their schools.

9. Sympathy with their subjects is essential for biographers; such sympathy, (however, otherwise), all too often leads to uncritical admiration.

10. One Nashville museum is Bill Monroe's Bluegrass Hall of Fame; (similarly, thus), Minnie Pearl's Museum features displays such as dolls in glass cases representing key moments in Minnie Pearl's career.

Avoiding Run-on Sentences with Conjunctive Adverbs

When writers use conjunctive adverbs, they must be sure to avoid creating run-on sentences. In a **run-on sentence** two sentences are incorrectly punctuated as a single sentence. When two sentences are joined without any punctuation, the run-on sentence is called a **fused sentence**. When the two sentences are linked by a comma, the error is called a **comma splice**.

A conjunctive adverb does not affect the kind of punctuation required between two independent clauses. However, in the following example the conjunctive adverb is mistakenly used to connect two independent clauses:

NOT: An archer fish can shoot a jet of water as far as five feet, *consequently*, it can knock an insect from an overhanging branch.

The comma after *consequently* correctly separates the conjunctive adverb from the main portion of the second clause. However, the comma after *feet* is an error; a comma is insufficient to separate two independent clauses. If the writer does not wish to divide the passage into two separate sentences by putting a period after *feet*, a semicolon is necessary:

> An archer fish can shoot a jet of water as far as five feet; *consequently*, it can knock an insect from an overhanging branch.

EXERCISE 17   **Directions:** Correct each run-on sentence below by adding a period and a capital letter or a semicolon where it belongs.

Example:

> On television commercials, pain usually lasts for about thirty seconds, [;] nevertheless, chronic pain makes everyday activities agonizing for many people.

1. To judges and juries, few types of evidence are as persuasive as fingerprints, however, law enforcement officers often miss fingerprints that might help ensure convictions.

2. Badminton was first played in England in the 1860s it then became popular among English army officers in India.

3. The first aerial photographs were taken by simple hand-held cameras, later, the entire surface of the earth was photographed from satellites at regular intervals, creating a huge amount of data.

4. During the blizzard of 1888, telephone and telegraph circuits were out, and even the carrier pigeons were grounded by the blinding snow, therefore, no storm warnings reached New York City.

5. Amulets are stone or metal objects worn to protect against sickness, moreover, such charms are believed to provide protection from witchcraft.

6. Butlers are trained to make daily life flow smoothly, furthermore, they have mastered details such as whether rose petals or lemon should be added to finger bowls.

7. When taking notes from a rare book, one should never use ink, likewise, only a velvet-covered beanbag or similar soft object should be used to prop the book open.

8. The simplest animals do not have blood to move the products of metabolism through the body, movement from cell to cell takes place instead by diffusion.

9. In the late 1800s more than 4,000 cattle brands were registered in the Western United States, however, most cattle rounded up in the spring and fall had brands from only a few nearby ranches.

10. Fire ants reached the U.S. from South America before World War II they have subsequently spread across the United States.

*A*djectives modify nouns and pronouns.

Adjectives can precede the words they describe, follow them or appear after linking verbs.

Present participles and past participles can function as adjectives.

Nouns can be used as adjectives to modify other nouns or pronouns.

Phrases and clauses can function as adjectives.

Coordinate adjectives are pairs of adjectives that can be reversed and that are separated by commas.

Compound adjectives are usually hyphenated when they precede the words they modify.

Proper adjectives, which are formed from proper nouns, are capitalized.

Adverbs modify verbs, adjectives, other adverbs, verbals, and whole sentences.

Modifiers should appear in sentences as close as possible to the words they describe.

Negatives are words such as no, not, neither, nor, never, none, no one, *and* nothing.

Double negatives should be avoided.

The comparative form of most adjectives and adverbs is usually formed by adding -er *or the word* more.

The superlative form of most adjectives and adverbs is usually formed by adding -est *or the word* most.

Conjunctive adverbs help guide readers from one idea to the next.

7

Conjunctions

Conjunctions connect words, phrases, and clauses. There are three kinds of conjunctions: coordinating conjunctions, correlative conjunctions, and subordinating conjunctions. They have the same forms wherever they appear in sentences.

Conjunctions both join elements within sentences and join entire sentences to produce more complicated sentences. Writing that contains few conjunctions tends to be choppy and vague. By using conjunctions skillfully, you can make your prose easier to read because conjunctions suggest relationships between ideas and clarify sequences of thought.

USING COORDINATING CONJUNCTIONS

There are seven **coordinating conjunctions**: *and, but, or, nor, yet, for, and so. And, but,* and *or* are the most common of the coordinating conjunctions. They connect words, phrases, and clauses of roughly equal importance. They can join nouns, pronouns, verbs, verbals, adjectives, adverbs, phrases, clauses, and whole sentences. *Nor* is similar to *or*, but it is used only in negative sentences. *Yet* does not usually join nouns or pronouns but can be used in all other situations that require coordinating conjunctions. *For* and *so* are more restricted; when they function as coordinating conjunctions, they join simple sentences but not words and phrases.

Using Coordinating Conjunctions to Join Words and Phrases

And, but, and *or* signal basic connections between words and phrases. *And,* meaning "in addition to," acts like a plus sign:

We ate <u>apples</u> *and* <u>pears</u>.

It was a picture of a <u>huge elephant</u> *and* a <u>tiny mouse</u>.

Shareen asked me <u>to come</u> *and* <u>look</u>.

But, meaning "however," introduces an exception or an apparent contradiction:

<u>Everyone</u> *but* <u>I</u> came to the party by car.

Manuel was <u>intelligent</u> *but* <u>careless</u>.

You spoke <u>quickly</u> *but* <u>clearly</u>.

Or offers alternatives (that is, it says that one of two things is possible, but not necessarily both):

<u>Elliott</u> *or* <u>Olivia</u> will definitely come.

Marta was <u>late</u> *or* <u>absent</u> every day last week.

Did we do <u>well</u> *or* <u>poorly</u> on the exam?

Nor is the negative form of *or.* It is used only in negative sentences. It must follow grammatically negative words such as *no, not, never,* and *neither*:

I never eat <u>snacks</u> *nor* <u>desserts.</u>

Yet means "nevertheless":

At the end of the day we were <u>tired</u> *yet* <u>happy</u>.

Sarah did the job <u>rapidly</u> *yet* <u>correctly</u>.

I <u>recognize</u> *yet* <u>neglect</u> my body's need for physical exercise.

EXERCISE 1

Directions: Underline the coordinating conjunctions in the sentences below.

Example:

This hair dryer dries my hair quickly <u>but</u> weighs too much.

1. Most bats catch and consume their prey on the wing.

2. A barrow is a mound of earth or stone covering a grave.

3. The postal service is advertising more rapid but more expensive package-delivery services.

4. I never smoke nor drink.

5. An item labeled "German silver" or "nickel silver" contains copper, zinc, and nickel yet contains no silver.

6. A television set with a three-inch screen is truly portable but is unlikely to have picture quality equal to that of a television set with a larger screen.

7. Baba, the grandmother of the devil according to Slavonic mythology, had an enormous nose, elongated teeth, and untidy hair.

8. A rising cloud of white dust or a roaring sound is a sign of an approaching avalanche.

9. Some kinds of bamboo grow more than 120 feet high yet are no more than five inches in diameter.

10. Graduation will be held outdoors or indoors, depending on the weather.

Writing Compound Sentences

All the coordinating conjunctions, including *for* and *so*, connect simple sentences to form larger sentence units. A sentence made up of two simple sentences joined by a coordinating conjunction is called a **compound sentence**. Simple sentences within compound sentences are called **independent clauses**.

For means "because" and connects two sentences when the second sentence explains the reason for an event or circumstance described in the first:

> independent clause
> The rain turned to snow after midnight, *for* a cold front
>
> independent clause
> had moved in from the north.

(*For* can also be a preposition, as in "for my mother.")
So means "therefore" and is used when the second sentence describes the result of an action or circumstance mentioned in the first sentence:

> independent clause   independent clause
> Fred was more than an hour late, *so* I decided to go by myself.

When two simple sentences are connected by a coordinating conjunction to form a compound sentence, a comma is used after the first sentence and immediately before the conjunction:

> independent clause
> The committee's work was completed in less than a week ,
>
> independent clause
> *and* its report was submitted to the governor by the first of the following month.

When the two sentences are short, the comma may be omitted:

> It started to rain *and* I ran for cover.

EXERCISE 2   **Directions:** Circle the word that correctly completes each sentence below.

Example:

Most flower bulbs must have good soil drainage, (and, or) they will rot.

1. Stanley, a black cat, won Friday's contest for the best cat adopted from an animal shelter, (but, for) he failed to place in the animal and owner look-alike contest on Saturday.

2. The Murrays plan to move, (for, yet) they have outgrown their one-room apartment.

3. My car's heater is noisy (and, nor) it heats very poorly.

4. Psychologists report that having one or more friends is important to a child's development, (but, for) being popular is not.

5. Head lice are only about the size of sesame seeds, (for, so) they can be hard to detect.

6. A foot-pound is used to measure energy, (but, nor) a pound-foot is used to measure torque.

7. One of the largest jigsaw puzzles ever completed contained 10,000 pieces, (and, or) it took 2,500 hours to complete.

8. At about eighteen miles into a race, marathon runners often feel that they cannot go on, (for, yet) they usually get a second wind and finish the race.

9. Rocky Mountain National Park contains 355 miles of trails, (nor, so) visitors can hike as far and as high as they wish.

10. Incandescent bulbs neither use as little electricity as fluorescent bulbs, (nor, yet) do they last as long.

UNDERSTANDING CORRELATIVE CONJUNCTIONS

Correlative conjunctions are paired connecting words that link words, phrases, and sentences. Below is a list of correlative conjunctions:

both . . . and
either . . . or

neither . . . nor
whether . . . or
not only . . . but also

The following examples show how correlative conjunctions work in sentences:

I have *neither* a picture of my great grandmother *nor* any information about her life.

Mr. Cabalo expects *either* a written report *or* an oral presentation.

The words that make up correlative conjunctions can also be used independently as other parts of speech:

coordinating
conjunction

I hit a single *and* a double in the game yesterday.

pronoun

Both of my brothers went to the game.

Using Correlative Conjunctions to Combine Sentences

Correlative conjunctions can link independent clauses to form longer sentences. Two clauses linked by *either . . . or* and *whether . . . or* retain their normal word order:

independent clause   independent clause
Either you come with me right now *or* I'll go alone.

independent clause   independent clause
I don't care *whether* you come along *or* you don't.

When *not only . . . but also* is used to link shorter sentences, *not only* can follow the subject, and *but* and *also* can be separated:

Carmelo *not only* bought an exercise bicycle *but* he *also* purchased a treadmill.

Another way to express this idea is to use the auxiliary verb *do*:

Not only did Carmelo buy an exercise bicycle *but* he *also* purchased a treadmill.

Using Neither . . . Nor

When two clauses are linked by *neither . . . nor*, the word order changes slightly. If *neither* and *nor* appear before the subjects of their clauses, the subjects appear after auxiliary verbs:

Neither do I want to go myself, *nor* do I want you to go.

If *neither* appears after the subject of its clause, the auxiliary verb comes before the subject only in the second clause:

I *neither* want to go myself, *nor* do I want you to go.

EXERCISE 3   **Directions:** Underline the correlative conjunctions in the sentences below.

Example:

I couldn't decide <u>whether</u> I preferred the spaghetti <u>or</u> the linguini.

1. Plastic water pipes can be both cut with a hand saw and tightened by hand.

2. Because sewage plants and industries had flushed so much waste into the bay, people joked that someone who fell into it would either drown or dissolve.

3. The door of the aircraft had both loose bolts and a faulty seal, so we removed the door and sent it to the repair shop.

4. Stainless-steel thermos bottles are not only heavy, but they also cost four or five times as much as glass thermos bottles.

5. Hot dogs contain large amounts of both water and fat.

6. Whether ocean breezes flow toward the land or away from it depends on whether the land is warmer or cooler than the ocean.

7. Neither the claims for Miracle Spot Remover made in television advertisements nor the recommendation of my neighbor persuaded me to buy it.

8. To make freeze-dried coffee, brewed coffee is not only frozen but also ground up, passed through a vacuum, and heated to remove the liquid.

9. During the hottest part of the day, the Indian buffalo prefers either to wallow in mud or to stand in water with only part of its head showing above the surface.

10. Joslyn not only cleaned the kitchen woodwork with a solvent intended for boat decks but also washed the windows with lukewarm water and vinegar.

USING PARALLEL FORM WITH COORDINATING AND CORRELATIVE CONJUNCTIONS

When two or more items in a list are in the same grammatical form, they are said to be **parallel**. Using parallel form signals readers that the items listed are about equally important.

Using Parallel Form with Coordinating Conjunctions

The elements joined by coordinating conjunctions should be grammatically identical (two nouns, two noun phrases, two verbs, two verbals, two clauses, and so on):

noun   noun
Inez and *Carlotta* are my sisters.

gerund phrase   gerund phrase
I would enjoy *seeing a movie* or *going shopping*.

independent clause   independent clause
I had it a minute ago, yet *now it's disappeared*.

If more items were added to any of the examples, they too would need to be in the same grammatical form.

An exception to the requirement that items connected by coordinating conjunctions should be parallel is that *and, but, or,* and *nor* can connect nouns and noun phrases with pronouns:

John and *I* are coming together.

Everyone but *Charlie* is here now.

She or *her older sister* will write the report.

Tell Bill I never want to see *him* nor *his cousin* again.

Using Parallel Form with Correlative Conjunctions

Sentence elements linked by correlative conjunctions should also be parallel. In the following sentence the two items "physical benefits" and "it can benefit people spiritually," linked by correlative conjunctions, are not parallel because the first one is a phrase and the second one is a clause:

NOT: Bathing in the Ganges is believed to have not only

phrase   clause
physical benefits *but also* it can benefit people spiritually.

Lining up the two items makes it easier to see that they are not in balance:

not only *physical benefits*

but also *it can benefit people spiritually.*

A version of the sentence that is properly parallel is easier to understand and remember:

Bathing in the Ganges is believed to have *not only* physical benefits *but also* spiritual ones.

EXERCISE 4   **Directions:**

1. Identify the sentences below as parallel or not parallel by using the following code:

P   parallel   NP   not parallel

2. Correct the sentences that are not parallel on the lines provided. There may be more than one way to correct the sentences that are not parallel.

Example:

NP   Using a finishing sander requires both a light touch and constantly keep moving the sander.

Using a finishing sander requires both a

light touch and constant movement of the sander.

_____ 1.   According to Tammy, saffron is both the most expensive spice and the most delicious one.

_____

_____

_____ 2.   Marcia does not know whether to put hot food directly into the refrigerator or letting it cool first.

_____

_____

_____ 3.   Many parents in our school district know neither how to make the school system work for them nor spotting problems before they get out of hand.

_____

_____

_____ 4.   I want a mattress that is firm both along the edges and in the middle.

_____

_____

_____ 5.　Will is not sure whether the rock he found is igneous or to be a sedimentary rock.

_____

_____

_____ 6.　In last names not only _Mc_ but also _Mac_ means "son of."

_____

_____

_____ 7.　Hollow enamel in teeth more than 30,000 years old is evidence of malnutrition or of starvation among our ancestors.

_____

_____

_____ 8.　Botanical gardens not only educate the public about plants but also centers for scientific investigation into botany.

_____

_____

_____ 9.　Ablution is ceremonial washing of a part of the body, such as the hands, or of the entire body.

_____

_____

_____ 10.　Amber can't remember whether a checkerboard has sixty-four squares or that it has forty-eight squares.

_____

_____

UNDERSTANDING SUBORDINATING CONJUNCTIONS

Subordinating conjunctions join **subordinate (dependent) clauses** to main (independent) clauses to form complex sentences. Subordinating conjunctions can clarify time sequences, express possibilities, compare ideas, add information on location and manner, and explain cause-and-effect relationships.

Some coordinating and subordinating conjunctions are equivalent in meaning (for example, *for* and *because* mean about the same thing). On the whole, however, subordinating conjunctions express more complicated relationships than coordinating conjunctions do.

Common Subordinating Conjunctions

Below is a list of the most common subordinating conjunctions grouped according to their meanings:

Common Subordinating Conjunctions

Time

after	once	when
as	till	whenever
before	until	while

Possibility

as if	if	unless
as though	provided (that)	whether

Comparison and Contrast

although	than	though

Manner and Location

how	where	wherever

Cause and Effect

because	whereas	why
since		

Relative Pronouns

A **relative pronoun** introduces one kind of subordinate clause, called a **relative clause**. Relative pronouns act as subordinating conjunctions:

relative clause

The woman *who called me last night* is my sister.

Relative clauses can function in sentences as nouns or adjectives. (For more on relative pronouns, see chapter 3.) Below is a list of relative pronouns:

who (whom — object case, whose — possessive case)
whoever (whomever — object case)
that
which
what
whatever
whichever

EXERCISE 5

Directions: Underline the subordinating conjunctions in the sentences below.

Example:

This spaghetti sauce tastes homemade <u>because</u> it is homemade.

1. If orange juice is not stored properly, its flavor and vitamin content can deteriorate.

2. We walked past a place where beavers had cut down aspens in an attempt to dam the Big Thompson River.

3. Shadows are longer in the winter than they are in the summer.

4. When the inner bark of fig trees is moistened and beaten, it is gradually transformed into bark cloth, a smooth, paperlike substance.

5. X-ray photographs of flowers reveal layers of plant tissue and petals, but the images are in black and white since there is no color at X-ray wave lengths.

6. Most fire companies order fast-food meals though some still make their own home-style food.

7. Baking soda, a substitute for yeast, produces a spongy texture in baked goods by releasing carbon dioxide while it is being heated.

8. Whenever Kiko walks her dog, the whole neighborhood seems to be asleep.

9. After George played baseball with the fishermen, they felt more comfortable with him.

10. Although an excited woodchuck can breathe as often as 100 times a minute, in hibernation the same animal may breathe as rarely as once every five minutes.

Writing Complex Sentences

Two closely connected ideas can be expressed in two separate sentences:

It was raining.

We called off the block party.

The two ideas can also be connected by a coordinating conjunction, producing a compound sentence:

independent clause   independent clause

It was raining,   *so*   we called off the block party.

But there is another way of showing the relationship between the two ideas. One of the two can be subordinated to the other:

dependent   independent
(subordinate) clause   (main) clause
Because it was raining, we called off the block party.

Of the two ideas, the one that can best stand alone is "We called off the block party." The fact that it was raining provides the reason for calling it off, and the subordinating conjunction *because* introduces this kind of explanation. Together, the subordinate clause and the main clause form a complex sentence. A **complex sentence** is a sentence consisting of an independent clause and one or more dependent clauses.

A clause introduced by a subordinating conjunction can appear within the main clause of a sentence as well as either before it or after it. Usually the position of the subordinate clause makes no difference to the meaning of the sentence. For example, the two sentences below mean about the same thing:

subordinate clause
Since George's new computer game came in the mail last week,

main clause
he has come out of his room only for trips to the refrigerator.

main clause
George has come out of his room only for trips to the

subordinate clause
refrigerator *since his new computer game came in the mail last week.*

When the subordinate clause comes first, the division between the two clauses is marked by a comma. No punctuation is used between the main clause and the subordinate clause when the main clause comes first.

EXERCISE 6   **Directions:** Underline the subordinate clauses in the sentences below.

Example:

<u>Although wild boars have a reputation for being ferocious</u>, they are normally not aggressive.

1. When a baby elephant first tries to drink its mother's milk, its trunk gets in the way.

2. Because statisticians do not keep records of how many engagements are broken, no one knows exactly how common broken engagements are.

3. Until the guillotine was invented, French nobles were decapitated, but common people were drawn and quartered.

4. While I drove through the center of Cleveland, I was surprised to see a red-tailed hawk circling overhead.

5. In mental hospitals, prisons, and soup kitchens, where few pleasures are available, cigarettes are distributed every day.

6. After a spectacular meteor fall occurred in 1803, scientists could no longer deny the reality of objects falling from the sky.

7. Before business schools graduate students specializing in international business, they should require each student to learn at least one foreign language.

8. Jennifer has been baking cookies since she was nine years old.

9. As the days become longer, many people in our neighborhood are spending more time outside.

10. Even in apparently unpromising northern waters, you can see hermit crabs, blue crabs, and whelks if you use a diving mask.

ADJECTIVE CLAUSES

Since a relative clause usually functions as an adjective to describe a noun or pronoun in the main clause, it often appears in the middle of the main clause (as near as possible to the word it describes):

relative clause

The people *who came to dinner last night* left their umbrella behind.

In this sentence the relative clause "who came to dinner last night" describes the noun *people*. Clauses that function in sentences as adjectives are called **adjective clauses**.

Restrictive Clauses. Sometimes an adjective clause provides information that is needed to identify the person or thing referred to in the main clause:

restrictive adjective clause

The players *who do not know the rules* should not criticize the referees.

According to this sentence, only some players do not know the rules; they are the ones who should not criticize the referees. The adjective clause "who do not know the rules" not only describes the noun *players* but specifies which of the players the writer means. Adjective clauses that provide information needed to identify the nouns or noun substitutes they modify are called **restrictive clauses**.

Nonrestrictive Clauses. Some adjective clauses, on the other hand, are not needed to identify the person or thing mentioned in the main clause:

nonrestrictive adjective clause

The players, *who do not know the rules*, should not criticize the referees.

This sentence asserts that none of the players knows the rules; consequently, none of them should criticize the referees. Adjective clauses providing additional details not necessary for identification are called **nonrestrictive clauses.**

Nonrestrictive clauses are marked off by commas from the rest of the sentence; restrictive clauses are not.

That and ***Which*.** The relative pronouns *that* and *which* both refer to things. In restrictive clauses, either *that* or *which* can be used:

> restrictive clause
>
> The necktie *that/which I wear to weddings and funerals* is purple with green dots.

In this sentence no commas are needed since the relative clause is necessary to identify the necktie the writer means.

However, *that* should not be used in nonrestrictive clauses:

> NOT: My only necktie, *that I wear to weddings and funerals*, is purple with green dots.

Here the clause "that I wear only to weddings and funerals" is nonrestrictive because it is not needed to identify the necktie (the writer has only one). In this sentence, *which* is the correct relative pronoun to use:

> nonrestrictive clause
>
> My only necktie, *which I wear to weddings and funerals*, is purple with green dots.

A good rule to remember is that relative clauses beginning with *that* are always restrictive, so they are not marked off by commas.

EXERCISE 7   **Directions:** Identify the underlined clauses as restrictive or nonrestrictive by using the following code:

> R   restrictive clause   N   nonrestrictive clause

Example:

N   Josie is a triskaidekaphobiac, <u>which means she has an abnormal fear of the number thirteen</u>.

_____ 1.   Mary Poppins, <u>who was created by P. L. Travers</u>, carries a perfectly rolled umbrella with a parrot handle.

_____ 2.   Sports drinks, <u>which are intended to replace fluids and nutrients lost during exercise</u>, can be high in calories.

_____ 3.   The gnomon of a sundial casts a shadow <u>that indicates the correct time</u>.

_____ 4. A multiple independently targetable re-entry vehicle, <u>which is known as a MIRV</u>, is a long-range missile with more than one warhead.

_____ 5. Anyone <u>who has a legitimate business reason</u> can run a credit check on you without your permission.

_____ 6. Milk <u>which has not been pasteurized</u> can cause sickness and even death.

_____ 7. The Becks' dish antennae, <u>which brings in hundreds of television channels</u>, was very expensive.

_____ 8. The habits <u>that are easiest to break</u> are the good ones.

_____ 9. Our toaster consistently makes toast <u>that is golden brown on one side and dark brown on the other</u>.

_____ 10. An electric guitar has a solid body, unlike an acoustic guitar, <u>which has a hollow body</u>.

EXERCISE 8 **Directions:** Add commas to set off the nonrestrictive clauses in the sentences below.

Example:

Micky's father , who lives with Micky and his wife , is a wonderful storyteller.

1. In Dr. Jamison's work with children which is a form of play therapy she uses puppets, blocks, and other toys to help young children cope with the stresses in their lives.

2. Al Hautzig who was the first person in our neighborhood to get a motorboat fished every weekend, regardless of the weather.

3. Mrs. Morgan whose dogs have been trained to protect sheep objects to the use of poison to control wolves.

4. An aria which is a solo vocal passage in an opera is usually expressive and moving.

5. Josef Jacobus whom I met at a fund-raising dinner last April announced today that he plans to run for mayor.

6. Father Time who is a mythical figure is usually pictured carrying an hourglass and a scythe.

7. Horatio Alger whose theme was always the rise from rags to riches wrote 135 novels.

8. Chopines which were shoes worn by European women in the 1600s were so high that women wearing them could not walk without the help of servants.

9. Our landlord whom we still owe for last month's rent refuses to fix our air conditioner until our rent is paid.

10. Edgar Allan Poe whose parents were actors was orphaned when he was three years old.

ADVERB CLAUSES

Many subordinate clauses function as adverbs to modify entire main clauses. They are called **adverb clauses**:

> adverb clause
>
> *After we find our seats*, we'll ask the conductor when the train arrives in St. Louis.

In this sentence the subordinate clause "After we find our seats" acts as an adverb to answer the question "When?"

Adverb clauses also answer other questions, such as "How?" "Where?" and "Why?" as in the following sentences:

> Zhi acts *as if he doesn't remember going to school with me*.

> I asked for help *wherever I could*.

> Lydia got the job *because she was the best-qualified applicant*.

EXERCISE 9   **Directions:** Indicate whether the underlined clauses in the sentences below function as adjectives or adverbs. Use the following code:

ADJ   adjective clause   ADV   adverb clause

Example:

ADV   The fruit of the breadfruit tree is usually baked or roasted <u>before it is eaten</u>.

_____ 1. <u>As the costs of synthetic fiber fillings decreased</u>, comforters became more affordable.

_____ 2. <u>When Abraham Lincoln was assassinated</u>, he was watching the play *Our American Cousin*.

_____ 3. Women <u>who share a household with another adult</u> report fewer chronic health problems than those who live alone.

_____ 4. <u>Because snow places heavy burdens on roofs</u>, the roofs in northern regions have steep pitches.

_____ 5. Progress <u>which was made in military psychiatry in World War II</u> led to optimism about the potential of psychiatry.

_____ 6. <u>Since computers function in some ways like human brains</u>, the use of computers can raise questions about the nature of the human mind.

_____ 7. Herrings were once such a valuable resource that they influenced world events in much the same way <u>that petroleum does today</u>.

_____ 8. <u>After knitted silk and wool stockings became fashionable for women in the eighteenth century</u>, the demand for stockings led to the invention of the knitting machine.

_____ 9. An aeolian harp has strings <u>which produce tones</u> when they are moved by the wind.

_____ 10. Children's rooms need paint <u>that washes well</u>.

NOUN CLAUSES

Subordinate clauses that function as nouns appear in sentences as subjects, objects, and complements, just as other nouns do. These clauses are known as **noun clauses**. In the following sentence, a subordinate clause is the subject:

noun clause

What I wanted for my birthday was a new radio.

Here the subordinate clause "What I wanted for my birthday" is the subject of the verb *was*. It fits the definition of a clause since it has a subject *(I)* and a verb *(wanted)*. The main clause of the sentence has a verb of its own *(was)*, but its subject is the relative clause itself. The sentence is actually a combination of two simpler sentences:

I wanted a present for my birthday.

It was a new radio.

In the complex sentence, the noun phrase *a present* is replaced by a relative pronoun *(what)* and the pronoun *it* of the second sentence is replaced by the first sentence.

Noun clauses can also function as objects and complements:

direct object

As object: I got *what I wanted for my birthday*.

subject complement

As complement: The present was *what I wanted*.

EXERCISE 10   **Directions:** Identify the underlined noun clauses in the sentences below as subjects, objects or complements by using the following code:

S   subject   O   object   C   complement

Example:

_____S_____   <u>Whoever plays a sport for love, not for money</u>, fits the literal definition of an amateur.

_____ 1.   Stanley often dreams <u>that he is swimming across a slowly moving river</u>.

_____ 2.   <u>Why people enjoy high-speed, bone-rattling roller coaster rides</u> is a mystery to me.

_____ 3.   We always know <u>where to find Neal</u>: in the barn among the dirty cobwebs and old farm tools.

_____ 4.   Joe's definition of art is <u>whatever appeals to him</u>.

_____ 5.   Hans is learning <u>how he can resolve conflicts without antagonizing people</u>.

_____ 6.   The winner will be <u>whoever creates packaging that best protects a raw egg dropped from a second-story window</u>.

_____ 7.   Yee-sun Wu, a Hong Kong businessman, told the group <u>what executives can do to improve productivity</u>.

_____ 8.   Our main hope is <u>that we can play today's music, not music that was first played back in the sixties and seventies</u>.

_____ 9.   <u>Whether a gull is judged by other gulls as dependable or not</u> determines whether or not that gull's warning cries are heeded.

_____10.   Please tell me <u>who did the landscaping for this building</u>.

A single subordinating conjunction can introduce clauses that function as nouns, adjectives or adverbs:

noun clause
I know *where I'm going*.

adjective clause
The building *where Mom used to work* is on Pine Street.

adverb clause
Avi found his keys *where he left them*.

EXERCISE 11   **Directions:** Identify the ways the underlined clauses function in the sentences below by using the following code:

N noun   ADJ adjective   ADV adverb

Example:

N   Scientists now believe that the <u>earth is about four and a half billion years old.</u>

_____ 1.   <u>After James left his hometown in Tennessee</u>, he lived in Mexico for a year and then moved to Florida.

_____ 2.   A badger's teeth are adapted for crushing rather than cutting its food, <u>which includes roots, berries, insects, young rabbits, and wasps' nests</u>.

_____ 3.   Mrs. McHale wants to know <u>why Ellen did not try out for the chess team this year</u>.

_____ 4.   <u>Where I take my vacation</u> is less important to me than who goes on the vacation with me.

_____ 5.   <u>If a television set's cabinet is not well made</u>, the sound quality can be affected.

_____ 6.   The woman <u>who called</u> wanted to remind you to vote today.

_____ 7.   I once traveled across the desert with a friend <u>whose car air conditioner had broken down</u>.

_____ 8.   Red maples grow well <u>where soil is compacted or poorly drained</u>.

_____ 9.   The clay targets <u>that are used in trap shooting</u> are called pigeons.

_____ 10.   <u>Whenever a lifeless area, such as the site of a volcanic eruption, is colonized</u>, lichens are the first living forms to occupy the area.

Improving Style by Using Subordinating Conjunctions

One way to make your writing interesting is to use a variety of sentence types. Short, simple sentences can be dramatic, focusing readers' attention or speeding up the pace of your writing. Longer sentences can slow the pace of your writing, making it seem more thoughtful. Too many sentences of any one type in a row, however, can be monotonous, so make an effort to vary your sentences.

A number of short, simple sentences in a row can make prose seem choppy and immature. On the other hand, a series of compound sentences may be uninteresting because each presents two ideas side by side without suggesting which of the two is more important. However, a complex sentence, which also presents two ideas, contains the additional feature that the more important idea is emphasized and the less important idea is subordinated to it. If you are dissatisfied with the style of something you have written, consider changing some simple and compound sentences into complex ones. Compare the two sentences below:

> independent clause
> Compound: The long day was finally over, and I was able to
>
> independent clause
> relax for the first time in nearly eighteen hours.
>
> subordinate clause
> Complex: When the long day was finally over, I was able to
>
> main clause
> relax for the first time in nearly eighteen hours.

Here, the second version is better since the subordinating conjunction "When" clarifies the relationships between the events described in it.

EXERCISE 12   **Directions:** Circle the word that correctly completes each sentence below.

Example:

Arthur wanted to go back home (because, that) two black cats crossed the street in front of his car.

1. (After, Than) the Hong Kong stock exchange's trading floor was completely computerized in 1986, traders no longer needed to shout or wave their arms.

2. Although Boyd has photographed poisonous snakes, mountain gorillas, and New York cab drivers, photographing bears in Alaska scared him more (than, which) any of his other assignments.

3. (If, Though) Verlyn is good at the technical side of astronomy, he is less interested in improving telescopes than in studying the sky with the equipment he has.

4. (Unless, Why) Tara calls me, I'll be home all evening.

5. Janeen was considered shy (because, until) she became involved in community theater presentations.

6. Greta has not seen her father (since, whenever) she was five years old.

7. (Unless, While) David finished making the minestrone, Edna frosted the birthday cake.

8. Jerry recently spent a week on the farm (if, where) he had worked as a teenager.

9. A book louse is an insect (that, whichever) eats mold and mildew, not books.

10. English, Spanish, French, and Italian are the languages (that, where) are spoken most widely in North America.

TRY IT OUT

Short, choppy sentences can be distracting to your readers. To eliminate choppiness, try using coordinating and subordinating conjunctions to combine short sentences and to clarify the connections between ideas. Adding conjunctions should make your writing easier and more interesting to read. Compare the following choppy, disconnected passage to the improved version which follows it:

A hurricane is a gigantic weather system. It is dangerous. A hurricane is the most destructive storm on earth. In a hurricane winds can exceed 155 miles an hour. The winds can topple trees. The winds can rip roofs and doors off houses. The winds can flatten small buildings. A hurricane has enormous power. It can toss trees through the walls of buildings. It can drive splinters of wood through sheet metal.

Adding coordinating and subordinating conjunctions to combine sentences results in the following improved version of the same passage:

A hurricane, which is a gigantic, dangerous weather system, is the most destructive storm on earth. In a hurricane, winds that can exceed 155 miles an hour topple trees, rip roofs and doors off houses, and flatten small buildings. The enormous power of a hurricane can toss trees through the walls of buildings and drive splinters of wood through sheet metal.

Now, choose a passage from your own writing in which short sentences give a choppy, disjointed impression. To improve the passage, combine sentences with conjunctions that provide smooth, logical connections between your ideas.

*C*onjunctions connect words, phrases, and clauses.

Coordinating conjunctions connect words, phrases, and clauses of roughly equal importance.

When a coordinating conjunction is used to connect two sentences, the result is a compound sentence.

Correlative conjunctions are paired connecting words that link words, phrases, and clauses.

When items in lists are joined by coordinating or correlative conjunctions, the items should be parallel, which means they should all be in the same grammatical form.

Subordinating conjunctions join dependent clauses to independent clauses.

A relative pronoun acts as a subordinating conjunction to introduce one kind of subordinate clause, a relative clause.

A complex sentence is a sentence consisting of an independent clause and one or more dependent clauses.

A clause introduced by a subordinating conjunction can appear within the main clause of a sentence, before it or after it.

Subordinate clauses can function in sentences as adjectives, adverbs or nouns.

Adjective clauses that provide information needed to identify a person or thing are restrictive clauses. They are not set off by commas.

Adjective clauses that provide information not needed to identify a person or thing are nonrestrictive clauses. They are set off by commas.

Using a variety of sentence types improves sentence style.

8

Prepositions

Prepositions *connect nouns, pronouns, and nounlike elements to other words in sentences. Prepositions indicate relationships, as illustrated in the following sentence:*

> preposition
> The bread is on the table.

Here the preposition on *indicates the relative positions of the bread and the table.*

IDENTIFYING PREPOSITIONS

One way to identify prepositions is to look for words that indicate connections between other words. Prepositions indicate not only space relationships (as in "The bread is *on* the table") but time relationships ("He was born just *after* World War II") and various other connections between ideas ("All the club members, *including* Isaac, agreed to go"). However, other kinds of words also indicate relationships. Therefore, the only practical way to identify prepositions is to memorize the most common ones.

Common Prepositions

Most prepositions are short words. Their forms never change, no matter where they appear in sentences. Below is a list of common one-word prepositions:

Common Prepositions

about	despite	over
above	down	past
across	during	regarding
after	except	since
against	excluding	through
along	for	throughout
among	from	till
around	in	to
as	including	toward
at	inside	under
before	into	underneath
behind	like	unlike
below	near	until
beneath	of	up
beside	off	upon
between	on	with
beyond	onto	within
by	out	without
concerning	outside	

Some of these words can also function as other parts of speech. For example, *for* is also a coordinating conjunction, *as* and *since* are also subordinating conjunctions, and *outside* is also an adverb.

EXERCISE 1   **Directions:** Underline the prepositions in the sentences below. Each sentence contains one preposition.

Example:

The first automobile race was won <u>by</u> an Oshkosh steamer.

1. Pierre is the capital of South Dakota.

2. Rick's book is about a young grizzly bear.

3. I drove past Marcy's house every evening last week.

4. Rhinoplasty is plastic surgery performed on a person's nose.

5. Australia accepted 75,000 convicts between 1790 and 1840.

6. X-rays can detect cracks in metal.

7.   Sleeping Beauty slept for 100 years.

8.   Bacteria are mostly composed of water.

9.   Gourds have been made into musical instruments, masks, and waterproof containers.

10.   Popeye has an anchor tattooed on his arm.

Compound Prepositions

Compound prepositions, which are phrases made up of prepositions and other words, function in the same way as other prepositions do. In the following sentence the compound preposition "in front of" shows a relationship just as a one-word preposition would:

Clara is the girl standing *in front of* Felice in the class picture.

Below is a list of commonly used compound prepositions:

Common Compound Prepositions

according to	except for	instead of
along with	in addition to	next to
apart from	in back of	on account of
as for	in case of	on behalf of
aside from	in front of	on top of
because of	in place of	out of
by means of	in regard to	regardless of
by way of	in spite of	with regard to

EXERCISE 2

Directions: Underline the compound prepositions in the sentences below. Each sentence contains one compound preposition.

Example:

Mr. Moore will welcome the crowd <u>on behalf of</u> the whole team.

1.   I'll meet you in front of the theater at seven o'clock.

2.   Americans continue to choose potato chips as their favorite snack in spite of repeated warnings against eating too much fat.

3.   Pam plans to quit her job regardless of her mother's objections.

4.   At a power station in Northern Ireland electricity is generated by incoming and receding waves instead of by fossil fuels.

5.   Please leave the cayenne pepper out of the chili this time.

6.   In addition to the Oscars awarded to people, at least one Oscar has been given to a cartoon character, Mickey Mouse.

7. I was late for work because of the heavy fog.

8. When an animal spends the summer in a dormant state, the term used is estivation instead of hibernation.

9. Larry Fine, along with Moe and Curly Howard, achieved fame as a member of the Three Stooges.

10. In case of a fire, do not use the elevator.

UNDERSTANDING PREPOSITIONAL PHRASES

The combination of a preposition, the noun, pronoun or nounlike element that follows it, and any intervening modifiers is called a **prepositional phrase.** "Across the street," "over the summer," and "despite the rising cost" are examples of prepositional phrases. The noun or noun substitute at the end of a prepositional phrase is the **object of the preposition.** In the following sentence, "flight" is the object of the preposition *in:*

prepositional phrase
An albatross can cover 10,000 miles *in a single flight.*

Here the preposition *in* shows the relationship between a flight and the distance covered (10,000 miles).

EXERCISE 3 **Directions:** Underline the prepositional phrases in the sentences below. The number of prepositional phrases is indicated in parentheses. Remember, an infinitive (*to* followed by the basic form of a verb) is a verbal, not a prepositional phrase.

Example:

Farmers used to smoke bacon <u>by hanging it</u> <u>in their chimneys</u>. (2)

1. One of the items on display at the museum is a large sculpture of the feet of King Cheops. (5)

2. The earth travels through space at 66,700 miles an hour. (2)

3. Tucking his briefcase under his arm, Leo carried the doughnut and cup of coffee onto the elevator. (3)

4. A refrigerator should be kept at thirty-seven degrees and a freezer at zero. (2)

5. Air vents over the gauze pads on adhesive bandages help air circulate around wounds. (3)

6. Animal acts were barred from the Miss America talent contest in 1948. (2)

7. During World War I balloons were used to watch for submarines. (2)

8. Aztec religion was dominated by a preoccupation with time. (2)

9. Reykjavik is the capital of Iceland. (1)

10. In 1901 Guglielmo Marconi transmitted the Morse code for the letter S (dot-dot-dot) from England to Newfoundland, marking the beginning of radio. (5)

TRY IT OUT

Practice creating your own prepositional phrases by writing phrases that begin with twenty different prepositions. Your list might include prepositional phrases like these:

behind the door	under the bed
until noon	regarding money
for my paycheck	near my car
with my sister	throughout the house
on the floor	unlike my brother

Next, write five sentences in which you use as many of your prepositional phrases as you can. Your sentences might be similar to this one:

> With my sister I searched throughout the house for my paycheck, which we finally found on the floor under the bed.

Using Prepositional Phrases in Sentences

Prepositional phrases function in sentences as adjectives, adverbs, and nouns. In the following sentence, the prepositional phrases "of Enterprise, Alabama" and "to the boll weevil" function as adjectives modifying the nouns *citizens* and *monument*:

noun   prepositional phrase   noun
The *citizens of Enterprise, Alabama*, erected a *monument*

prepositional phrase
to the boll weevil.

In the next sentence, the prepositional phrase "to a rifle muzzle" functions as an adverb modifying the past participle *attached*, which is used as an adjective:

adjective   prepositional phrase

A bayonet is a short blade *attached*   *to a rifle muzzle*.

In the following sentence, the prepositional phrase "From Jacksonville to Key West" functions as a noun. The whole prepositional phrase is the subject of the verb *is*:

prepositional phrase

From Jacksonville to Key West is more than 500 miles.

Using a prepositional phrase as a noun is rare, perhaps because such usage can seem awkward.

EXERCISE 4   **Directions:** Circle the abbreviation that identifies the way each prepositional phrase functions in the sentences below. Use the following code:

    ADJ   adjective phrase   ADV   adverb phrase   N   noun phrase

Example:

(ADJ) ADV N   Meltdown is the disintegration <u>of a nuclear reactor's core</u>.

ADJ ADV N 1. Among the earliest adhesives were glues made <u>by carpenters</u> from animal hides and bones.

ADJ ADV N 2. The selection <u>of a new pope</u> is announced through the release of white smoke.

ADJ ADV N 3. An aardvark's tongue can be as long <u>as eighteen inches</u>.

ADJ ADV N 4. <u>Out the door</u> is where you'll be if you keep bouncing that ball in here.

ADJ ADV N 5. Why did so many U.S. presidents come <u>from Virginia</u>?

ADJ ADV N 6. <u>At one feeding</u> a hippopotamus may eat as much as 100 pounds of food.

ADJ ADV N 7. <u>Between five and six o'clock</u> is our busiest time.

ADJ ADV N 8. Sand is the main ingredient <u>in glass</u>.

ADJ ADV N 9. A dragonfly feeds and mates <u>on the wing</u>.

ADJ ADV N 10. <u>Beyond Washington</u> is too far away from here for a weekend trip.

Putting Prepositional Phrases Where They Belong

Like other modifiers, prepositional phrases should appear in sentences as close as possible to the words they describe. Accurately placed, prepositional phrases can make sentences more vivid and precise:

> The tired children lay down *on the grass under the shade of an old oak tree* and fell asleep.

In this sentence the three prepositional phrases "on the grass," "under the shade," and "of an old oak tree" allow a reader to picture a scene which would otherwise remain vague.

If prepositional phrases are misplaced, however, they can make a sentence confusing or unintentionally comic:

> NOT: The crowd applauded wildly after the great trapeze artist did a triple somersault *for five minutes*.

No matter how great a trapeze artist may be, he or she cannot remain suspended in the air turning somersaults for five minutes. An enthusiastic crowd can applaud that long, and this is probably what the writer intended to convey. The revised version is clearer:

> The crowd applauded wildly *for five minutes* after the great trapeze artist did a triple somersault.

EXERCISE 5

Directions:

1. Identify the underlined prepositional phrases according to the following code:

    C   correctly placed   I   incorrectly placed

2. Correct the sentences with incorrectly placed prepositions on the lines provided.

Example:

_____   After he failed his third quiz in a row, Harry decided to quit school and become a circus clown <u>in the biology lab</u>.

After he failed his third quiz in a row in the biology lab,
Harry decided to quit school and become a circus clown.

_____ 1.   Water boils <u>at 100 degrees centigrade</u>.

_____

_____

_____ 2.   The women <u>in Portuguese</u> were singing "Happy Birthday."

_____

_____

_____ 3. Writing helped Mona to understand her fully for the first time <u>about her grandmother</u>.

_____

_____

_____ 4. Acrophobia is the fear <u>of heights</u>.

_____

_____ 5. Moslems fast <u>during the month</u> of Ramadan.

_____

_____ 6. <u>Of advertising campaigns</u> humor is a well-established part.

_____

_____ 7. Patsy <u>on a jogging trail</u> met her future husband.

_____

_____

_____ 8. Sri Lanka was once connected to India <u>by a land bridge</u>.

_____

_____

_____ 9. <u>In mosquitos</u> record rainfalls led to an increase this year.

_____

_____

_____ 10. The capital <u>of New Zealand</u> is Wellington.

_____

_____

AVOIDING MISTAKES WITH PREPOSITIONS

Sometimes two or more prepositions could appear in the same place in a sentence with very little difference in meaning. The two sentences below, for example, mean about the same thing:

Professor Shaw is an expert *in* marine biology.

Professor Shaw is an expert *on* marine biology.

Most of the time, however, prepositions are not interchangeable. Using one preposition when another one is needed is a mistake. In the following sentence, using the wrong preposition produces confusion:

NOT: Last evening, my wife and I went over to the Hoffners' and helped put *down* their new drapes.

Up, not *down,* is the preposition needed here.

Understanding Omitted Prepositions

Sometimes prepositions can be omitted without changing the meaning of a sentence. In the following sentence, for example, the meaning does not change whether the preposition *in* is included or not:

A mosquito can travel more than ten miles *(in)* a day.

Most of the time, however, the correct preposition should be included:

NOT: Would you like to come over my house on Saturday afternoon?

In this sentence, the preposition *to* is required in formal writing:

Would you like to come over *to* my house on Saturday afternoon?

A common cause of omitted prepositions is faulty proofreading. Prepositions are so familiar that writers sometimes see them in their sentences even when they are not there. Writers should be careful to ensure that the words they intended actually appear on the page in front of them.

Avoiding Unnecessary Prepositions

Sometimes speakers or writers include prepositions where they are not needed. For example, the preposition *off* is sufficient by itself and does not require the help of the additional word *of*:

NOT: Take your feet off *of* the table!

Here, "Take your feet *off* the table!" is correct.
Another preposition that is often added unnecessarily is *at*:

NOT: Where's my briefcase *at*?

Here, "Where's my briefcase?" requests the same information in better English.

Using Between and Among

Between is a proposition usually used to describe the relationship of a person or thing to one other person or thing:

> Let's keep this information a secret *between* the two of us.

In addition, it is used to indicate the space separating two points:

> My brother is the one standing *between* the man in the gray suit and the woman in the red dress.

Between is also used for time:

> We finished cleaning up *between* eight and nine o'clock.

Among is usually used when three or more people or things are involved:

> Choosing a flavor of ice cream *among* so many possibilities isn't easy.

Avoiding Incorrect Use of Prepositions

Some verbs and adjectives are followed by specific prepositions, not because the two are logically connected but because good speakers and writers have always used them that way. For example, the preposition used with the adjective *capable* is *of*, as in the following sentence:

> Ralph is *capable of* doing much better work than he has done so far.

Using another preposition in place of *of* (such as "capable *to*") would be awkward. Below is a list of several verbs and adjectives and the prepositions that accompany them:

center on	different from
common to	inferior to
compatible with	rely on
consist of	substitute for
capable of	susceptible to
detract from	

If you are in doubt about which preposition is needed with a particular word, consult a good dictionary.

Many words can be followed by more than one preposition; however, combining the same word with different prepositions can result in very different meanings. For example, the combination *differ from* means "be unlike," as in the following sentence:

> A house cat *differs from* a tiger in size but not in temperament.

The combination *differ with* means "disagree," as in this sentence:

> I *differed with* my husband about where to go on our vacation this year, so we compromised and stayed home.

Sometimes two words, each requiring its own preposition, occur in the same sentence. Omitting one of the two prepositions is an error:

NOT: We will always *rely and have confidence in* you.

The writer of this sentence used the preposition *in* with both *rely and confidence*, but *rely in* is incorrect. *Rely* requires the preposition *on*. A correct version of this sentence contains both prepositions:

We will always *rely on and have confidence in* you.

EXERCISE 6   **Directions:** Correct the sentences below by crossing out unnecessary prepositions, adding needed prepositions, and replacing incorrect prepositions. Each sentence contains one error.

Example:

The albatross is the largest / *of* the web-footed birds.

1.   Wildflowers can be substituted with mowed grass on highway shoulders and medians.

2.   To clear deep snow off of a sidewalk or driveway, shovel the snow in layers, starting with the top few inches.

3.   You can rely to Southerners never to agree about politics, religion or barbecuing.

4.   Among dark and light turkey meat, the dark meat has more calories.

5.   Chocolate is different to mocha, which is a combination of chocolate and coffee.

6.   The "new, improved" cereal is neither different nor cheaper than the old one.

7.   Unfortunately, my new computer is not compatible to my old computer printer.

8.   Bricks made of sun-dried mud have been used as building materials since before 3,400 B.C., but such bricks are durable only warm, dry climates.

9.   Cats are capable to living thirteen or fourteen years.

10.   Arab countries the Red Cross is known as the Red Crescent.

*P*repositions connect nouns, pronouns, and nounlike elements to other words in sentences.

Compound prepositions, phrases made up of prepositions and other words, function in the same way as one-word prepositions do.

A prepositional phrase includes a preposition, the noun, pronoun or nounlike element that follows it, and any intervening modifiers.

The noun or nounlike element at the end of a prepositional phrase is the object of the preposition.

Prepositional phrases function in sentences as adjectives, adverbs, and nouns.

Prepositional phrases should be located as close as possible to the words they describe.

Omitting necessary prepositions and adding unnecessary prepositions should be avoided.

Some prepositions are always used with specific verbs and adjectives.

Glossary

An **absolute phrase** is a group of words that modifies an entire sentence rather than a specific word in the sentence.

Abstract nouns name things that cannot be perceived with the senses. *Democracy* and *love* are examples of abstract nouns.

The **active voice** is a way of expressing an idea in which the performer of the action is the subject of the verb. "I hit a stop sign" is in the active voice.

Adjective clauses are subordinate clauses (groups of words containing subjects and predicates) that function in sentences as adjectives.

Adjectives are words that describe (modify) nouns and pronouns.

Adverb clauses are subordinate clauses (groups of words containing subjects and predicates) that function in sentences as adverbs.

Adverbs are words that modify verbs, adjectives, other adverbs, verbals, and whole sentences. Adverbs answer questions such as "How?" "When?" and "Where?" They often end in *-ly.*

Agreement is the correspondence in person and number between subjects and verbs and the correspondence in person, number, and gender between pronouns and their antecedents. For example, if a pronoun's antecedent is singular and masculine, the pronoun must be singular and masculine in order to agree with it.

Antecedents are the words to which pronouns refer.

Appositives are nouns, noun phrases or adjectives which immediately follow nouns or nounlike elements and rename or identify the same people or things. In "My sister, Luella Sanders," *Luella Sanders* is an appositive.

Articles introduce nouns. *The* is the definite article and *a* and *an* are the indefinite articles.

Auxiliary or **helping verbs** are verbs that do not appear alone in sentences but always accompany one or more other verbs. Examples of auxiliary verbs are *be, can, have, may, should,* and *might.* Auxiliary verbs combine with basic forms of verbs, present participles, and past participles to form verb phrases.

Basic forms of verbs are the forms verbs are listed under in dictionaries. *Walk* is an example of a basic form of a verb.

Cardinal numbers are numbers used as adjectives, such as *three* in "three oranges." Cardinal numbers answer the question "How many?"

Case is the classification of pronouns and nouns according to whether they are subjects or objects or show possession.

Clauses are groups of words that contain subjects and predicates.

Collective nouns are words that name groups considered as wholes. *Family* and *class* are examples of collective nouns.

A **comma splice** is a type of run-on sentence in which two independent clauses (two separate sentences) are incorrectly linked by a comma.

Common nouns are words that name any, some or all members of groups. All nouns that are not proper nouns are classified as common nouns.

A **comparative form** of an adjective or adverb, such as *larger* or *more easily,* is used to show that one person or thing has more of some quality than another.

A **complement** is a word or phrase that completes the meaning of another word. Sentences can have subject complements or object complements.

Complete subjects include simple subjects and all the words that modify them.

A **complex sentence** is a sentence consisting of an independent clause and one or more dependent clauses.

A **compound adjective** is made up of two or more words that form a unit describing one noun or pronoun. The words in the group may belong to any part of speech. When a compound adjective appears before the word it describes, a hyphen is usually used between the words of the compound. In "clear-cut objective," *clear-cut* is a compound adjective.

A **compound noun** is a combination of two or more words that form a new word or phrase functioning as a single noun. *Ice cream* is an example of a compound noun.

Compound prepositions are phrases made up of prepositions and other words. They function in the same way as other prepositions do to connect nouns, pronouns, and nounlike elements to other words in sentences and indicate the relationships between them. *According to, except for,* and *instead of* are examples of compound prepositions.

A **compound sentence** is a single sentence made up of two independent clauses joined by a coordinating conjunction.

A **compound subject** contains two words, phrases or clauses which are both the subjects of a single verb.

A **compound-complex sentence** is a sentence consisting of two or more independent clauses and at least one dependent clause.

Concrete nouns are words naming things that can be perceived with the senses. *Table* and *bottle* are examples of concrete nouns.

The **conditional** verb forms are the auxiliary verbs *would* and *could*. They tell what would be true in imagined situations: "I *would* like to live in Hawaii"; "I wish I *could* remember Tonya's telephone number."

Conjunctions are words that connect other words, phrases, and clauses. There are three kinds of conjunctions: coordinating conjunctions, correlative conjunctions, and subordinating conjunctions.

A **conjunctive adverb** is a word that indicates the relationship between ideas but that does not connect one independent clause to another to form a complete sentence. *However, meanwhile,* and *therefore* are examples of conjunctive adverbs.

A **contraction** is a combination of two words in which an apostrophe marks the place of one or more omitted letters. A pronoun often forms part of a contraction, as in *it's* ("it is").

Coordinate adjectives are two or more adjectives in a row that describe the same word and that can be reversed without seeming awkward. In "competent, enthusiastic staff" *competent* and *enthusiastic* are coordinate adjectives.

Coordinating conjunctions are words that connect other words, phrases, and clauses of roughly equal importance. *And, but, or, nor, yet, for,* and *so* are the coordinating conjunctions.

Correlative conjunctions are paired connecting words that link words, phrases, and clauses. The correlative conjunctions are *both . . . and, either . . . or, neither . . . nor, whether . . . or,* and *not only . . . but also.*

Count nouns are words that name things that can be counted, at least in theory. *Cup* is an example of a count noun.

A **dangling participial phrase** is a participial phrase modifying a word that does not appear in the same sentence as the participial phrase. This error can be corrected by adding the missing word to the sentence.

Declarative sentences are sentences that make statements.

The **definite article** is *the*.

The **demonstrative pronouns** are *this, that, these,* and *those.* They point out people and things.

Dependent clauses are groups of words that contain subjects and predicates but cannot stand alone as sentences.

A **direct object** names the person, thing or idea directly acted upon by the action described by a verb.

A **double negative** is the use of two negative words when one of them is unnecessary. "I do*n't* have *no* money" is an example of a double negative.

Exclamatory sentences are sentences that express emotions. They end in exclamation points.

Feminine gender is the classification of pronouns (and a few nouns) that refer only to females. The pronoun *she* refers only to a female person or animal, so it is feminine. A few objects, such as ships, are sometimes considered to be feminine.

A **finite verb** is any verb that functions as the main verb of a sentence.

A **fused sentence** is a type of run-on sentence in which two sentences are incorrectly joined without any punctuation between them.

The **future tense** is a verb form describing an action or condition that will take place after it is described. An example of the future tense is *will be walking*.

Gender is the classification of pronouns (and of a few nouns, such as *man* and *woman* or *rooster* and *hen*) according to whether they refer to males (masculine gender), females (feminine gender) or neither (neuter gender).

Gerunds are verb forms ending in -*ing* that are used as nouns.

The **imperative mood** is the manner of expressing the action of a verb used for requests and commands.

Imperative sentences are sentences that give orders.

The **indefinite articles** are *a* and *an*.

Indefinite pronouns refer to unspecified people or things. They include words that end in -*body*, -*one*, and -*thing*, such as *anybody, anyone,* and *anything*.

Independent clauses are clauses (groups of words containing subjects and predicates) that can stand alone as sentences.

The **indicative mood** is the manner of expressing the action of a verb used to state facts or ask questions about them. Most sentences are in the indicative mood.

Indirect objects are objects of verbs that can be changed into phrases beginning with the prepositions *to* and *for*. To find an indirect object, ask the question "To or for whom or what?"

An **infinitive** is the basic form of a verb preceded by the word *to*. *To study* is an example of an infinitive.

Intensive pronouns are identical in form to reflexive pronouns. They emphasize or intensify a noun or pronoun in the same sentence. In "She did it herself," *herself* is an intensive pronoun.

Interjections are members of a class of words that express emotions and are unrelated grammatically to the sentences in which they appear. *Wow* and *oh* are examples of interjections.

Interrogative pronouns are pronouns used to ask questions: "*Who* was that masked man?" "*What* are you looking for?" Except for *that,* which is a relative pronoun but not an interrogative one, interrogative pronouns and relative pronouns are identical in form.

Interrogative sentences are sentences that ask questions.

Intransitive verbs are verbs that describe actions but are not followed by direct objects or complements.

Irregular verbs, such as *sing* and *think,* are verbs that do not follow the standard patterns that regular verbs follow. Irregular verb forms such as *sang, sung,* and *thought* must be memorized.

Linking verbs are words that describe conditions, not actions. The forms of *be* (such as *am, is,* and *are*) are examples of linking verbs. Linking verbs are followed not by objects but by subject complements—words, phrases or clauses that rename or describe subjects.

A **main verb** describes an action or condition with reference to a specific subject.

Masculine gender is the classification of pronouns and a few nouns that refer only to males. The pronoun *he* refers only to a male person or animal, so it is masculine.

Mass nouns are words naming things that cannot be counted. *Love* and *sugar* are examples of mass nouns.

Modal auxiliaries are auxiliary verbs such as *can, could, may, might, must, ought, shall, should, will,* and *would.* They are used with the basic forms of other verbs to express writers' attitudes toward what they are writing.

Modifiers make words more specific by describing or limiting them in some way. Adjectives and adverbs are modifiers.

Mood is the use of verbs to indicate a person's attitude toward what he or she is saying or writing.

Negatives are words such as *no, not, neither, nor, never, none, no one, nothing, barely, hardly,* and *scarcely.*

Neuter is the classification of a word that is neither masculine nor feminine in gender. *It* is an example of a pronoun that is neuter in gender.

Nonrestrictive clauses are clauses (groups of words containing subjects and predicates) that provide additional details about the words they modify. These details are not necessary for identification. Nonrestrictive clauses are marked off by commas from the rest of the sentences in which they appear.

Noun clauses are subordinate clauses (groups of words containing subjects and predicates) that function as nouns. They appear in sentences as subjects, objects, and complements, just as other nouns do.

Noun phrases are groups of words that function in sentences as single nouns do and that do not contain verbs. Typically, a noun phrase contains a noun and the words that modify it.

Nouns are names. They indicate people *(George Washington, Dracula),* places *(New York, Zambia),* objects *(table, mountain),* and abstract ideas *(friendship, biology).*

Number is the classification of words according to whether they refer to one person or thing or to more than one.

The **object case** is the class of pronouns that can be used as objects of verbs or prepositions. *Us* is an example of a pronoun in the object case.

Object complements are words that follow direct objects and provide additional information that describes or clarifies them. In "We elected Cindy chairperson," *chairperson* is an object complement. Object complements can be nouns or adjectives.

Objects of prepositions are the nouns, pronouns or nounlike elements that end prepositional phrases.

Ordinal numbers are numbers functioning as adjectives that answer the question "Which one?" *Fourth* is an example of an ordinal number.

Parallel items are items in a list or in a pair that are in the same grammatical form. In "I like swimming and fishing," *swimming* and *fishing* are parallel.

Parts of speech are categories into which words are divided according to the roles they play in sentences. The parts of speech are nouns, articles, pronouns, verbs, verbals, adjectives, adverbs, conjunctions, prepositions, and interjections.

The **passive voice** is a way of expressing an idea in which the target of the action is the subject of the verb. *"The stop sign was hit"* is in the passive voice.

Past participles are verb forms that follow the verb *have* in verb phrases such as *have walked.* For regular verbs, past participles are identical with the past tense forms (the basic forms plus the ending *-d* or *-ed*). Past participles function in sentences as parts of verb phrases or as adjectives.

The **past tense** is a verb form describing an action or condition that took place before it was described. A regular verb indicates the past tense by adding *-ed* to the basic form for all persons and both numbers.

The **perfect tenses** are verb forms used to describe how events in the present, past or future continue to be relevant at a later time. The present perfect is also used to describe events that started in the past and continue into the present: "Leontyne *has shopped* at that store since she was a child." The past perfect describes an event in the past and shows that it was still relevant at a later time: "Mario *had* already *arrived* home when his mother walked in." The future perfect describes an event in the future and shows its relevance to another event in the future: "I *will have returned* by eleven o'clock."

Person is the distinction between the speaker (first person), the person or people spoken to (second person), and the person or people spoken about (third person).

Personal pronouns are pronouns that refer to specific people or things. They have different forms to indicate differences in person, number, gender, and case. *I, her,* and *our* are examples of personal pronouns.

Phrases are combinations of words that belong together because they express a single idea.

The **possessive case** is the class of nouns and pronouns that show possession. *Mary's* and *our* are examples of words in the possessive case.

A **predicate** is the part of a sentence that says something about the subject. It contains the verb and other words needed to complete its meaning, such as objects, complements, and modifiers. Everything in a sentence that is not part of the complete subject is part of the predicate.

A **predicate adjective** is an adjective functioning as a subject complement. A predicate adjective follows a linking verb and describes the subject of the linking verb.

A **prepositional phrase** is the combination of a preposition, the noun, pronoun or nounlike element that follows it, and any intervening modifiers.

Prepositions are words that connect nouns, pronouns and nounlike elements to other words in sentences and indicate the relationships between them. *In, from*, and *between* are examples of prepositions.

Present participles (basic verb forms ending in *-ing*) appear in sentences as parts of verb phrases or as adjectives. *Walking* is an example of a present participle.

The **present tense** is a verb form describing an action that takes place at the same time as it is being described. In addition, the present tense is used to indicate a time in the future, to describe habitual actions, to tell general truths, to write about books, movies, and other narratives, and to tell stories more vividly. *Walks* is an example of a verb in the present tense.

The **principal parts** of a verb are the basic form, the past tense form, and the past participle. Knowing these forms enables one to create all the other forms.

The **progressive** is a verb form which emphasizes that an event being described is in progress. It combines the auxiliary verbs *be, have*, and *will* with the present participle (which ends in *-ing*): *am walking, was walking, will be walking, have been walking, had been walking, will have been walking.*

Pronouns are words that replace nouns in sentences.

Proper adjectives are adjectives formed from proper nouns. *American* is an example of a proper adjective.

Proper nouns are nouns that name specific members of a group. Proper nouns are always capitalized. *America* is an example of a proper noun.

The **reciprocals** are the pronouns *each other* and *one another*. They express shared feelings or actions.

Reflexive pronouns are pronouns used as objects when subjects both perform the action of verbs and are acted upon. A reflexive pronoun reflects the subject like a mirror. In "I hurt myself," *myself* is a reflexive pronoun. Reflexive pronouns can appear in prepositional phrases when they refer to people or things mentioned earlier: "Nora ate by *herself*."

Regular verbs are verbs for which all the forms are predictable once the basic forms are known. *Walk* is an example of a regular verb.

A **relative clause** is a kind of dependent clause that begins with a relative pronoun such as *who, which* or *that*. Relative clauses may function in sentences as nouns or adjectives.

A **relative pronoun** is a pronoun that incorporates one kind of dependent clause, called a relative clause, into a sentence. The relative pronouns are *who, whom, whose, whoever, that, which, what, whatever*, and *whichever*.

Restrictive clauses are clauses that provide information needed to identify the nouns or noun substitutes they modify. Restrictive clauses are not set off by commas from the sentences in which they appear.

A **run-on sentence** is two sentences incorrectly punctuated as a single sentence.

The **sentence** is the basic unit of grammar. In writing, each new sentence opens with a capital letter and closes with an end mark, such as a period or a question mark. Sentences contain subjects (that is, they mention someone or something) and predicates (that is, they tell something about their subjects). A sentence expresses a complete idea.

A **sentence fragment** appears to be a sentence but is missing a vital sentence element, sometimes a main verb and sometimes both a subject and a verb. When a dependent (subordinate) clause stands alone, it is also a sentence fragment.

Sequence of tenses refers to the time relationships between verbs, which should reflect the order in which the events described by the verbs took place.

A **simple sentence** is a sentence consisting of a single independent clause.

A **simple subject** is the noun at the heart of a noun phrase that serves as the subject of a sentence.

A **split infinitive** is an infinitive in which *to* and the basic form of the verb are divided by one or more other words.

A **subject** mentions a person, place or thing. A subject is almost always found in the first part of a sentence. To find the grammatical subject of a sentence (not what the sentence seems to be about), ask "Who or what?" with the verb.

The **subject case** is the class of pronouns that can be used as subjects. *We* is an example of a pronoun in the subject case.

A **subject complement** is a word or phrase that follows a linking verb and renames or describes its subject. A subject complement can be a noun, a pronoun or an adjective.

The **subjunctive mood** is the manner of expressing the action of a verb to indicate desires, requests or suggestions. It also indicates imaginary or hypothetical conditions (sometimes called conditions contrary to fact). In the present subjunctive, the verbs appear in their basic forms. In the past subjunctive, the verb forms are identical with those in the past tense.

Subordinate clauses are dependent clauses joined to main (independent) clauses to form complex sentences. Subordinate clauses begin with subordinating conjunctions.

Subordinating conjunctions are words that connect clauses and indicate that one of the two clauses is more important than the other. *After, because, if, since, unless,* and *while* are some of the subordinating conjunctions. A subordinating conjunction appears at the beginning or in the middle of a sentence.

A **superlative form** of an adjective or adverb, such as *largest* or *most easily,* is used to show that one person or thing has more of some quality than two or more others.

Tenses are verb forms that indicate when actions take place, either in general or in relation to other actions. Examples of tenses are the present tense and the future tense.

Transitive verbs are verbs that require direct objects to complete their meanings.

Verb phrases are closely related groups of verb forms that function in sentences the same way single verbs do.

Verbals are derived from verbs, but they function in sentences as nouns, adjectives, and adverbs. Infinitives, gerunds, and participles are verbals.

Verbs are words that name actions (both physical and mental) and conditions.

Voice is a way of expressing an idea that indicates whether a subject is acting or is acted upon.

Answers to Exercises — Chapter 1

Exercise 1

1. INT
2. E
3. IMP
4. D
5. D
6. INT
7. E
8. INT
9. IMP
10. D

Exercise 2

1. Lidia / often
2. buses / are
3. Paulette / wore
4. divers / retrieved
5. people / choose
6. sweeteners / are
7. New York / spent
8. puzzles / is
9. water / flooded
10. battery / sprays

Exercise 3

1. Martin, clothes, catalogues
2. guests, show, opinions
3. concerts, quality, sound
4. supermarket, products
5. outside, building
6. flea, eggs
7. Mike, quarterback, team
8. Caryl, rug, sides
9. Squirrels, bulbs, nests, attics
10. Aluminum, steel, use, aluminum, cars, costs, fuel

Exercise 4

1. The, a, an
2. the, the, the, the
3. the, the
4. the, a
5. the, a, the, a
6. a, a
7. the, a
8. the
9. the, a
10. the, the

Exercise 5

1. You, yourself, you
2. their
3. I, my
4. she, her
5. their, their, they
6. she, her
7. her, she
8. he, his
9. their, their
10. he

Exercise 6

1. dangled
2. met
3. wrote
4. makes
5. contains
6. hide
7. prefers
8. removes
9. bought
10. owns

Exercise 7

1. flat, fresh
2. watery, itchy, runny
3. quick, powerful
4. Bright, big, young
5. fine, younger, new
6. good
7. old, large
8. excellent
9. black, rotary
10. wooden, dusty

Exercise 8

1. finally
2. previously, very
3. recently
4. typically, much
5. never
6. already
7. less, now, once
8. heavily, solidly
9. entirely
10. Extremely

Exercise 9

1. but
2. when
3. If
4. unless
5. when
6. and
7. Although
8. or
9. before
10. as

Exercise 10

1. in, on
2. from, to, of
3. by, from, to
4. on, in
5. In, of, for, of, in
6. After, to, from
7. in, in
8. for, in
9. on, in, of, of
10. In, in, by

Exercise 11

1. Great
2. Aha
3. well
4. Yech
5. Wow

6. Ouch
7. Shh
8. Hey
9. Darn
10. Whew

Exercise 12

1. adjective
2. verb
3. noun
4. adverb
5. conjunction
6. pronoun
7. verb
8. noun
9. article
10. preposition

Exercise 13

1. N
2. V
3. ADV
4. N
5. ADJ
6. ADJ
7. N
8. ADJ
9. V
10. ADJ

Exercise 14

1. PP
2. NP
3. VP
4. NP
5. PP
6. NP
7. PP
8. VP
9. PP
10. VP

Exercise 15

1. I
2. I
3. D
4. I
5. D
6. I
7. D
8. D
9. D
10. D

Exercise 16

1. simple
2. compound
3. simple
4. compound-complex
5. compound
6. complex
7. simple
8. complex
9. complex
10. compound

Exercise 17

1. S
2. V
3. V
4. V
5. S
6. V
7. S
8. S
9. V
10. V

Exercise 18

1. the gutters
2. the gate
3. his mortgage
4. the ground
5. his car
6. some insurance
7. stock
8. his own glass-cleaning liquid
9. the leaves
10. forty-five cents

Exercise 19

1. ADJ
2. N
3. ADJ
4. N
5. ADJ
6. ADJ
7. N
8. N
9. ADJ
10. ADJ

Exercise 20

1. Rita
2. his sisters
3. the trainer
4. the mayor
5. her son
6. Larry
7. Stan
8. my sister
9. her lawyer
10. Susie

Exercise 21

1. N
2. ADJ
3. N
4. ADJ
5. ADJ
6. N
7. ADJ
8. N
9. ADJ
10. ADJ

Try It Out: Answers will vary.

Exercise 22

1. S
2. F
3. S
4. F
5. S
6. F
7. F
8. S
9. F
10. F

Exercise 23

1. S
2. F
3. F
4. S
5. S
6. S
7. F
8. F
9. F
10. F

Exercise 24

1. F
2. S
3. F
4. S
5. F
6. S
7. S
8. F
9. S
10. F

Exercise 25

1. F
2. S
3. F
4. F
5. S
6. S
7. F
8. F
9. S
10. S

Exercise 26

1. RO
2. RO
3. S
4. RO
5. S
6. S
7. RO
8. S
9. RO
10. S

Exercise 27

1. RO
2. RO
3. S
4. RO
5. S
6. S
7. RO
8. S
9. RO
10. RO

Answers to Exercises — Chapter 2

Exercise 1

1. girls, vegetables, dinners
2. campaigns, voters, politics
3. baskets, straw, bark, roots
4. winter, duckling, swan
5. Chicory, coffee, caffeine
6. class, Juanita, collage, shoes, silverware, clippings, newspapers
7. people, pillow, place, rooms, effort, closets
8. Vera's, salsa, calories
9. Detectors, places, alarms
10. Osteoporosis, loss, bone

Exercise 2

1. proper noun
2. common noun
3. concrete noun
4. abstract noun
5. mass noun
6. mass noun
7. concrete noun
8. proper noun
9. compound noun
10. count noun

Try It Out: Answers will vary.

Exercise 3

1. noun phrase
2. noun clause
3. noun phrase
4. noun phrase
5. noun clause
6. noun clause
7. noun phrase
8. noun clause
9. noun phrase
10. noun clause

Exercise 4

1. step
2. employees
3. men
4. breakup
5. Belle
6. numbers
7. Bicycling
8. people
9. Wool
10. law

Exercise 5

1. Weddings, teas
2. films, comedies
3. cars, convertibles
4. dinners, potatoes
5. cupful, photograph
6. friends, relatives
7. Shanghai, Mexico City
8. Fission, fusion
9. hotlines, counseling
10. pedaling, braking

Exercise 6

1. DO
2. IO
3. IO
4. DO
5. IO
6. DO
7. DO
8. IO
9. DO
10. DO

Exercise 7

1. night
2. movie
3. robbery
4. album
5. budget
6. fare
7. camp
8. closet
9. films
10. case

Exercise 8

1. sun, cause
2. letters, notes
3. Uncle Julius, man
4. request, programming
5. Ross, electrician
6. regulations, rules
7. Tara Pederson, choice
8. name, Blibber-Blubber
9. Phyllis, cousin
10. friends, Toby, Cheryl

Exercise 9

1. Lori, player
2. Norbert, uncle
3. program, challenge
4. city, center
5. Eileen Mulder, vice president
6. shopping, waste
7. Louis Finney, chairperson
8. fish, Winifred
9. Claire, fool
10. Alex, executive

Exercise 10

1. earth, the fifth largest planet
2. Hindenburg, an enormous German dirigible
3. Himalayas, the greatest concentration of high mountains in the world
4. dome, a structure invented by R. Buckminster Fuller
5. conditioners, products intended to make hair easier to manage
6. Holocaust, the destruction of approximately 6 million Jews by the Nazis
7. Travel Tapes, recordings describing the history and geology of the area through which they are riding
8. waffles, big waffles with large, deep indentations

9. Armory Show, an art exhibit held in New York in 1913.
10. Patricia Hearst, the daughter of publisher Randolph Hearst

Exercise 11

1. fields
2. taxes
3. officials
4. princesses
5. shoes
6. classes
7. topazes
8. newspapers
9. inches
10. crashes

Exercise 12

1. cities
2. monkeys
3. candies
4. turkeys
5. warranties
6. communities
7. cherries
8. plays
9. destinies
10. ploys

Exercise 13

1. congressmen
2. nuclei
3. cellos
4. axes
5. algae
6. cupfuls
7. brothers-in-law
8. cacti or cactuses
9. bacteria
10. sanatoriums or sanatoria

Exercise 14

1. the book's preface
2. the mirror's frame
3. Russ's hand
4. the fly's wings
5. the pool's depth
6. the dress's hem
7. Oklahoma's capital
8. the summer's beginning
9. the waitress's tray
10. the sun's effects

Exercise 15

1. the trucks' cost
2. the children's complaints
3. the carpets' colors
4. the nurses' salaries
5. the babies' home
6. the stores' alarm systems
7. the mothers-in-law's dinners
8. the men's hobbies
9. the actresses' costumes
10. the workers' goals

Exercise 16

1. the women's credit cards
2. the girls' birthdays
3. the plan's benefits
4. the chairs' backs
5. the week's events

6. the clubs' meetings
7. the movies' plots
8. the company's laboratories
9. the alumni's reunion
10. the managers' techniques

Exercise 17

1. a
2. an
3. an
4. a
5. an
6. A
7. an
8. a
9. a
10. an

Exercise 18

1. a
2. the
3. X
4. a
5. the
6. the
7. the
8. X
9. a
10. the

Answers to Exercises — Chapter 3

Exercise 1

1. you, me, your
2. Somebody
3. I, I, I, her
4. their
5. This, my
6. I('d), I, I, anyone, me
7. its, it
8. nobody, her
9. his
10. she

Exercise 2

1. he
2. his, him
3. it
4. they
5. my
6. I, your, I('ll)
7. he, his
8. their, her
9. her, she
10. he, I

Exercise 3

1. N, themselves
2. C
3. N, me
4. C
5. N, yourselves
6. N, themselves
7. C
8. N, himself
9. C
10. C

Exercise 4

1. D
2. IND
3. I
4. D
5. IND

6. R
7. D
8. I
9. R
10. IND

Exercise 5

1. Who
2. Whoever
3. whom
4. whomever
5. who
6. whom
7. whomever
8. who
9. Whoever
10. whom

Exercise 6

1. N, hers
2. N, ours
3. C
4. N, yours
5. C
6. N, theirs
7. C
8. N, his
9. C
10. N, theirs

Exercise 7

1. Whose
2. they're
3. It's
4. their
5. its
6. your
7. whose
8. they're
9. Who's
10. You're

Exercise 8

1. me
2. us
3. he
4. We
5. her, me
6. us
7. her
8. He
9. We
10. him

Exercise 9

1. they: cleansers
2. she: Nancy; her: Nancy
3. it: object
4. their: teenagers; them: teenagers
5. his: Joshua; he: Joshua
6. him: Keith; his: Keith
7. her: Claudia
8. it: parrot; him: Paul
9. she: Gwendolyn; his: Dionysios
10. her: Mrs. Wilkowski; their: assistants

Exercise 10

1. C
2. C
3. U
4. U
5. C
6. U
7. C
8. U
9. C
10. C

Exercise 11

1. C
2. N, it
3. C
4. N, it
5. C
6. N, they
7. C
8. N, they
9. C
10. N, its

Exercise 12

1. C
2. N
3. N
4. C
5. C
6. N
7. C
8. N
9. N
10. C

Exercise 13

1. its
2. her
3. its
4. their
5. their
6. its
7. she
8. its
9. its
10. his

Exercise 14

1. Hikers should be especially alert when they are in bear country.
2. District managers should be sure that they are detail oriented and prudent.
3. Self-employment can give parents some flexibility while they are raising their children.
4. Doctors use small hammers to check their patients' reflexes.
5. When players spike a volleyball, they hit it sharply downward.
6. Financial planners may earn their living from commissions on the products they sell.
7. With light meters photographers can accurately determine the correct settings for their cameras.
8. Riders sit more nearly upright on all-terrain bicycles than they do on ordinary racing bikes.
9. The balloons cartoonists draw for characters' thoughts differ from those they use for dialogue.

10. Company directors should recognize that free fitness programs can reduce their companies' medical costs.

Exercise 15

1. C
2. C
3. N, If someone is removing an old muffler, he or she may also have to remove the pipes on either side of it. Or: If people are removing an old muffler, they may also have to remove the pipes on either side of it.
4. N, A painter should use a tack cloth to clean a surface he or she is about to paint. Or: Painters should use tack cloths to clean surfaces they are about to paint.
5. C
6. N, When people bag grass clippings, their lawns will look better, but there may be no good way to dispose of the clippings.
7. C
8. N, In a joint checking account, nothing prevents one owner from emptying the account without telling the other one.
9. C
10. C

Try It Out: Answers will vary.

Answers to Exercises — Chapter 4

Exercise 1

1. PAST
2. PRES
3. PRES
4. PAST
5. PRES
6. PAST
7. PRES
8. PAST
9. PRES
10. PAST

Exercise 2

1. 3 P
2. 1 P
3. 3 S
4. 1 S
5. 2 P
6. 3 S
7. 2 S
8. 1 S
9. 3 P
10. 1 P

Exercise 3

1. became
2. kept
3. got
4. spun, spun
5. wept
6. built
7. met
8. ate, rode
9. worn
10. arose, arisen

Exercise 4

1. leaves
2. have
3. visited
4. caused
5. rescued
6. attend
7. hides
8. bought
9. keep
10. spent

Exercise 5

1. sat
2. retires
3. celebrated
4. fell
5. participated
6. smiled
7. improved
8. blew
9. arrived
10. continued

Exercise 6

1. lies
2. set
3. laid
4. sat
5. lie
6. sat
7. sat
8. lain
9. sets
10. lay

Exercise 7

1. seems
2. looks
3. is
4. feels
5. was
6. was
7. seem
8. appeared
9. are
10. is

Exercise 8

1. F
2. N
3. F
4. N
5. F
6. F
7. N
8. F
9. F
10. N

Exercise 9

1. am
2. should
3. did
4. can
5. will
6. may
7. had
8. would
9. can, has
10. is

Exercise 10

1. L
2. T
3. L
4. A
5. T
6. A
7. I
8. A
9. I
10. I

Exercise 11

1. orders
2. hates
3. is
4. end
5. turns
6. is
7. takes
8. compliment
9. emphasizes
10. hopes

Exercise 12

1. refused
2. was, had
3. wanted
4. discussed, made
5. had, put, inhaled
6. accepted
7. lighted or lit, carried
8. used
9. planned, liked
10. resembled

Exercise 13

1. will benefit
2. will bring
3. will keep
4. will hold
5. will bloom
6. will be
7. will help
8. will be
9. will contain
10. will cause

Exercise 14

1. had forgotten or had forgot
2. will have driven
3. had climbed
4. had won
5. have measured
6. had learned
7. will have spent
8. has taken
9. will have built
10. has inspired

Exercise 15

1. is looking
2. will have been caring
3. have been protesting
4. is riding
5. will be leaving
6. had been collecting
7. were crawling
8. had been looking
9. were working
10. have been refusing

Exercise 16

1. took
2. lasted
3. wants
4. won
5. tastes
6. wrote
7. started
8. has
9. weighed
10. puts

Exercise 17

1. The indentation below the nose is known as the philtrum?
2. How do robot arms assemble products such as automobiles and television sets?
3. Does lightning cause millions of dollars in home and property damage each year?
4. Was Nero, the Roman emperor, only thirty-one when he died?
5. Has Maria read all 38 of Shakespeare's plays?
6. Can taking aspirin reduce the chances of heart attacks in men over fifty?
7. Emily's television set receives 105 channels?
8. Is the covering on the end of a shoelace called an aglet?
9. Why was Janet reading the advertising panels on the walls of the subway car?
10. Is Martin one of the students watching the Senate debate from the galleries?

Exercise 18

1. is
2. use
3. is
4. gives
5. are
6. plans
7. follow
8. are
9. are
10. cause

Exercise 19

1. ask
2. pastes
3. do
4. are
5. seem
6. causes
7. are
8. takes
9. checks
10. do

Exercise 20

1. are
2. is
3. are
4. are
5. is
6. is
7. is
8. are
9. is
10. are

Exercise 21

1. was
2. was
3. are
4. is
5. is
6. was
7. were
8. is
9. was
10. is

Exercise 22

1. have
2. is
3. buys
4. dislike
5. is
6. benefits
7. remembers
8. stop
9. ends
10. pass

Exercise 23

1. is
2. accepts
3. is
4. remains
5. is
6. is
7. was
8. is
9. are
10. is

Exercise 24

1. is
2. interests
3. are
4. become

5. cost
6. is
7. are
8. is
9. are
10. is

Exercise 25

1. P
2. A
3. A
4. P
5. A
6. P
7. P
8. P
9. A
10. P

Exercise 26

1. Vacuum cups gently lift commercially baked bread from its baking pan.
2. The band parents' organization compiled a cookbook to sell as a fund raiser.
3. One of the windows in Washington National Cathedral contains a piece of rock from the moon.
4. Bradley perfected his clowning skills at Clown Camp in La Crosse, Wisconsin.
5. Cathleen ordered boiled hard-shell crabs.
6. Russell criticizes every suggestion I make.
7. If you wear boots for hiking, break them in before taking a long hike.
8. The Laytons painted their house inside and out every other year.
9. Gwen and Bradford bought a stroller, a crib, a playpen, a bassinet, and a high chair.
10. I had reported safety violations as early as June 1990.

Try It Out: Answers will vary.

Exercise 27

1. I
2. S
3. S
4. IMP
5. S
6. I
7. IMP
8. S
9. I
10. IMP

Exercise 28

1. were
2. stop
3. prepare
4. were
5. be
6. were
7. come
8. be
9. leave
10. owned

Exercise 29

Tenses and Moods of Hunt and See
Indicative Mood
The Present Tense: Active Voice
singular/plural
first person: I hunt, see we hunt, see
second person; you hunt, see you hunt, see
third person: he, she, it hunts, sees they hunt, see
The Present Tense: Passive Voice
singular/plural
first person: I am hunted, seen we are hunted, seen
second person: you are hunted, seen you are
  hunted, seen
third person: he, she, it is hunted, seen they are
  hunted, seen
The Past Tense: Active Voice
singular/plural
first person: I hunted, saw we hunted, saw
second person: you hunted, saw you hunted, saw
third person: he, she, it hunted, saw they hunted,
  saw

The Past Tense: Passive Voice
singular/plural
first person: I was hunted, seen we were hunted,
  seen
second person: you were hunted, seen you were
  hunted, seen
third person: he, she, it was hunted, seen they
  were hunted, seen
The Future Tense: Active Voice
singular/plural
first person: I will hunt, see we will hunt, see
second person: you will hunt, see you will hunt,
  see
third person: he, she, it will hunt, see they will
  hunt, see
The Future Tense: Passive Voice
singular/plural
first person: I will be hunted, seen we will be
  hunted, seen
second person: you will be hunted, seen you will
  be hunted, seen
third person: he, she, it will be hunted, seen they
  will be hunted, seen
The Present Perfect Tense: Active Voice
singular/plural
first person: I have hunted, seen we have hunted,
  seen
second person: you have hunted, seen you have
  hunted, seen
third person: he, she, it has hunted, seen they
  have hunted, seen
The Present Perfect Tense: Passive Voice
singular/plural
first person: I have been hunted, seen we have
  been hunted, seen
second person: you have been hunted, seen you
  have been hunted, seen
third person: he, she, it has been hunted, seen
  they have been hunted, seen
The Past Perfect Tense: Active Voice
singular/plural
first person: I had hunted, seen we had hunted,
  seen
second person: you had hunted, seen you had
  hunted, seen
third person: he, she, it had hunted, seen they had
  hunted, seen

The Past Perfect Tense: Passive Voice
singular/plural

first person: I had been hunted, seen we had been hunted, seen

second person: you had been hunted, seen you had been hunted, seen

third person: he, she, it had been hunted, seen they had been hunted, seen

The Future Perfect Tense: Active Voice
singular/plural

first person: I will have hunted, seen we will have hunted, seen

second person: you will have hunted, seen you will have hunted, seen

third person: he, she, it will have hunted, seen they will have hunted, seen

The Future Perfect Tense: Passive Voice
singular/plural

first person: I will have been hunted, seen we will have been hunted, seen

second person: you will have been hunted, seen you will have been hunted, seen

third person: he, she, it will have been hunted, seen they will have been hunted, seen

The Present Progressive: Active Voice
singular/plural

first person: I am hunting, seeing we are hunting, seeing

second person: you are hunting, seeing you are hunting, seeing

third person: he, she, it is hunting, seeing they are hunting, seeing

The Present Progressive: Passive Voice
singular/plural

first person: I am being hunted, seen we are being hunted, seen

second person: you are being hunted, seen you are being hunted, seen

third person: he, she, it is being hunted, seen they are being hunted, seen

The Past Progressive: Active Voice
singular/plural

first person: I was hunting, seeing we were hunting, seeing

second person: you were hunting, seeing you were hunting, seeing

third person: he, she, it was hunting, seeing they were hunting, seeing

The Past Progressive: Passive Voice
singular/plural

first person: I was being hunted, seen we were being hunted, seen

second person: you were being hunted, seen you were being hunted, seen

third person: he, she, it was being hunted, seen they were being hunted, seen

The Future Progressive: Active Voice
singular/plural

first person: I will be hunting, seeing we will be hunting, seeing

second person: you will be hunting, seeing you will be hunting, seeing

third person: he, she, it will be hunting, seeing they will be hunting, seeing

The Future Progressive: Passive Voice
singular/plural

first person: I will be being hunted, seen we will be being hunted, seen

second person: you will be being hunted, seen you will be being hunted, seen

third person: he, she, it will be being hunted, seen they will be being hunted, seen

The Present Perfect Progressive: Active Voice
singular/plural

first person: I have been hunting, seeing we have been hunting, seeing

second person: you have been hunting, seeing you have been hunting, seeing

third person: he, she, it has been hunting, seeing they have been hunting, seeing

The Present Perfect Progressive: Passive Voice
singular/plural

first person: I have been being hunted, seen we have been being hunted, seen

second person: you have been being hunted, seen you have been being hunted, seen

third person: he, she, it has been being hunted, seen they have been being hunted, seen

The Past Perfect Progressive: Active Voice
singular/plural

first person: I had been hunting, seeing we had been hunting, seeing

second person: you had been hunting, seeing you
  had been hunting, seeing

third person: he, she, it had been hunting, seeing
  they had been hunting, seeing

The Past Perfect Progressive: Passive Voice

singular/plural

first person: I had been being hunted, seen we
  had been being hunted, seen

second person: you had been being hunted, seen
  you had been being hunted, seen

third person: he, she, it had been being hunted,
  seen they had been being hunted, seen

The Future Perfect Progressive: Active Voice

singular/plural

first person: I will have been hunting, seeing we
  will have been hunting, seeing

second person: you will have been hunting,
  seeing you will have been hunting, seeing

third person: he, she, it will have been hunting,
  seeing they will have been hunting, seeing

The Future Perfect Progressive: Passive Voice

singular/plural

first person: I will have been being hunted, seen
  we will have been being hunted, seen

second person: you will have been being hunted,
  seen you will have been being hunted, seen

third perso:n: he, she, it will have been being
  hunted, seen they will have been being
  hunted, seen

The Subjunctive Mood

The Present Subjunctive: Active Voice

singular/plural

first person: (he, she insists) I hunt, see (he, she
  insists) we hunt, see

second person: (he, she insists) you hunt, see (he,
  she insists) you hunt, see

third person: (he, she insists) he, she, it hunt, see
  (he, she insists) they hunt, see

The Present Subjunctive: Passive Voice

singular/plural

first person: (he, she insists) I be hunted, seen
  (he, she insists) we be hunted, seen

second person: (he, she insists) you be hunted,
  seen (he, she insists) you be hunted, seen

third person: (he, she insists) he, she, it be
  hunted, seen (he, she insists) they be hunted,
  seen

The Past Subjunctive: Active Voice

singular/plural

first person: (if) I hunted, saw (if) we hunted, saw

second person: (if) you hunted, saw (if) you
  hunted, saw

third person: (if) he, she, it hunted, saw (if) they
  hunted, saw

The Past Subjunctive: Passive Voice

singular/plural

first person: (if) I were hunted, seen (if) we were
  hunted, seen

second person: (if) you were hunted, seen (if) you
  were hunted, seen

third person: (if) he, she, it were hunted, seen (if)
  they were hunted, seen

The Imperative Mood

singular/plural

second person: hunt, see hunt, see

Answers to Exercises — Chapter 5

Exercise 1

1. to get
2. to find
3. to iron
4. to finish
5. to reduce
6. to turn
7. to learn
8. to take
9. to overreact
10. to sell

Exercise 2

1. to make her stone sculptures.
2. to be drawing remarkably different conclusions from the same data.
3. to adjust to unfamiliar foods
4. to have been embittered against the company
5. to watch for meteors
6. to be comprehended easily by the general public.
7. to read the headlines of the tabloids to each other.
8. to lift cooked spaghetti from boiling water.
9. to appear in print
10. to have been looking for another job

Exercise 3

1. ADV
2. N
3. ADV
4. ADJ
5. ADV
6. ADJ
7. ADJ
8. N
9. ADJ
10. ADV

Exercise 4

One way to rearrange each sentence is suggested. Other versions are also possible.

1. necessarily; not necessarily need
2. definitely; Antonina definitely hopes
3. finally; Kay finally went
4. safely; skate safely, a
5. immediately; Puerto Rico immediately after
6. severely; managers severely and
7. sometimes; is sometimes able
8. dramatically; Heaven dramatically.
9. directly; appeal directly to
10. immediately; lawyer immediately.

Exercise 5

1. proposed
2. created
3. tilted
4. colored
5. unaccompanied
6. grouped
7. hissing
8. compressed
9. flashing
10. taken

Exercise 6

1. blown through jets in the underside of its hull.
2. swimming among the sharks.
3. wearing shorts, a blouse, a tailored jacket, sheer hose, and flat shoes.
4. decorated with cartoon characters.
5. labeled as an atrium; called a mud room.
6. covering the earth's surface.
7. sought by early Spanish explorers in the New World.
8. connecting points with equal barometric pressure.
9. worn by soldiers in the Revolutionary War.
10. transmitting messages as far away as the moon.

Exercise 7

One way to rewrite each absolute phrase as a subordinate clause is given. Other ways to rewrite the absolute phrases are also possible.

1. Time having been called
    When time was called, Marcella flipped through her program to find the names of the players.
2. The monkeys making their distinctive alarm calls
    As the monkeys made their distinctive alarm calls, the leopard moved silently through the grass.
3. The litter having been removed from the roadside
    After the litter had been removed from the roadside, the Scouts returned to their bus.
4. The electricity having gone off
    After the electricity went off, we went to bed.
5. The weather being good
    Because the weather is good, the picture will be taken outdoors.
6. The luncheon having ended
    After the luncheon ended, everyone began to leave the conference.
7. All things considered
    After we considered everything, we concluded that the bake sale was a success.
8. the gas overflowing from the car's tank
    Jeff absent-mindedly watched the traffic pass while the gas overflowed from the car's tank.
9. The fireworks exploding overhead
    While the fireworks exploded overhead, I watched the celebration from my rented house on the hillside.

10. The times being bad
    Because the times are bad, we should save more money.

Exercise 8

1. Containing a bullet pouch, mace holder, pen holder, and handcuff case, a policeman's belt stores much more than a gun.
2. Putting in many extra hours at the supermarket, Gary no longer makes the fire company his first priority.
3. By changing the designs of U.S. coins, the government would probably raise millions of dollars though sales to coin collectors.
4. The Romans called a land north of Britain, now believed to be Iceland, Ultima Thule.
5. Spreading drops of honey through the hive and fanning them with their wings, bees reduce the amount of water in nectar.
6. Considering the Bacharach's property too small for the number of donkeys they have, the neighbors filed a protest at city hall.
7. Using the computerized sewing machines, Johanna sewed elaborate lettering and decorative patterns.
8. Running to my car, I found a ring.
9. Wearing a morning coat and striped trousers, the butler brought in tea on a silver tray.
10. Using a metal detector, May and Frederick searched for the lost class ring.

Exercise 9

1. C
2. I
3. I
4. C
5. I
6. C
7. I
8. I
9. C
10. C

Try It Out: Answers will vary.

Exercise 10

1. F
2. C
3. F
4. C
5. C
6. F
7. C
8. F
9. F
10. F

Exercise 11

1. Packing
2. accounting
3. refusing
4. accepting
5. manufacturing
6. Eating
7. choosing
8. bumping
9. standardizing
10. pureeing

Exercise 12

1. G
2. P
3. P
4. G
5. P
6. G
7. G
8. G
9. P
10. P

Exercise 13

1. To blend two words, Blending
2. to look into the safety mirror above his crib, looking
3. to refrigerate it, refrigerating
4. to descend even 1,000 feet, descending
5. To advertise job openings, Advertising
6. to be shy, being
7. To play the national anthem before sporting events, Playing
8. to install a prefabricated disappearing attic staircase, installing
9. To move a camera from side to side, Moving
10. To get ahead in business, Getting

Exercise 14

1. Marcy's
2. their
3. Your
4. Jessie's
5. my
6. Clay's
7. dentist's
8. his
9. Lucy's
10. her

Exercise 15

1. to thicken them, to help their ingredients combine smoothly, and to preserve them.
2. to push earth and to grade it.
3. for bathing, soaking their clothing, and even giving their horses a more pleasant odor.
4. for encouraging mildew, warping wood, and rusting metal.
5. not being at home during the fire and having removed valued belongings before the fire.
6. to gauge stress and to alert a computer
7. Removing the front door and carrying the four-poster bed upstairs
8. making french fries and cleaning washrooms.
9. Increasing dietary intake of calcium and exercising regularly
10. for taping his traveler's checks to the back of the mirror in his motel room and then forgetting to take them with him the next day.

Answers to Exercises — Chapter 6

Exercise 1

1. only
2. good, good, personal
3. more
4. compulsive, psychic
5. sugary
6. same, six
7. parasitic
8. universal, various
9. three
10. top, big

Exercise 2

1. PA
2. OC
3. PA
4. OC
5. PA
6. PA
7. OC
8. PA
9. OC
10. PA

Try It Out: Answers will vary.

Exercise 3

1. ADJ, shifts
2. N
3. ADJ, ant
4. N
5. ADJ, telephone
6. ADJ, signs
7. N
8. ADJ, waves
9. ADJ, book
10. N

Exercise 4

1. P, bird
2. C, animals
3. P, trunk
4. P, holes

5. C, lever
6. P, defense
7. P, budget
8. P, truth
9. C, girl
10. C, building

Exercise 5

1. NC
2. NC
3. C soft, light
4. NC
5. C faded, deteriorating
6. C shiny, silky
7. NC
8. NC
9. C deep, rich
10. C safe, inexpensive

Exercise 6

1. all-talking
2. low lying
3. baked-apple
4. two-mile
5. prize-winning
6. largest selling
7. fiber-optic
8. battery-powered
9. four-inch
10. toll-free

Exercise 7

1. African
2. Asian
3. Egyptian
4. English
5. Hindi
6. Alcan
7. Brazilian
8. American
9. Pennsylvania
10. Broadway

Exercise 8

1. cleaned, V
2. important, ADJ
3. bake, V
4. hard, ADV
5. effortlessly, ADV
6. causes, V
7. one, ADJ
8. was considered, V
9. generous, ADJ
10. too, ADV

Exercise 9

1. formerly
2. quickly
3. well
4. chemically
5. extremely
6. very
7. today
8. only
9. most
10. reasonably

Exercise 10

1. really
2. surely
3. well
4. everyday
5. badly
6. all ready
7. bad
8. good
9. already
10. perfectly

Exercise 11

Answers may vary somewhat. Two possible ways to make each sentence negative are given below.
1. I cannot afford a new dishwasher this year.
   > I can't afford a new dishwasher this year.
2. Brent believes that nausea and lightheadedness are not good reasons to stop an exercise workout.
   > Brent does not believe that nausea and lightheadedness are good reasons to stop an exercise workout.
3. A local check will not clear this bank in three days.
   > A local check will never clear this bank in three days.
4. A smoke detector cannot determine whether smoke is coming from frying food or from a house fire.
   > A smoke detector has no way to determine whether smoke is coming from frying food or from a house fire.
5. Mr. Gowers's children did not give him flowers for Father's Day.
   > Mr. Gowers's children never gave him flowers for Father's Day.
6. The temperature does not fall below zero in Hawaii.
   > The temperature never falls below zero in Hawaii.
7. A flea market is not held every Saturday and Sunday at the Englewood Farmers' Market.
   > No flea market is held every Saturday and Sunday at the Englewood Farmers' Market.
8. Professor Furness does not study seabirds.
   > Professor Furness never studies seabirds.
9. I do not want to visit Pamplona to see the running of the bulls through the streets of the town.
   > I never want to visit Pamplona to see the running of the bulls through the streets of the town.
10. Lee does not plan to enter the watermelon-seed-spitting contest in Paul's Valley, Oklahoma.
    > Lee never plans to enter the watermelon-seed-spitting contest in Paul's Valley, Oklahoma.

Exercise 12

1. C
2. I, Scarcely any train stations are larger than Grand Central Station in New York City.
3. I, I don't have anything in my purse, so I don't care if it's stolen.
4. C
5. I, Jerry never visited any place he liked better than home, so he finally started staying home most of the time.
6. C
7. C
8. I, We will never accept any new production standards.
9. I, Manx cats have hardly any tails.
10. I, Vultures do not make any noises except for occasional hisses.

Exercise 13

1. most mysterious
2. most valuable
3. higher
4. strongest
5. smallest
6. most important
7. more crunchy
8. higher, greater
9. largest
10. more organized

Exercise 14

1. more carelessly, most carelessly
2. faster, fastest
3. more quickly, most quickly
4. more adequately, most adequately
5. harder, hardest
6. more obviously, most obviously
7. more quietly, most quietly
8. more consistently, most consistently
9. sooner, soonest
10. more neatly, most neatly

Exercise 15

1. C
2. I, Please take the bigger of these two pieces of cake.
3. C
4. C
5. I, Of all the written records people have made, the earliest are accounts of financial transactions.
6. I, Michael and Ralph both talk a great deal, but Ralph is the more talkative of the two.
7. I, Nanette is the most unusual person I have ever known.
8. C
9. I, In this suit I feel as if I could win an award for worst-dressed person of the year.
10. I, Of the twins, Len weighs more and is taller.

Exercise 16

1. also
2. likewise
3. subsequently
4. Furthermore
5. nevertheless
6. however
7. finally
8. hence
9. however
10. similarly

Exercise 17

Each sentence can be corrected either with a semicolon or a period and a capital letter.

1. fingerprints; however,   fingerprints. However,
2. 1860s; it   1860s. It
3. cameras; later,   cameras. Later,
4. snow; therefore,   snow. Therefore,
5. sickness; moreover,   sickness. Moreover,
6. smoothly; furthermore,   smoothly. Furthermore
7. ink; likewise,   ink. Likewise,
8. body; movement   body. Movement
9. States; however,   States. However
10. World War II; they   World War II. They

Answers to Exercises — Chapter 7

Exercise 1

1. and
2. or
3. but
4. nor
5. or, and, yet
6. but
7. and
8. or
9. yet
10. or

Exercise 2

1. but
2. for
3. and
4. but
5. so
6. but
7. and
8. yet
9. so
10. nor

Exercise 3

1. both . . . and
2. either . . . or
3. both . . . and
4. not only . . . but . . . also
5. both . . . and
6. Whether . . . or, whether . . . or
7. Neither . . . nor
8. not only . . . but also
9. either . . . or
10. not only . . . but also

Exercise 4

One way to correct each incorrect sentence is provided. Other ways to correct the sentences are also possible.

1. P
2. NP Marcia does not know whether to put hot food directly into the refrigerator or let it cool first.
3. NP Many parents in our school district know neither how to make the school system work for them nor how to spot problems before they get out of hand.
4. P
5. NP Will is not sure whether the rock he found is igneous or sedimentary.
6. P
7. P
8. NP Botanical gardens not only educate the public about plants but also serve as centers for scientific investigation into botany.
9. P
10. NP Amber can't remember whether a checkerboard has sixty-four squares or forty-eight squares.

Exercise 5

1. If
2. where
3. than
4. When
5. since
6. though
7. while
8. Whenever
9. After
10. Although

Exercise 6

1. When a baby elephant first tries to drink its mother's milk
2. Because statisticians do not keep records of how many engagements are broken
3. Until the guillotine was invented
4. While I drove through the center of Cleveland
5. where few pleasures are available
6. After a spectacular meteor fall occurred in 1803
7. Before business schools graduate students specializing in international business
8. since she was nine years old
9. As the days become longer
10. if you use a diving mask

Exercise 7

1. N
2. N
3. R
4. N
5. R
6. R
7. N
8. R
9. R
10. N

Exercise 8

1. In Dr. Jamison's work with children, which is a form of play therapy, she uses puppets, blocks, and other toys to help young children cope with the stresses in their lives.
2. Al Hautzig, who was the first person in our neighborhood to get a motorboat, fished every weekend, regardless of the weather.
3. Mrs. Morgan, whose dogs have been trained to protect sheep, objects to the use of poison to control wolves.
4. An aria, which is a solo vocal passage in an opera, is usually expressive and moving.
5. Josef Jacobus, whom I met at a fund-raising dinner last April, announced today that he plans to run for mayor.
6. Father Time, who is a mythical figure, is usually pictured carrying an hourglass and a scythe.
7. Horatio Alger, whose theme was always the rise from rags to riches, wrote 135 novels.
8. Chopines, which were shoes worn by European women in the 1600s, were so high that women wearing them could not walk without the help of servants.
9. Our landlord, whom we still owe for last month's rent, refuses to fix our air conditioner until our rent is paid.
10. Edgar Allan Poe, whose parents were actors, was orphaned when he was three years old.

Exercise 9

1. ADV
2. ADV
3. ADJ
4. ADV
5. ADJ
6. ADV
7. ADJ
8. ADV
9. ADJ
10. ADJ

Exercise 10

1. O
2. S
3. O
4. C
5. O
6. C
7. O
8. C
9. S
10. O

Exercise 11

1. ADV
2. ADJ
3. N
4. N
5. ADV
6. ADJ
7. ADJ
8. ADV
9. ADJ
10. ADV

Exercise 12

1. After
2. than
3. Though
4. Unless
5. until
6. since
7. While
8. where
9. that
10. that

Try It Out: Answers will vary.

Answers to Exercises — Chapter 8

Exercise 1

1. of
2. about
3. past
4. on
5. between
6. in
7. for
8. of
9. into
10. on

Exercise 2

1. in front of
2. in spite of
3. regardless of
4. instead of
5. out of
6. In addition to
7. because of
8. instead of
9. along with
10. In case of

Exercise 3

1. of the items, on display, at the museum, of the feet, of King Cheops
2. through space, at 66,700 miles an hour
3. under his arm, of coffee, onto the elevator
4. at thirty-seven degrees, at zero
5. over the gauze pads, on adhesive bandages, around wounds
6. from the Miss America talent contest, in 1948
7. During World War I, for submarines
8. by a preoccupation, with time
9. of Iceland
10. In 1901, for the letter S (dot-dot-dot), from England, to Newfoundland, of radio

Try It Out: Answers will vary.

Exercise 4

1. ADV
2. ADJ
3. ADV
4. N
5. ADV
6. ADV
7. N
8. ADJ
9. ADV
10. N

Exercise 5

1. C
2. I The women were singing "Happy Birthday" in Portuguese.
3. I Writing about her grandmother helped Mona to understand her fully for the first time.
4. C
5. C
6. I Humor is a well-established part of advertising campaigns.
7. I Patsy met her future husband on a jogging trail.
8. C
9. I Record rainfalls led to an increase in mosquitos this year.
10. C

Exercise 6

1. ~~with~~ for
2. ~~of~~
3. ~~to~~ on
4. Among ~~Between~~
5. ~~to~~ from
6. from (add between *different* and *nor*)
7. ~~to~~ with
8. in (add between *only* and *warm*)
9. ~~to~~ of
10. In (add before *Arab*)

Index

OTHER BOOKS IN THE HARPERCOLLINS COLLEGE OUTLINE SERIES

ART
History of Art 0-06-467131-3
Introduction to Art 0-06-467122-4

BUSINESS
Business Calculus 0-06-467136-4
Business Communications 0-06-467155-0
Introduction to Business 0-06-467104-6
Introduction to Management 0-06-467127-5
Introduction to Marketing 0-06-467130-5

CHEMISTRY
College Chemistry 0-06-467120-8
Organic Chemistry 0-06-467126-7

COMPUTERS
Computers and Information Processing 0-06-467176-3
Introduction to Computer Science and Programming
   0-06-467145-3
Understanding Computers 0-06-467163-1

ECONOMICS
Introduction to Economics 0-06-467113-5
Managerial Economics 0-06-467172-0

ENGLISH LANGUAGE AND LITERATURE
English Grammar 0-06-467109-7
English Literature From 1785 0-06-467150-X
English Literature To 1785 0-06-467114-3
Persuasive Writing 0-06-467175-5

FOREIGN LANGUAGE
French Grammar 0-06-467128-3
German Grammar 0-06-467159-3
Spanish Grammar 0-06-467129-1
Wheelock's Latin Grammar 0-06-467177-1
Workbook for Wheelock's Latin Grammar
   0-06-467171-2

HISTORY
Ancient History 0-06-467119-4
British History 0-06-467110-0
Modern European History 0-06-467112-7
Russian History 0-06-467117-8
20th Century United States History 0-06-467132-1
United States History From 1865 0-06-467100-3
United States History to 1877 0-06-467111-9
Western Civilization From 1500 0-06-467102-X

Western Civilization To 1500 0-06-467101-1
World History From 1500 0-06-467138-0
World History to 1648 0-06-467123-2

MATHEMATICS
Advanced Calculus 0-06-467139-9
Advanced Math for Engineers and Scientists
   0-06-467151-8
Applied Complex Variables 0-06-467152-6
Basic Mathematics 0-06-467143-7
Calculus with Analytic Geometry 0-06-467161-5
College Algebra 0-06-467140-2
Elementary Algebra 0-06-467118-6
Finite Mathematics with Calculus 0-06-467164-X
Intermediate Algebra 0-06-467137-2
Introduction to Calculus 0-06-467125-9
Introduction to Statistics 0-06-467134-8
Ordinary Differential Equations 0-06-467133-X
Precalculus Mathematics: Functions & Graphs
   0-06-467165-8
Survey of Mathematics 0-06-467135-6

MUSIC
Harmony and Voice Leading 0-06-467148-8
History of Western Music 0-06-467107-7
Introduction to Music 0-06-467108-9
Music Theory 0-06-467168-2

PHILOSOPHY
Ethics 0-06-467166-6
History of Philosophy 0-06-467142-9
Introduction to Philosophy 0-06-467124-0

POLITICAL SCIENCE
The Constitution of the United States 0-06-467105-4
Introduction to Government 0-06-467156-9

PSYCHOLOGY
Abnormal Psychology 0-06-467121-6
Child Development 0-06-467149-6
Introduction to Psychology 0-06-467103-8
Personality: Theories and Processes 0-06-467115-1
Social Psychology 0-06-467157-7

SOCIOLOGY
Introduction to Sociology 0-06-467106-2
Marriage and the Family 0-06-467147-X

Available at your local bookstore or directly from HarperCollins at 1-800-331-3761.